DREAMING IN PUBLIC

Building the Occupy Movement

D0111872

Edited by Amy Schrager Lang
& Daniel Lang/Levitsky

About the Editors

Amy Schrager Lang taught U.S. literature and culture for thirty-five years and remains on the faculty of Syracuse University. She is the author of scholarly books and articles and the co-editor of *What Democracy Looks Like: A New Critical Realism for a Post-Seattle World*. She co-edits the book series Class : Culture for the University of Michigan Press.

Daniel Lang/Levitsky is a puppeteer, designer, organizer, and agitator based in Brooklyn. Raised radical, grew up queer & gendertreyf; a founding member of the NYC Direct Action Network, Jews Against the Occupation/NYC, and the Aftselokhes Spectacle Committee. Presently a board member of Jews For Racial & Economic Justice, a dancer with the Rude Mechanical Orchestra's Tactical Spectacle, and organizer of Just Like That (an affinity group and research collective).

DREAMING IN PUBLIC

Building the Occupy Movement

Edited by Amy Schrager Lang
& Daniel Lang/Levitsky

Dreaming In Public: Building the Occupy Movement
First published in 2012 by
New Internationalist Publications Ltd
55 Rectory Road
Oxford OX4 1BW, UK
newint.org

This book has been compiled by Amy Schrager Lang and Daniel
Lang/Levitsky. Copyright over the contributions to the book is held
by the individual authors. Their work appears here under a Creative
Commons Attribution-NonCommercial-ShareAlike license.

Front cover photograph and design: Tim Simons
Design: Andrew Kokotka and Ian Nixon.
Series editor: Chris Brazier

Printed by Versa Press, Peoria, Illinois, US.

British Library Cataloguing-in-Publication Data
A catalogue record for this book is available from the British
Library.

Library of Congress Cataloguing-in-Publication Data
A catalogue record for this book is available from the Library of
Congress.

ISBN 978-1-78026-084-6

FSC
www.fsc.org
MIX
Paper from
responsible sources
FSC® C005010

Contents

Preface

Occupy Wall Street took everyone by surprise! That surprise was felt by those who initiated the action as well as by others who, like myself, joined in later.

No doubt like other observant participants, in trying to understand what was happening I used previous experience as a template. The experience that came to my mind was that of the New Left of the early 1960s.

From 1960 to 1967 or 1968, the Student Nonviolent Coordinating Committee (SNCC) and Students for a Democratic Society (SDS) professed belief in nonviolence and in what we called 'participatory democracy'. We believed that we are all leaders, and, although we did not use the term, our practice expressed horizontalism. We sought to influence each other by exemplary action rather than by ideological harangue. History, it seemed to us, might come about because Rosa Parks refused to go to the back of a bus, because four young men 'sat in' at a segregated lunch counter, or because David Mitchell refused to be drafted for a war in Vietnam that he considered a war crime.

The Occupy movement exhibits these same characteristics to an astonishing degree. Who would have believed that this 'structure of feeling' could reappear after SNCC and SDS crashed and burned in the late Sixties? It is as if beneath the charred surface of the forest floor all manner of seeds, sprouts, networks of green and growing things, somehow survived and now have reappeared.

Thus SNCC and SDS on the one hand, and Occupy on the other, are alike in their commitment to certain values.

There are particular problems that we in the Sixties failed to resolve and must therefore pass on, in that unhappy state, to protagonists of Occupy.

The first has to do with demands. We had demands in the Sixties: Yes to the right to vote in the Deep South, No to military service in Vietnam. We knew that behind these problems stood an economic system, capitalism. We did not know how to make specific demands that, if acted on, could change capitalism into something better. We passed on this conundrum to those who came after us, who turned out to be Occupy.

We failed in creating an appropriate process of representative government within our Movement as its numbers grew.

We did not know, and proved unable to learn, how to deal with an intransigent minority in the course of Movement decision-making.

This is a formidable collection of unresolved matters!

Sorry about that, brothers and sisters.

But in effect, history has given all of us a second chance. There is excitement in recognizing that the activists in Movements all around the world, gathered, as we have, in downtown public squares (Wenceslas Square in Prague, Tahrir Square in Cairo), are struggling with the same problems.

In the Sixties we supposed that somewhere there was a society that had found solutions to the issues we experienced. If not the Soviet Union, then surely the intrepid guerrillas of Latin America, Algerian women with their battle cry, the Chinese in seeking to pass on the spirit of revolution to a new generation, even the students of Paris, had found the Answers. Painfully, we discovered that was not the case.

We are all in this together.

Staughton Lynd
Longtime US activist, lawyer, historian and author.

Foreword

All of the writing and images we have included in this collection were created and circulated by their authors as part of their active participation in Occupy/Decolonize. Some have been read widely and are understood as key contributions to the movement's evolution – Manissa McCleave Maharawal's 'So Real It Hurts', for example. Others have reached far fewer people, like the Mortville Declaration of Independence, but are no less significant for that. Still others are part of the ferment of largely anonymous cultural production that has accompanied Occupy – photoshopped graphics featuring Lieutenant John Pike (the 'Pepper Spray Cop') or 'Occupy Sesame Street' images. The selections are strikingly different in tone: earnest, ironic, hilarious, somber, enraged, or all of these by turns. What they share is intensity of feeling; what they do, collectively, is create the movement.

Without these cultural producers, without their work, and without the commitment to social protagonism that animates it, Occupy would not exist, any more than it would without the cooks, trash-haulers, librarians, livestreamers, medics and residents of the encampments. This is no less true of the thousands of other writers, photographers, photoshoppers and so on whose work we have not included. We have chosen these particular works because we feel that they, together, show the scope and the depth of the whole.

Among these selections can be found:

Celebrations of the range of Occupy's success – from Sara Marcus' appreciation of the OWS livestream to Jaime Omar Yassin's love letter to the Occupy Oakland kitchen to photographs documenting the range of creative responses to tent bans from Melbourne to Berkeley.

Diagnoses and analyses of the movement's recurrent problems, internal and external – for instance, Emma Rosenthal's indictment of the inaccessibility of Occupy LA to disabled would-be participants, and the Occupy Boston Women's Caucus statement on behalf of the 52 per cent.

Assessments of the strategies that Occupy/Decolonize has used, and strategies that have been proposed to it – Mike Konczal on Occupy Foreclosures, the 'Clarification on Nature of Call for West Coast Port Blockade' and low end theory's discussion of Occupy Oakland in relation to class politics within African-American communities.

Interventions in the movement's internal debates – such as Morrigan Phillips' 'Room for the Poor', Sonny Singh's assessment of the OWS Spokes Council from the perspective of the People of Color Caucus, and the American Indian Movement of Colorado's indigenous platform proposal.

And work that does several of these at once, and other things entirely.

* * *

We have borrowed the names of OWS Working Groups to organize the sections of this book. They provide a loose thematic structure, across which other threads of discussion emerge. So, for example, the fraught relationship between Occupy and pre-existing homeless populations runs through work appearing in the sections titled 'Safer Spaces', 'Sustainability' and 'Town Planning', among others. Our object is not to turn the reader's attention away from the pervasive concerns of the movement, but to highlight the ways in which these flow into all working groups and caucuses, whatever their precisely defined purview.

Two sections require additional comment. The 'Arts & Culture' section brings together verbal and visual material showcasing the creativity of Occupy/Decolonize manifested in internet memes, in propaganda posters, in street actions and in the never-quite-explicable catchphrases that bind together what Anne Tagonist calls 'the tribe'.

The one section not named for a working group – 'Elsewhere' – is intended to intimate the global reach of the movement. In part, it takes up Occupy as it has appeared in the UK. From London to Wigan, a distinct movement grounded in the anti-austerity organizing and popular unrest of the past few years has, like others around the world, adopted 'Occupy' as a gesture of solidarity with the US movement. The work we have included here makes clear both the particularities of the UK movement and its affiliation with movements elsewhere. Another part of the section glimpses the real and affective history of the movement. Accounts of Spain's 15-M plaza occupations in 2011 and the protest camping tradition that includes the feminist anti-nuclear Greenham Common encampment that lasted from 1981 to 2000 offer different useable pasts for Occupy/Decolonize, as does a short history of masking as a protest tactic. Finally, Emmanuel Iduma's writing makes no mention of Occupy. When he describes needing 'this revolution', however, he evokes the affinities that knit Nigeria to the global phenomenon of Occupy and the Arab Revolutions that began in

North Africa in 2011.

* * *

The work in this collection appears in the form in which it originally circulated (with a few exceptions noted in the text). The one change made throughout has been to bring the texts into conformity with the style of our UK-based publishers.

However, one of the unavoidable difficulties in presenting in paper form texts which originally appeared online is dealing with the specific structures of online writing: both its social aspects and the intertextual possibilities it affords writers.

In only one case have we included any of the comments which accompany a piece originating on a blog. While we have included pieces that originated on Tumblr, we have not traced their re-postings and comment streams. We have included no tweets except those quoted in more extended pieces of writing.

We have included as footnotes some of the links that appear in these texts – primarily those that serve as citations and those that point to material that expands the reach of a piece. We have omitted those that direct readers to reference material – the websites of organizations named in the text; wikipedia definitions of terms of political theory; etc – and those that are more narrowly illustrative examples. We encourage you to look at the pieces in their original forms, and to follow the links, comment streams, and trails of breadcrumbs you will find.

The images we have included are, likewise, drawn primarily from online sources. Many of them make that origin visible in their resolution and clarity, despite our attempts to use the highest-quality versions we could locate. We make no apology for this; we've chosen the images that we feel are important, revealing, or typical, rather than the ones available at a high resolution. And, as with the writing we've selected, we encourage you to seek out the many alternative versions, remixes, and other developments of the same memes towards which these images can lead you.

* * *

Without the generosity of the tireless chroniclers of the Occupy movement, this volume would not have been possible. Our first and greatest thanks are to them, for their words, their pictures, their suggestions, and their advice on this project.

All the work here appears courtesy of its creators, under Creative Commons Attribution-NonCommercial-ShareAlike licenses. Details of the license terms can be found at http://creativecommons.org/ licenses/. The creators retain all rights to their work.

A number of publications and organizations have allowed us to reprint materials they originally published. We would like to express our particular gratitude to:

> *The Los Angeles Review of Books* for Sara Marcus's 'C-SPAN for Radicals'
> *Alternet* for Sarah Jaffe's 'Occupy Wall Street Prepares for Crackdown – Will Bloomberg Try to Tear It All Down?'
> *Rabble.ca* for Harsha Walia's 'Letter to Occupy Together Movement'

And the other publications which first presented this work: *Black Agenda Report, Black Looks, The Boston Review, Bully Bloggers, ColorLines, El Enemigo Común, Hyphen Magazine, In Front & Center, Jadaliyya, Left Turn, N+1, The Nation, New Internationalist, The Occupied Times of London, Occupy Writers, Possible Futures, Social Text, Z Communications.*

We were not able to identify the creators of some of the images we've included. If you can put us in touch with any of these creators, we would be very grateful, and pleased to be able to give them the credit they deserve.

Friends, comrades, and relations have supplied us with a stream of postings, videos, and reports from their own encounters with Occupy – from the activities of the women's caucus in Boston to the tent boat in the 2011 Los Angeles Harbor Holiday Afloat parade. To Emily Achtenberg, Emily Forman, Grace Goodman, Michele Hardesty, Jamie Kelsey-Fry, Emma Lang, Bill V Mullen, Lenny Olin, Lily Paulina, Jane Queller, Jen Ridgley, John Simon, 'Pirate' Jenny Smith, Megan Wolff – our thanks.

Our love and gratitude go especially to Julie Abraham who, in addition to supplying our private encampment with all the comforts of home, lent us her skill as editor and photographer.

Amy Schrager Lang and **Daniel Lang/Levitsky**

Anonymous

NO I'M THE POET

NO YOU'RE THE POET

NO HE'S THE POET

NO THEY'RE THE POET

NO SHE'S THE POET

NO THAT'S THE POET

NO THIS IS THE POET

NO I'M THE POET

(repeat)

Eileen Myles
Over the human microphone at Liberty Plaza.

Introduction

The Politics of the Impossible
Amy Schrager Lang & Daniel Lang/Levitsky

I know that what I am asking is impossible. But in our time, as in every time, the impossible is the least that one can demand . . . .
– James Baldwin, *The Fire Next Time* (1963)

Zuccotti Park lies about halfway between Wall Street and New York's City Hall, across the street from the construction site where the World Trade Center once stood. A dim, one-block-square paved plaza caught on all sides between looming office towers, it was constructed by US Steel in 1968 in exchange for a height bonus on an adjacent building. Once named and now again referred to by its occupiers as Liberty Plaza, Zuccotti Park is a 'privately owned public space', one of New York's many POPS, as they are dubbed, built in return for zoning variances granted to real-estate developers beginning in the 1960s as the wholesale privatization of public space transformed New York and other US cities.

On 17 September 2011, it was the fallback position for that day's planned action in the New York financial district to protest the dramatic and rapidly growing economic inequality and the equally dramatic increase in the political influence and impunity of corporations and financial institutions for which Wall Street is a metonym. Unlike city-owned parks (and most POPS), which have a curfew allowing the police to remove homeless New Yorkers, and anyone else, Zuccotti Park had no posted rules about hours of access.

The Occupy Wall Street encampment – which began as soon as it became apparent that the city could not order instant eviction and lasted until 15 November when, in a co-ordinated effort to disband Occupy sites all over the US, it was sacked by the police – grew steadily from September on. Locals and new arrivals to the city slept in the plaza; even larger numbers of people spent hours there each day. Working groups formed to meet the encampment's needs for food, sanitation, medical care, cultural and intellectual sustenance; a general assembly convened daily as the central decision-making body. In a remarkably short time, hundreds of Occupy encampments sprang up across the United States and elsewhere, particularly but not only in Europe. In some places, organizations or clusters of individuals initiated planning meetings; in others, an online call brought people together for an initial action. While local histories, individual experiences, and specific strategies varied wildly, the first move in most places was to reclaim a public space and establish a full-time presence there in an effort to make concrete the outrage, hopes, despair and dreams of those who answered the call.

Our aim in this volume is neither to compile a narrative history of the events that began in the fall of 2011 nor to assemble contributions from the enormous and rich pool of writing about Occupy in journalistic, academic and other venues outside the movement. Nor do we mean to claim what can only be, especially at this stage of the movement, a fictional comprehensiveness. The multiplication of Occupy sites within and outside the United States alone would prohibit any such attempt but so, too, does the historical moment at which we are gathering these documents. With most Occupy encampments banned and dispersed, the open-ended communal space in which Occupy figured a politics of what we are told is impossible is, at least temporarily, gone. The question now is how to carry forward what we learned there. We are convinced that bringing together documents (verbal and visual) about Occupy by participants in Occupy – by those who are Occupy – will help mark the way.

Throughout this collection, we use 'Occupy' and 'Occupy/ Decolonize' interchangeably to designate this new movement as a whole. Our reasons are multiple. We want, first, to credit the arguments against 'occupation' and the ways in which the word Occupy erases both histories of colonialism and experiences of military rule. But beyond this, our own active opposition to existing military occupations – in Palestine, in Afghanistan, in Iraq – means the unmodified term 'Occupy' makes us queasy, even though OWS is, as a sign at Zuccotti Park says, 'an occupation a radical Jew can get behind.' Nonetheless, 'Occupy' has become the commonplace name for the movement, no matter how many of its participants feel, as we do, that 'Reclaim' or 'Decolonize' better suit its realities and aims.

Dreaming in Public is, then, an assemblage of documents, both texts and images, produced within the political movement that emerged in the wake of Occupy Wall Street largely for its own use. What binds these documents together is their producers' efforts to address their own role in the development of a new politics. They record interventions in the movement's actions and its understanding of itself, and articulate essential, if often painful, disagreements among participants. They recount attempts on the part of individuals to explain what they, themselves, are doing in the movement. They capture and reflect both the ethic of participation that drives Occupy and its remarkable inventiveness. They grow out of, and feed, the crucial sense shared by individual actors in Occupy of their own centrality to the movement – and their commonality.

* * *

If we appear to seek the unattainable, as it has been said, then let it be known that we do so to avoid the unimaginable.
– Port Huron Statement (1962)

Once, it might be argued, progressive political discourse in the United States was dominated by the idea that the Truth, if revealed with sufficient force, would not only set us free but also return us to a path immanent in the founding documents of the nation. Martin Luther King Jr's promised land was, after all, 'promised', there to be seen from the mountaintop by a new Moses, and guaranteed moreover by the national rhetoric of civil rights, human equality and justice; were the Constitution only respected, the war in Vietnam, being both immoral in its conduct and illegal in its basis, would, of necessity, be ended; women having at long last attained full legal citizenship, their rights would seem to be self-evident. In short, a 'true' America was lurking within the real one, if we could only recover it. The political Jeremiad, with its appeal to the nation to return to its 'ideals' and thereby avert imminent downfall – now intoned primarily and vociferously by the Right – was, if nothing else, politically useful to progressives at a time when reform seemed possible, when to demand voting rights, the end to an unauthorized war, political and social equality was only, after all, to ask America to be 'America' again.

If this account seems to impute naïveté to 20th-century social movements, that is emphatically not our intent: the architects and the actors in these movements were hardly ignorant of either the reality of power relations in the United States or the difficulty of the tasks they assumed – or, for that matter, the lengths to which their opposition would go in order to thwart them. Likewise, we do not mean to imply some monolithic agreement within or among movements on the Left about the nature (or plausibility) of 'demands,' much less about the most effective language of political persuasion. Nonetheless, the invocation of a 'true' America, which defined the political and social landscape for so long, is precisely what Occupy steps away from, however tentatively.

If there is one consensus apparent in the documents in this volume, it is that 'demands' cannot be made, that they are not meaningful in a time when an apparently seamless social and economic order is able to absorb and sell back to us anything that can be contained and marketed. As relentlessly global in its scope as it is intensely personal in its reach, this all-encompassing world system can, after all, appropriate a demand as easily as it can a political icon, a 'subversive' lifestyle, a 'progressive' ideal. As the 'Declaration of the Occupation of New York City' proclaims, its hand, no longer invisible, can be seen everywhere in a country in which extremes of poverty and wealth have reached historic levels without any attention to their redress, in which the electoral process has been sold to the highest bidder, in which both unemployment and actual or prospective homelessness are understood as problems to be solved by the private corporate interests that now control the greater part of the national wealth, in which 'government of the people, by the people, and for the people' seems, in fact, to have perished from the earth. 'This list,' as the Declaration is careful to remind its readers, 'is not all-inclusive.'

If ideas of the 'general welfare' or 'the common good' have been met and vanquished by the privatization of everything from prisons, utilities, schools and social services to emotional life; if contingent (or, in the case of interns, unpaid) labor is an increasingly acceptable norm; if retirement pensions and healthcare are luxuries to be bargained away by unions or flatly withdrawn by employers; if Congress need not declare war or acknowledge peace, US citizens can be summarily executed without trial, and non-citizens held in 'indefinite detention' at Guantánamo or in Immigration and Customs Enforcement detention centers; if clean water, food, and air – or even planetary survival – are no longer matters of governmental concern, then what? If everything and, therefore, nothing constitutes a 'community', which is to say a target market for commodities, policies, or both – from 'the Intelligence community' to 'the Public Broadcasting community' to 'the knitting community' – if, in short, there is nothing but *this*, what is there to demand except everything?

Part, then, of what has been taken by insiders and outsiders alike as radically new in the Occupy movement is its stalwart refusal to proclaim an authoritative set of putatively answerable demands. To yield to the demand for 'demands' would be to credit existing social and political institutions with the will and the ability to correct the ills that afflict us. It would be to put faith in the self-correcting power of the state or of capitalism, in the ameliorative power of NGOs or the mythical transcendent force of 'civil society'. And this in the absence of all evidence.

In this respect, the rejection of demands on the part of Occupy mirrors a broader rejection of older terms of political struggle. Rather than assuming that the shape of the world we want to build can be found in a pre-existing blueprint – the Constitution, *Das Kapital*, or the Algerian, Cuban, Nicaraguan revolutions – Occupy offers 'continuous practice' in the present – that is, a process of trying things out, seeing what works, and changing direction based on the results – as a method both for letting go of existing structures of living and for devising new ones. Unlike 'progressive' movements that work to prefigure a particular improved future, Occupy assumes neither a single answer nor an endpoint to social transformation.

Which is not to say Occupy is unprecedented. The history of its various elements can, needless to say, be traced back into the 19th century and before, but Occupy draws most directly on forms within US social justice movements since World War Two. The emphasis on daily practice, on experimentation with new structures for directly meeting the needs of participants and communities, follows examples set by the Black Panther Party's citizens' patrols and free breakfast programs, the Women's Liberation Movement's autonomous feminist health clinics and safe houses, and other similar projects in the 1960s and 1970s. Its insistence on total transformation rather than a list of demands echoes the Gay Liberation Front and the Women's Liberation Movement of the same period, as well as projects inspired by the May 1968 uprising of students and workers in Paris and the Situationist politics connected to it. The principles and practices of participatory democracy that have become a hallmark of Occupy have a long history, most conspicuously in Students for a Democratic Society and among second-wave feminists. Finally, the ways in which Occupy/Decolonize weaves together global and local scales of struggle and analysis mirror the practices developed in the 1990s and 2000s by parts of the radical environmental movement, by No Borders collectives and encampments that combine analyses of the economics that drive migration and the state policies that seek to control it, and by ACT UP-Philadelphia, which, far more than other chapters, has successfully addressed global access to treatment for HIV/AIDS alongside local access to services.

More immediately, however, the reclamation of public spaces, and the language of 'occupying' them, that gave Occupy its initial shape emerged from a strategic shift that took place over the late 2000s. After the crest of the urban squatting movement of the 1980s, building and space reclamation actions became much less common in the US. When they did happen, they were almost always symbolic, looking to media impact or public visibility as the source of their effectiveness. From corporate and government office takeovers to university building occupations, holding space indefinitely was a largely rhetorical goal, not part of these actions' concrete strategy. Longer-term reclamation and squatting continued, but almost never as public actions.

Soon after the start of the foreclosure wave of 2008, however, several groups – most notably Miami's Take Back the Land – began a public campaign of moving evicted families into vacant houses. Other projects focusing on housing and homelessness took inspiration from Take Back the Land and brought its strategies to bear elsewhere in the country. The tactic emerged in other movements as well, to a limited degree – in 2008, the workers at Chicago's Republic Windows and Doors held a 10-day sit-down strike to prevent a plant closure, the first in decades; and in February 2011, workers, students and community supporters set up a fully functioning community of occupiers within the Wisconsin state capitol building in an attempt to block anti-union legislation proposed by Governor Scott Walker.

Each of these uses of long-term reclamation – of 'occupation' – wears on its sleeve connections to movements outside the US. Take Back the Land (and other housing justice organizations like New York City's Picture the Homeless) takes the ongoing Brazilian Landless Movement (MST: Movimento dos Trabalhadores Sem Terra), begun in 1985, as a model and reference point. The workers at Republic cited as a precedent the many factories reclaimed in Argentina after the 2001 financial crisis alongside the US auto and steel sit-down strikes of the 1930s. And at the Wisconsin state capitol, the Egyptian revolution, taking place simultaneously, was frequently invoked. This desire to understand what's happening as part of something international, to think of local events as intimately linked to movements outside the US, carries on into Occupy/Decolonize.

In other aspects of the movement as well, local and international prehistories intertwine. Many of the specific methods used in Occupy's participatory democratic structure come from particular recent histories in the US. The hand-gestures used at OWS to show agreement and make various kinds of process intervention, which have come to signify Occupy's process as a whole, are a good example. They were adapted from those used in 1999-2002 by the NYC Direct Action Network, which in turn extended the adoption of American Sign Language applause by activist groups in California to speed up meetings by replacing clapping (which cuts off spoken discussion) with a silent show of approval. Similarly, Occupy/Decolonize working group and spokescouncil structures come directly out of a lineage leading back through the global justice movement of the early 2000s through ACT UP and the continuing movement to close the School of the Americas (now called the Western Hemisphere Institute for Security Co-operation) to feminist anti-militarist organizing of the 1970s and 1980s.

But, again, international sources abound: the non-hierarchical leadership structures the Zapatistas have developed in the years since their rebellion against the Mexican state began in 1994; the Popular Assemblies through which neighborhoods in Argentina organized themselves against austerity measures and international debt in 2001, ousting four presidents along the way; the subsequent, rather different, forms of assemblies developed in Oaxaca, Spain and Italy. These models share Occupy's approach of building towards an unknown other world through continuous practice, perhaps best summarized in the words of Antonio Machado adopted as a motto by many Zapatista-inspired groups: *se hace el camino al andar* – 'we make the road by walking'.

Just as the interweaving of recent local and international influences on Occupy/Decolonize reflects resistance to neoliberal economics, to Structural Adjustment Programs imposed by the International Monetary Fund, and to 'austerity' budgets both within the US and elsewhere, so too were the local post-World War Two movements which make up the movement's earlier prehistory intertwined with those abroad – the US face of anti-colonial struggles from Vietnam to Algeria to South Africa, student uprisings from Paris to Tokyo to Mexico City, and so on. The felt affinity that has produced the slogan 'Arab Spring, European Summer, American Fall' is the same affinity alluded to in the phrase 'Two, Three, Many Vietnams', drawn from a 1966 speech by Che Guevara. But the basis of that affinity is radically different. Whereas the earlier phrase announces solidarity against a common enemy – colonialism and US imperialism – the current one evokes the shared *form* of struggle: participatory, leaderless, horizontally structured, inclusive and demanding everything.

* * *

In the day I would be reminded of those men and women
Brave, setting up signals across vast distances,
Considering a nameless way of living, of almost unimagined values.
– Muriel Rukeyser, 'Poem' (1968)

If the problem with 'having no demands' is that a movement can slide – or be thought of as sliding – into demanding nothing, Occupy suggests that the antidote lies in building something, together, that can begin to provide what people feel is missing from their lives. The names of some of the first OWS Working Groups speak to those lacunae: Comfort; The People's Kitchen; Town Planning; The People's Library; Sustainability; Sanitation.

Many of the essays and photographs in this collection detail the infrastructure of Occupy encampments, which are widely understood to embody the movement's strengths and its ethos. The effectiveness of this infrastructure at meeting the basic needs of participants in Occupy/Decolonize – food, clothing, medicine, human connection, intellectual and cultural excitement – has made it possible for the movement to devote its energy to stubborn problems that many political movements shelve. In the absence of 'a demand', and in the presence of an ethic of participation, there is no need – or excuse – to postpone addressing these lasting tensions until after the moment of struggle. The shared assumption is not merely that there is no value in deferring conflict, but rather that fully engaging conflict is itself generative, necessary and valuable.

Perhaps the biggest tension afflicting the movement – as an internal matter and a constantly repeated challenge from outside – revolves around the meaning of 'the 99%', as a rhetorical device and as a description of Occupy's constituency. In New York City, for example, where the slogan originated, the 53 per cent of New Yorkers who are women, the 67 per cent who are people of color, the 37 per cent who are immigrants, pose a demographic complication to any assumed common interest or shared experience. The very things the slogan implicitly appeals to as a basis of unity – unemployment, debt, foreclosure and eviction, 'middle class' status – weigh so differently in different communities that fractures appear, however strongly felt is the desire for unity.

But, as this volume makes clear, the problem exceeds demography. Who counts as the 99%? Cops? Ron Paul libertarians? Sectarian leftists? Can a movement committed to inclusivity draw a political boundary around itself? Must it allow full participation to all comers? By what means can these questions be decided, and how can a decision, once reached, be enforced?

Beyond demographic complexity and political boundary-marking lies another facet of this same tension – one in relation to which the slogan of 'the 99%' is never invoked. One of the most fraught and contentious debates over inclusion within Occupy concerns 'disruptive behavior' – what constitutes it, who is understood to engage in it, and who can be excluded from what because of it. Undoubtedly, the heat of these debates is generated in part because they conjure up questions of demography and boundary-marking yet allow decisions about exclusion to be presented as wholly individual, and by this means depoliticized. So, for example, from Oakland to London, 'bad behavior' is ascribed more often than not to participants in Occupy/Decolonize encampments who arrived already 'homeless' or impoverished, who are people of color, who are (or are assumed to be) substance users, who are read as disabled. The greater the number of these descriptions that can be applied to a given person, the more likely their actions are to be labeled as 'disruptive'.

Which is not to say that Occupy's decision-making processes and daily practice are immune to genuinely problematic behavior or the genuine misuse of process. Both problems do indeed exist. But the terms in which 'disruption' are usually broached mask their deeply political nature and allow 'bad behavior' to be dealt with as an issue of etiquette.

If the meaning of the 99% is one broad question through which the tensions within Occupy play out, the value of encampment – of holding public space, in full view, with no planned end-point – is another. First of all, there is deep disagreement over the strategic value of encampment as opposed to other forms of activity – over putting in place a new kind of space to demonstrate (on however small a scale) the viability of change, as opposed to movement-building strategies not tied to a specific location, such as direct actions, closer relationships with labor unions, neighborhood assemblies, popular education projects, and so on.

Beyond that strategic difference, some see the daily life of the encampments as checking antagonisms and building unity by creating an arena in which strangers meet and talk under a presumption of easy, direct communication across a wide range of differences, and in which resources are owned by no one and available to everyone. Others see the encampments as a source of division. From their point of view, the silver lining to the wholesale eviction of Occupy encampments during the winter was that it put to rest disputes between those for whom the movement's future centers on the encampments and those advocating movement-building in other forms.

Behind both of these positions lies the question of space itself. The unquestionable impact of maintaining a long-term physical presence in public space is what allowed Occupy/Decolonize to capture the world's imagination and proliferate with such astonishing rapidity. In part, defying the apparent impossibility of successfully taking control of public space away from its usual corporate and government keepers both literalized and symbolized the power of the people, of the 99%. Taking space in this way also made participation – working in the kitchen, hauling trash, screenprinting t-shirts, amplifying someone else's voice during a mic check – the basis of the movement, rather than adherence to a political platform or social compact. By allowing the lines between observer, visitor and active participant to become permeable, by reclaiming space and time, Occupy encampments simultaneously instantiated a better future and spoke clearly to the present.

But what happens when a material space reclamation – one that insists on and defends its permanent autonomous control of its terrain – becomes symbolic, that is, temporary, existing as an idea not a place? We don't yet know. That, in large part, is the question that Occupy/Decolonize faces in 2012. We do know, however, that the relationships between Occupy and other movements and organizations will change as the structure of their activities becomes, in some respects at least, more similar. How those relationships play out will itself affect the movement's decisions about re-establishing encampments, and indeed may make available wider possibilities. The continuities between Occupy as encampment, as direct-action movement, as educational and organizing project, as cultural force, remain an open question, one that participants will work out through practice and argument over the next few months and in the longer term – finding different answers as the movement's needs and conditions change.

*   *   *

Thus we presume to write, as it were, upon things that exist not, and travel by maps yet unmade, and a blank.
– Walt Whitman, *Democratic Vistas* (1871)

It's tempting to see Occupy as a 'prefigurative' project. We've become accustomed to using that phrase for endeavors that are based on participation, and that point to concrete possibilities for a different, better, world. And Occupy can look like that.

But implicit in 'prefiguration' is the idea that the present can only be a foreshadowing of a future reality, not a reality itself. It assumes a fundamental separation between our present work and the world we hope to bring into being. We want to argue that what Occupy has accomplished is not the shadowing forth of a promised future, but rather the creation, on however small a scale, of a present reality.

Not an act of prefiguration but an act of construction. That is to say, its energy – in encampments, in meetings and in street actions – is devoted to building present alternatives to failed structures and policies. However utopian, Occupy does not proceed in accordance with an abstract blueprint for the future; on the contrary, its design emerges from daily process and practice.

What Occupy creates, though its participatory ethos and its commitment to continuous and self-conscious reconsideration of what it does and how, is a sense of social protagonism: a sense that each of us is at the center of an ongoing and, crucially, a *collective* history. Neither the mediated communication of cyberspace nor the putative individualism of the corporate marketplace will do; we must all talk face to face and together about how to reshape a world gone awry.

None of us knows what comes next; we will build it together.

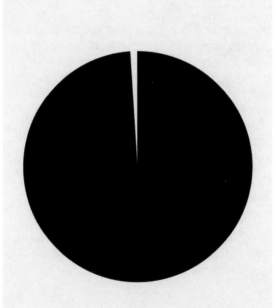

OCCUPY EVERYTHING

Information Desk

This section is meant as an overview, moving through Occupy Wall Street from the smallest scale of effects and possibilities to the largest – from new structures for everyday life to a new political engagement to a new politics.

Richard Kim's introduction to Occupy Wall Street leads us from the story of Joe Therrien, a member of the OWS Puppetry Guild, to a description of the radical structures of the movement. In recounting Therrien's now commonplace economic and social precariousness, Kim illuminates a crucial part of what drives Occupy's creation of spaces that resist 'the money-form and hierarchy'. Ira Livingston, by contrast, in Twitter-inspired 140-character lines echoing the way information circulates about Occupy, meditates on the impossibility of inhabiting neoliberal late capitalism. Deploying the fantasies of omnipotence that in US commercial culture carry fascist overtones, but in lived experience provide the possibility for social agency, he considers how we move from a sudden sense of political vitality to an active political stance. Naomi Klein, recalling the successful direct action that shut down the 1999 World Trade Organization Ministerial Conference in Seattle and the less successful subsequent actions at international financial institution summits that followed, addresses the difference that unlimited time and a changed target makes.

The Audacity of Occupy Wall Street

Richard Kim
2 November 2011

A few years ago, Joe Therrien, a graduate of the NYC Teaching Fellows program, was working as a full-time drama teacher at a public elementary school in New York City. Frustrated by huge class sizes, sparse resources and a disorganized bureaucracy, he set off to the University of Connecticut to get an MFA in his passion – puppetry. Three years and $35,000 in student loans later, he emerged with degree in hand, and, because puppeteers aren't exactly in high demand, he went looking for work at his old school. The intervening years had been brutal to the city's school budgets – down about 14 per cent on average since 2007. A virtual hiring freeze has been in place since 2009 in most subject areas, arts included, and spending on art supplies in elementary schools crashed by 73 per cent between 2006 and 2009. So even though Joe's old principal was excited to have him back, she just couldn't afford to hire a new full-time teacher. Instead, he's working at his old school as a full-time 'substitute'; he writes his own curriculum, holds regular classes and does everything a normal teacher does. 'But sub pay is about 50 per cent of a full-time salaried position,' he says, 'so I'm working for half as much as I did four years ago, before grad school, and I don't have health insurance... It's the best-paying job I could find.'

Like a lot of the young protesters who have flocked to Occupy Wall Street, Joe had thought that hard work and education would bring, if not class mobility, at least a measure of security (indeed, a master's degree can boost a New York City teacher's salary by $10,000 or more). But the past decade of stagnant wages for the 99% and million-dollar bonuses for the 1% has awakened the kids of the middle class to a national nightmare: the dream that coaxed their parents to meet the demands of work, school, mortgage payments and tuition bills is shattered. Down is the new up.

But then in these grim times, something unexpected happened: at first scores met in parks around New York City this summer to plan an occupation of Wall Street, then hundreds responded to their call, then thousands from persuasions familiar and astonishing, and now more than 100 cities around the country are Occupied. In the face of unchecked capitalism and a broken, captured state, the citizens of Occupy America have done something desperate and audacious – they put their faith and hope in the last seemingly credible force left in the world: each other.

Sometime during the second week of the Occupation, Joe took that leap. Within his first hour at Liberty Park, he was 'totally won over by the Occupation's spirit of co-operation and selflessness'. He has been going back just about every day since. It took him a few days to find the Arts and Culture working group, which has its roots in the first planning meetings and has already produced a museum's worth of posters (from the crudely handmade to slicker culture-jamming twists on corporate designs), poetry readings, performance-art happenings, political yoga classes and Situationist spectacles like the one in which an artist dressed in a suit and noose tie rolled up to the New York Stock Exchange in a giant clear plastic bubble to mock the speculative economy's inevitable pop.

Alexandre Carvalho, a Brazilian doctor who worked in Rio's *favelas* and was one of the original organizers of Arts and Culture, explains that the group's praxis revolves around two principles. 'First – autonomy, horizontalism and collectivism. We're non-hierarchical, self-regulating, self-deliberating and self-organizing. Everyone is creating their own stuff, but we're connected to a larger hub through the Arts and Culture group.' The second principle is something Alexandre calls 'virgeo,' a mashup of 'virtual' and 'geographical'. 'We try to have both an on-the-ground conversation and an online conversation so that people all over the world can send their ideas and respond to our work.' The same concepts apply, more or less, to the other culture working groups at OWS – from Media (which shoots video for OWS's livestream, documents direct actions and produces educational videos) to the Library (which has received more than 3,500 books, all logged in an online card catalog, from the nearly complete works of Noam Chomsky to *Creative Cash: How to Sell Your Crafts, Needlework, Designs and Know-How*).

At one of Arts and Culture's meetings – held adjacent to 60 Wall Street, at a quieter public-private indoor park that's also the atrium of Deutsche Bank – it dawned on Joe: 'I have to build as many giant puppets as I can to help this thing out – people love puppets!' And so Occupy Wall Street's Puppet Guild, one of about a dozen guilds under the Arts and Culture working group, was born. In the spirit of OWS, Joe works in loose and rolling collaboration with others who share his passion for puppetry or whose projects somehow momentarily coincide with his mission. With the help of a handful of people, he built the 12-foot Statue of Liberty puppet that had young and old alike flocking to him on 8 October in Washington Square Park. Right now, he's working with nearly 30 artists to stage Occupy Halloween, when his newest creations, a 12-foot Wall Street bull and a 40-foot Occupied Brooklyn Bridge inspired by Chinese paper dragons – along with a troupe of dancers playing corporate vampires – will inject a little bit of countercultural messaging into the annual parade of Snookis and True Blood wannabes strutting down Sixth Avenue.

Those of harder head or heart may tweet – giant puppets, #srsly? Yes, it's hard to draw a straight line from something like Occupy Halloween to the overthrow of global capitalism or a financial transactions tax or student debt relief or any number of goals – some of world-historical magnitude, some straight from the playbook of reformist thinktanks – that swirl around Liberty these days. But it's creative types, either shoved into crisis by the precarious economy or just sick of making things under the corporate system, who have responded most enthusiastically to Occupy Wall Street's call. It's not where one might have looked for a revolt to emerge organically. In subsequent Occupations like the one in Oakland, anti-racist organizers have been a dominant force; and in Rust Belt towns across the Midwest, blue-collar types have led the way. But the first spark, here in New York, was generated when artists, students and academics hooked up with activists from Bloombergville, a three-week occupation near City Hall to protest the mayor's budget cuts. This unlikely mix has proved to be a tactical boon, says Alexandre: 'Artists are in a privileged position to take the terrain without too much repression. It's harder for the police to move against you when you are clearly doing something nonviolent and artistic.'

When I ask Joe if he thinks Occupy Wall Street should make repealing budget cuts like the ones that struck New York's public schools a priority, he replies that the thought hadn't really crossed his mind. 'I hope there are groups of people who are working on that specific issue,' he says, but for the moment he's 'prioritizing what I'm most passionate about.' Which, he explains, is 'figuring out how to make theater that's going to help open people up to this new cultural consciousness. It's what I'm driven to do right now, so I'm following that impulse to see where it leads.'

*   *   *

Since 17 September, the first day of the Occupation, thousands of people have flocked to Liberty to follow this impulse to live life anew. To stay for even a few days there is to be caught up in an incredible delirium of talking, making, doing and more talking – a beehive in which the drones have overthrown the queen but are still buzzing about furiously without any immediately apparent purpose. Someone might shout over the human microphone, 'Mic check! (Mic check!) We need! (We need!) Some volunteers! (Some volunteers!) To go to Home Depot! (To go to Home Depot!) And get cleaning supplies! (And get cleaning supplies!)' A handful of people might perk up and answer the call – or not, in which case it is made again and again. Sometimes too many show up and are sent away; sometimes an Occupier jumps to attention but gets distracted by something or someone shiny in Liberty's evolving alleyways, and instead of shopping for the revolution is next seen discussing the politics of microfinance. Somehow, some way – brooms and mops, bleach and scrub brushes show up. They mysteriously vanish, and an ad hoc committee is organized to replenish them and then to guard them. To this day, Liberty is kept relatively clean, which keeps the cops out; the mums in the planters still bloom, hardy by stock but made hardier by the Occupation's life-sustaining and downwardly distributed ethic of care.

One of the first working groups that the original organizers created was simply called Food, and its first budget aspired to raise just $1,000 for peanut butter sandwiches. It now takes in donations from around the world and dishes out up to 3,000 meals a day; nobody is turned away as long as there is a morsel left, and there almost always is. Pizzas arrive by bike or car, many sent by labor unions; canned and dry goods are shipped to OWS's UPS address (118A Fulton St. #205, New York, NY 10038); oatmeal, quinoa and rice come in large sacks and small supermarket packages; chicken and beef, apples and seasonal root vegetables are trucked in from organic farms upstate. Trained chefs were quick to volunteer their time and have even opened up their kitchens.

Once the Occupation took root in Liberty, new working groups formed to meet its growing human needs: Sanitation; Comfort (which collects and distributes sleeping bags, tarps and warm clothes); Medics (which is staffed by nurses, doctors, therapists, acupuncturists and emergency workers, and sees up to 100 patients a day); Security (yes, there is some form of 'law' at OWS, including guidelines against public urination and defecation); and Sustainability (which composts 100 pounds of food waste each day and handles Liberty's recycling program). Each day, the race to reproduce life itself at Liberty begins, and each day it is largely met, in theory at least, without the use of two things – the money-form and hierarchy. ◆

thenation.com/article/164348/audacity-occupy-wall-street

Darth Vader and Occupy Wall Street: A Twitter Essay

Ira Livingston
13 November 2011

1

There's a new Volkswagen ad in which a child dressed as Darth Vader tries to use 'The Force' to control objects in the world.

Dad comes home from work and, standing with mom at the kitchen window, sees his child

trying to mind-control the family car in the driveway. The car starts as if by magic,

then you see that dad has secretly started it with a remote-control device, validating the child's belief in his own super powers.

This is a classic postmodern ad in that the viewer is shown exactly how the trick is played but made to believe it anyway.

Presumably, even for dad (whose role is otherwise limited to going back and forth to work), starting one's car remotely still bestows the feeling of having superpowers. But just ask *power to do what?* and you see

that what's being sold as magical omnipotence is just the ability to start a car with a button instead of a key.

At worst, this pitch is allied with what is recognizable as the fascist tendencies of capitalism

insofar as fascism is defined by the way it offers people an inflated, mythic sense of themselves – and a phantasmatic sense of belonging –

while systematically stripping them of any real agency and political power. Go to work. Buy a new car. You're a superhero!

Of course I'm not suggesting a fine company like Volkswagen could now have or could ever have had anything to do with fascism!

But there is another side of this. What makes the ad work is its psychological validity.

Unless parents serve their children's sense of magical omnipotence, their kids will be pathologically depressed at best, or simply dead.

The infant cries and food appears. He squirms in frustration because he wants a toy but lacks the strength and co-ordination to reach it,

and mom or dad see this and magically make it happen. The fantasy of sovereign agency and omnipotent power

precedes, is necessary to, and continues to underlie the acquisition of actual agency and power – the alternative is *learned helplessness.*

Given these two opposed perspectives, how can we think through this?

Even if you consider the ad a trivial matter, the contradiction is stark and the stakes seem pretty high.

To take the question to another register: do Occupy Wall Street and related actions empower people?

Do they contribute to mobilizing and opening up political discourse? Or can they be described as simple venting, or worse,

part of some systemic damage control mechanism that offers aesthetic or symbolic shows at the expense of real political mobilization?

As if the revolution were a car and OWS the remote-control device that will turn it on?

2

As you'd expect, many right-wingers but also some so-called leftists are bending over backwards to assure us

that this is just an infantile display, that we are clutching at straws, that no sustained movement can come from it.

In the face of contradiction, or even just because it's early days, how can they be so sure?

What makes these little Darth Vaders pretend to knowledge that one couldn't possibly have at this stage?

As philosopher Jacques Derrida put it, 'coherence in contradiction expresses the force of a desire'.

Whatever else its content, the desire seeks 'a reassuring certitude' by which 'anxiety can be mastered'.

The anxiety comes from 'being implicated', from being 'at stake in the game' – as it seems to me we are all at stake here.

Taking off from Derrida, we can speculate that what the dismissers desire, what they have to lose, is the structuring fantasy of a single center, a single origin or ground or goal, a single line of causality,

a single kind of political agency, a single public sphere, a single rationality and discourse, a single left and right –

all of what Occupy Wall Street defies.

A famous prayer asks for courage, serenity, and 'the wisdom always to know the difference' between what can be changed and what can't.

Better pray instead for the folly not to know the difference!

And as my old pal William Blake put it, 'if the fool would persist in his folly he would become wise'.

3

What if politics – what if the world – did not work exactly as we know?

What if things were more intricately, globally and locally networked in a complex ecology,

so that we could not necessarily predict how events in one realm might reverberate in another?

What if the Flap of a Butterfly's Wings in Brazil could Set Off a Tornado in Texas?

What if a mathematician's algorithms could trigger a stock-market collapse?

What if tiny, hyperlocalized genetic mutations could, through a process of natural selection, lead to collective evolution?

Wouldn't that be incredibly *weird*?

What if Occupy Wall Street could be described as a metaphor (the usual phrase is *merely a metaphor*)

for the movement in which we are hoping it will participate, meaning that the occupations of particular places,

such as Zuccotti Park near Wall Street, resonate with how one tries to establish a livable foothold in any inhospitable space –

whether it be the economy, the academy, the family, identity, theory? And what if these resonances are real and contagious?

What if The Coming Insurrection will take 'the shape of a music, whose focal points,

though dispersed in time and space,

succeed in imposing the rhythm of their own vibrations'?

What if what we consider solid realities – like bridges of steel and concrete – could one fine day begin to undulate and break apart?

And when we ask why, what if it turned out that the answer, my friend, is blowing in the wind? And what if, in the present conjuncture,

we could gain more leverage not by asserting knowledge but by persistently asking questions (as that song famously does)?

What if even God appeared to his faithful out of a whirlwind and addressed them with an epic series of questions,

designed to expose their presumption to knowledge they could not possibly have?

4

Occupy Wall Street has never suffered from a lack of rational plans and proposals, as some allege.

Here's some for you: progressive taxes, financial regulation, healthcare, jobs, socialism. Take your pick. I have more.

If the left suffers from anything now it seems more like the lack of emotional coherence,

part of what Raymond Williams called a 'structure of feeling'. This is part of what OWS is helping to discover, to invent.

Assorted already-existing emotional coherences are available, of course.

The sober left intellectuals, with their reassuring certitude that Occupy Wall Street is a flash in the pan,

have their manly stoicism and depressive clarity. The Tea Party has its righteous indignation,

or as historian Joan Scott translated the Tea Party stance into psychoanalytic terms, the outcry 'they've stolen our *jouissance*!'

As for the rest of us: well, at least nobody has stolen our *jouissance*! If you visit Occupy Wall Street,

you will hear hundreds of lively political conversations – in fact, this is one of the hallmarks of the occupation –

and among them will be careful analysis, magic thinking, policy proposals, paranoid ramblings, theorizing, new-age spiritualism, and so on,

but over them all, under them all, behind them all, running through them all is not exactly righteous indignation,

which comes from more privilege – more wounded sense of right and dignity – than most of those present possess.

There is the ever-present tenor of surrealism, which comes from the sense that dominant discourse is so thoroughly locked down –

so *foreclosed* – and political speech so narrowly defined that one cannot restrict oneself to the use of these tools

without undermining from the outset what one hopes to accomplish. Ultimately, as Audre Lorde said,

'the master's tools will never dismantle the master's house.' But this is not only a matter of tools, of instrumental strategies.

Surrealism arises when what counts as reality itself is so impoverished,

when what passes for intelligible politics, viable social identities, reasonable careers and aspirations are so hobbling, corrosive and suffocating as to make the reality of neoliberal late capitalism uninhabitable.

When you can't inhabit it, occupy it!

5

Over all the conversations, under them all, behind them all, running through them all

there is at least – a *vitality*.

As Brooklyn artist Dread Scott said about OWS: 'there's oxygen in the room again'.

Of course, I have to point out, you can't recognize constructive politics by vitality alone.

I recently watched a Wagner opera and was struck by the histrionics, tragic gender politics, erotic intensities

of hierarchy and duty and family: very lively indeed! I was mesmerized– but I also understood for the first time

something about the aliveness and emotional intensity captured by Nazism.

Much of the work of politics is *affective labor*, the work of translating vitality into a *stance*.

Lately I've been listening to old Woody Guthrie songs (more my style, admittedly) and marveling at how seamlessly

the songs combine the stances of worker, empathic ally of immigrants and outlaws, socialist, proud patriot, anti-fascist –

a combination mostly unthinkable today. But I bring this up not at all to say *those were the days*.

For one thing, they never were the days – and for another, they're *still* the days:

Rich man took my home and drove me from my door

And I ain't got no home in this world any more.

In any case, fascism remains and will remain one of the ongoing tendencies of capitalism, and not only as a distant specter.

Even if you were inclined to discount clearer and nearer dangers that demagogues can be elected, scapegoats systematically targeted,

people mobilized in favor of symbolic but deadly wars, or perpetual warfare sold as Manichaean good-versus-evil struggle –

what about the demagogues, scapegoating, symbolic and perpetual wars we *already have?*

What about the mazes we run to get the cheese and avoid the shocks, the levers we push to get the pellets

of whatever it is, the simulacra of identity and belonging being sold to us, and behind all that, underneath it all,

the dark energy pushing all of us apart?

What if, at the most fundamental level, we are engaged not so much in an attempt to enact specific reforms

nor to foment a one-off revolution, but in an ongoing struggle against fascism, to make the world livable,

and what if, in this, we are most aligned with the everyday work of various other queers, workers, culture-crossers, women,

immigrants, and other displaced people? What if, in our own lifetimes, we will only know small and local victories,

that resonate only faintly, sparks that crackle and wink out, glowing embers that never burst into flame?

Would that warmth be enough to sustain us?

6

In the interests of full disclosure, let me acknowledge where I'm coming from: I'm a writer. It's an interesting moment for me.

The presidency of George W Bush, as you may be aware, was also a nightmare for anyone who cares about language.

Language itself seemed to be in the process of being continually, systematically evacuated of meaning and life.

After that, to hear Obama speak with intelligence and presence – even with precise grammar – could bring tears to my eyes.

That's not enough, but it is something. So it's interesting to me to discover that the discursive spaces at Occupy Wall Street

are mostly not my spaces. Even though I make my living speaking (as a teacher, anyway), I'm not inclined to speak there, and the intellectuals I have heard speak there seem somewhat out of their element too.

In fact, the durational performance – the occupation – at the heart of OWS seems actively somehow to disturb and displace speech,

to make it plural (like the human microphone), to make no one iteration definitive. But although I'm not inclined to speak,

it feels *good* to me! This is partly because the massive, single acoustic space of traditional protest rallies always felt to me

like Hitler or Mussolini should be haranguing the crowd from a balcony. You *really* want a unified public sphere?

I experience this displacement of speech, of all that it is now possible to say, as something more like thinking,

more like writing, a process of reaching for what wants to be said but is not yet possible to say.

You there, with your head bent down! Why are you mumbling inarticulately to yourself?

I'm thinking.

7

If the fantasy of magic superpowers underlies all agency, then yes, at some level I must believe the world turns around my words

and around all words that move me. On the other hand, I know Auden was right:

'poetry makes nothing happen'.

If language can be understood as a parasite or a symbiotic entity that co-evolved with our brains, then yes,

I am one of those traitors to my species that serve the entity known as language. That's the extreme version, anyway.

But what if writers and intellectuals are also neither servants nor traitors nor leaders but just one kind of life-form among many,

each of which, even in the name of simple diversity, has a claim to life,

or even more simply, what if a text makes no claim at all but the bare fact of its aliveness in the moment of its being written and read?

This is why I want to say to those occupying Wall Street, and occupying and animating these words and thoughts, *thank you*.

As a Word Person, it's taken me 50 years to admit — as various therapists and lots of less verbal people have been telling me —

that the words themselves are always trumped by the ways they are wielded, the feelings that animate them.

'In those days,' as Virginia Woolf wrote wistfully about the days before the First World War,

'every conversation seemed to have been accompanied by a sort of humming noise,

not articulate, but musical, exciting, which changed the value of the words themselves.'

So what is it, over all the conversations at Occupy Wall Street, under them all, behind them all, running through them all?

Perversely, one of the most notoriously difficult writers of all time, psychoanalyst Jacques Lacan, gives me slogans for the placards with which I want to march out of here:

THE FUNCTION OF LANGUAGE IS NOT TO INFORM BUT TO INVOKE.

WHAT CONSTITUTES ME AS A SUBJECT IS MY QUESTION. ◆

(Acknowledgments: Many thanks to Thad Ziolkowski for insight into the VW ad, Jennifer Miller for citing Dread Scott, and apologies to Jayna for the Woody Guthrie references!)

bullybloggers.wordpress.com/2011/11/13/darth-vader-and-occupy-wall-street-a-twitteressay-by-ira-livingston/trackback/

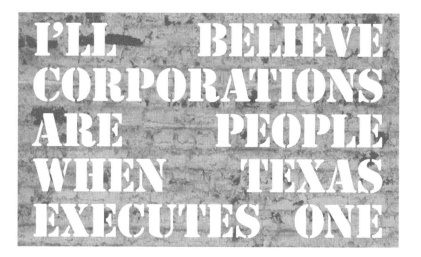

The Most Important Thing in the World

Naomi Klein
6 October 2011

I was honored to be invited to speak at Occupy Wall Street on Thursday night. Since amplification is (disgracefully) banned, and everything I say will have to be repeated by hundreds of people so others can hear (aka 'the human microphone'), what I actually say at Liberty Plaza will have to be very short. With that in mind, here is the longer, uncut version of the speech.

I love you.

And I didn't just say that so that hundreds of you would shout 'I love you' back, though that is obviously a bonus feature of the human microphone. Say unto others what you would have them say unto you, only way louder.

Yesterday, one of the speakers at the labor rally said: 'We found each other.' That sentiment captures the beauty of what is being created here. A wide-open space (as well as an idea so big it can't be contained by any space) for all the people who want a better world to find each other. We are so grateful.

If there is one thing I know, it is that the 1% loves a crisis. When people are panicked and desperate and no one seems to know what to do, that is the ideal time to push through their wish list of pro-corporate policies: privatizing education and social security, slashing public services, getting rid of the last constraints on corporate power. Amidst the economic crisis, this is happening the world over.

And there is only one thing that can block this tactic, and fortunately, it's a very big thing: the 99%. And that 99% is taking to the streets from Madison to Madrid to say 'No. We will not pay for your crisis.'

That slogan began in Italy in 2008. It ricocheted to Greece and France and Ireland and finally it has made its way to the square mile where the crisis began.

'Why are they protesting?' ask the baffled pundits on TV. Meanwhile, the rest of the world asks: 'What took you so long?' 'We've been wondering when you were going to show up.' And most of all: 'Welcome.'

Many people have drawn parallels between Occupy Wall Street and the so-called anti-globalization protests that came to world attention in Seattle in 1999. That was the last time a global, youth-led, decentralized movement took direct aim at corporate power. And I am proud to have been part of what we called 'the movement of movements'.

But there are important differences too. For instance, we chose summits as our targets: the World Trade Organization, the International Monetary Fund, the G8. Summits are transient by their nature, they only last a week. That made us transient too. We'd appear, grab world headlines, then disappear. And in the frenzy of hyper patriotism and militarism that followed the 9/11 attacks, it was easy to sweep us away completely, at least in North America.

Occupy Wall Street, on the other hand, has chosen a fixed target. And you have put no end date on your presence here. This is wise. Only when you stay put can you grow roots. This is crucial. It is a fact of the information age that too many movements spring up like beautiful flowers but quickly die off. It's because they don't have roots. And they don't have long-term plans for how they are going to sustain themselves. So when storms come, they get washed away.

Being horizontal and deeply democratic is wonderful. But these principles are compatible with the hard work of building structures and institutions that are sturdy enough to weather the storms ahead. I have great faith that this will happen.

Something else this movement is doing right: You have committed yourselves to nonviolence. You have refused to give the media the images of broken windows and street fights it craves so desperately. And that tremendous discipline has meant that, again and again, the story has been the disgraceful and unprovoked police brutality. Which we saw more of just last night. Meanwhile, support for this movement grows and grows. More wisdom.

But the biggest difference a decade makes is that, in 1999, we were taking on capitalism at the peak of a frenzied economic boom. Unemployment was low, stock portfolios were bulging. The media was drunk on easy money. Back then it was all about start-ups, not shutdowns.

We pointed out that the deregulation behind the frenzy came at a price. It was damaging to labor standards. It was damaging to environmental standards. Corporations were becoming more powerful than governments and that was damaging to our democracies. But to be honest with you, while the good times rolled, taking on an economic system based on greed was a tough sell, at least in rich countries.

Ten years later, it seems as if there aren't any more rich countries. Just a whole lot of rich people. People who got rich looting the public wealth and exhausting natural resources around the world.

The point is, today everyone can see that the system is deeply unjust and careening out of control. Unfettered greed has trashed the global economy. And it is trashing the natural world as well. We are overfishing our oceans, polluting our water with fracking and deepwater drilling, turning to the dirtiest forms of energy on the planet, like the Alberta tar sands. And the atmosphere cannot absorb the amount of carbon we are putting into it, creating dangerous warming. The new normal is serial disasters: economic and ecological.

These are the facts on the ground. They are so blatant, so obvious, that it is a lot easier to connect with the public than it was in 1999, and to build the movement quickly.

We all know, or at least sense, that the world is upside down: we act as if there is no end to what is actually finite – fossil fuels and the atmospheric space to absorb their emissions. And we act as if there are strict and immovable limits to what is actually bountiful – the financial resources to build the kind of society we need.

The task of our time is to turn this around: to challenge this false scarcity. To insist that we can afford to build a decent, inclusive society – while at the same time respecting the real limits to what the earth can take.

What climate change means is that we have to do this on a deadline. This time our movement cannot get distracted, divided, burned out or swept away by events. This time we have to succeed. And I'm not talking about regulating the banks and increasing taxes on the rich, though that's important.

I am talking about changing the underlying values that govern our society. That is hard to fit into a single media-friendly demand, and it's also hard to figure out how to do it. But it is no less urgent for being difficult.

That is what I see happening in this square. In the way you are feeding each other, keeping each other warm, sharing information freely and providing healthcare, meditation classes and empowerment training. My favorite sign here says, 'I care about you.' In a culture that trains people to avoid each other's gaze, to say, 'Let them die,' that is a deeply radical statement.

A few final thoughts. In this great struggle, here are some things that don't matter:

§ What we wear.

§ Whether we shake our fists or make peace signs.

§ Whether we can fit our dreams for a better world into a media soundbite.

And here are a few things that do matter:

§ Our courage.

§ Our moral compass.

§ How we treat each other.

We have picked a fight with the most powerful economic and political forces on the planet. That's frightening. And as this movement grows from strength to strength, it will get more frightening. Always be aware that there will be a temptation to shift to smaller targets – like, say, the person sitting next to you at this meeting. After all, that is a battle that's easier to win.

Don't give in to the temptation. I'm not saying don't call each other on shit. But this time, let's treat each other as if we plan to work side by side in struggle for many, many years to come. Because the task before us will demand nothing less.

Let's treat this beautiful movement as if it is the most important thing in the world. Because it is. It really is. ◆

thenation.com/article/163844/occupy-wall-street-most-important-thing-world-now

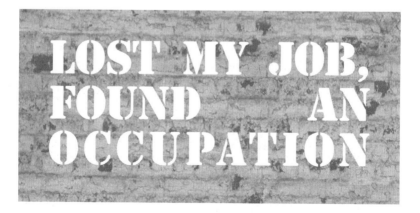

Media

Many public documents have circulated both within Occupy and in the news media more generally. These include declarations, statements of solidarity, and open letters to Occupy from movements abroad.

Under tremendous pressure to provide 'demands' to satisfy corporate media's limited imagination, OWS instead adopted a **Declaration of the Occupation of New York City** outlining principles and grievances. The process of drafting and arriving at consensus on this document was complicated and contentious, in particular around the question of how to articulate an anti-racist politics in the context of this emerging movement. Other declarations followed as the 'Occupy' label was used to focus an issue or name a thematic campaign. One of the first of these was **Occupy Student Debt**. Originating among students at notably expensive private universities, it addresses the cost of higher education across public and private sectors. In a different register, the queer camp at Occupy Baltimore produced the **Mortville Declaration of Independence**. The name of the camp, Mortville, is taken from the neoliberal queendom in John Waters' *Desperate Living*, where all 'must live in constant mortification' under a monarch who takes no responsibility for her subjects' 'income... living conditions, or... personal happiness', providing instead a spectacle for the amusement of tourists.

The **Council of Elders' Occupy Wall Street Statement of Solidarity** states what other veterans of previous US social movements had already expressed by their presence and participation in Occupy. This gathering of the 'architects of the nonviolent civil rights movements' of the 20th century publicly allied themselves with Occupy and urged the movement to develop in the tradition of the 'beloved community'. The Oakland General Strike of 2 November 2011 had strong support from organized labor in the Bay Area, officially or informally, depending on the political position of union staff members and in some cases the legal restrictions on members' actions. The **UAW Local 2865 Resolution in Support of Occupy Oakland General Strike**, from the local union branch representing graduate student employees at the University of California,

Berkeley, is one of the strongest official statements, explicitly recognizing the Occupy Oakland action as a formal picket line which no unionized workers should cross or disrupt. From a very different vantage-point, the **American Library Association's Occupy Wall Street Library Resolution** expresses its members' dismay at the destruction by the New York Police Department of the Occupy Wall Street Library, widely seen as one of the most important elements of the OWS encampment.

The Occupy/Decolonize movement has, likewise, received many statements of support from outside the US. The three included here are chosen because they make visible specific relationships between the US context of Occupy and other locations: the Zapatista uprising that marked the beginning of the US-initiated North American Free Trade Agreement; the Egyptian revolution against the US-funded regime of Hosni Mubarak; and the two decades of US sanctions and military occupation of Iraq frame these statements.

Declaration of the Occupation of New York City

Occupy Wall Street
29 September 2011

As we gather together in solidarity to express a feeling of mass injustice, we must not lose sight of what brought us together. We write so that all people who feel wronged by the corporate forces of the world can know that we are your allies.

As one people, united, we acknowledge the reality: that the future of the human race requires the co-operation of its members; that our system must protect our rights, and upon corruption of that system, it is up to the individuals to protect their own rights, and those of their neighbors; that a democratic government derives its just power from the people, but corporations do not seek consent to extract wealth from the people and the Earth; and that no true democracy is attainable when the process is determined by economic power. We come to you at a time when corporations, which place profit over people, self-interest over justice, and oppression over equality, run our governments. We have peaceably assembled here, as is our right, to let these facts be known.

They have taken our houses through an illegal foreclosure process, despite not having the original mortgage.

They have taken bailouts from taxpayers with impunity, and continue to give Executives exorbitant bonuses.

They have perpetuated inequality and discrimination in the workplace based on age, the color of one's skin, sex, gender identity and sexual orientation.

They have poisoned the food supply through negligence, and undermined the farming system through monopolization.

They have profited off of the torture, confinement, and cruel treatment of countless nonhuman animals, and actively hide these practices.

They have continuously sought to strip employees of the right to negotiate for better pay and safer working conditions.

They have held students hostage with tens of thousands of dollars of debt on education, which is itself a human right.

They have consistently outsourced labor and used that outsourcing as leverage to cut workers' healthcare and pay.

They have influenced the courts to achieve the same rights as people, with none of the culpability or responsibility.

They have spent millions of dollars on legal teams that look for ways to get them out of contracts in regards to health insurance.

They have sold our privacy as a commodity.

They have used the military and police force to prevent freedom of the press.

They have deliberately declined to recall faulty products endangering lives in pursuit of profit.

They determine economic policy, despite the catastrophic failures their policies have produced and continue to produce.

They have donated large sums of money to politicians supposed to be regulating them.

They continue to block alternate forms of energy to keep us dependent on oil.

They continue to block generic forms of medicine that could save people's lives in order to protect investments that have already turned a substantive profit.

They have purposely covered up oil spills, accidents, faulty bookkeeping, and inactive ingredients in pursuit of profit.

They purposefully keep people misinformed and fearful through their control of the media.

They have accepted private contracts to murder prisoners even when presented with serious doubts about their guilt.

They have perpetuated colonialism at home and abroad.

They have participated in the torture and murder of innocent civilians overseas.

They continue to create weapons of mass destruction in order to receive government contracts.*

To the people of the world,

We, the New York City General Assembly occupying Wall Street in Liberty Square, urge you to assert your power.

Exercise your right to peaceably assemble; occupy public space; create a process to address the problems we face, and generate solutions accessible to everyone.

To all communities that take action and form groups in the spirit of direct democracy, we offer support, documentation, and all of the

resources at our disposal.
Join us and make your voices heard! ◆

* These grievances are not all-inclusive.

occupywallst.org/forum/first-official-release-from-occupy-wall-street/

First announcement of core text:
nycga.net/2011/09/29/declaration-of-the-occupation-of-new-york-city/

Original approval in GA minutes:
nycga.net/2011/09/29/general-assembly-minutes-929-7pm/

Current official version:
nycga.net/resources/declaration/

Occupy Student Debt

21 November 2011

The Four Principles/Beliefs

Tuition-Free Public Higher Education

The single, largest step we could take to alleviate future student loan debt would be to guarantee tuition-free education for students enrolled at public colleges and universities.

Zero-Interest Student Loans

Student loans are not consumer loans, and they should not be packaged as if they were consumer credit debt.

Private Colleges Must Open Their Books

Students at private and for-profit universities and colleges have a fundamental right to know how their tuition dollars are being allocated and spent.

Student Debt Written Off In The Spirit of Jubilee

The student loan industry has profited from borrower vulnerability through predatory lending practices such as compounding interest rates, high collection fees, and few consumer protections.

Debtors' Pledge

As members of the most indebted generations in history, we pledge to stop making student loan payments after one million of us have signed this pledge.

Student loan debt, soon to top $1 trillion, is poisoning the pursuit of higher education. With chronic underemployment likely for decades to come, we will carry an intolerable burden into the future. The time has come to refuse this debt load. Debt distorts our educational priorities and severely limits our life options.

Education is not a commodity and it should not be a vehicle for generating debt, or profit for banks. Education at all levels – pre-K through PhD – is a right and a public good.

* We believe the federal government should cover the cost of tuition at public colleges and universities.

* We believe that any student loan should be interest-free.

* We believe that private and for-profit colleges and universities, which are largely financed through student debt, should open their books.

* We believe that the current student debt load should be written off.

In acknowledgment of these beliefs, I am signing the Debtors' Pledge of Refusal. ◆

occupystudentdebtcampaign.org/pledges/

occupystudentdebtcampaign.org/our-principles/

Forever a loan

The Mortville Declaration of Independence

5 October 2011

We, the people of Mortville, reject global capitalism and the consumer-based identities it imposes upon the populace. We acknowledge that race, class, gender and sexual orientation have been systematically transformed into marketing schemes to sell us our identities at the expense of the global poor and the human spirit. Mortville shall exist indefinitely as a laboratory in which we create recombinant personas from the detritus of corrupt corporate constructs. We shall embarrass capitalism by exposing its lies and subverting its strategy of spectacle. In the shadow of Urban Outfitters, we will illuminate the plight of those who toil in sweatshops to line the pockets of republican scum. We strive to alternately parody the excesses of consumer culture and set an example of living free of them. We declare the self-definition of glamor to be a human right and not a privilege of the 1%. Constantly reinventing ourselves as a hybrid of identities, we will look how we feel, say what we wish, fuck who we want, act as we should(n't), vogue like a queen, and walk like an Egyptian.

The first action of the un-government of Mortville shall be to impose economic sanctions upon the tyrannical regime of the status quo and its allies. Sanctions shall be lifted when the wealth is redistributed, the military industrial complex dismantled, the police disempowered, and the public sector fulfilling its obligations to the people. We demand education, housing, public transportation, dignified employment, energy that neither spoils our planet nor supports oppressive theocracies, abortions, human rights, arts programming, a secular and transparent democracy, free healthcare (including sex-change operations), and legal residency for all! Until our demands are met, we shall cast our glittery high-heeled sabots into the mechanism of complacency and laugh as the gears shatter! ◆

occupybmore.org/users/dazzlestorm/blog/queer-camp-mortville

Occupy Wall Street Statement of Solidarity

Council of Elders
20 November 2011

The Council of Elders, a newly organized, independent group of leaders from many of the defining American social-justice movements of the 20th century, declared today that we stand in basic solidarity with the national Occupy Wall Street movement and the committed young people who give guidance to this important quest for justice in the 21st century. We wish to explore every possible, helpful way in which we can connect together the continuing flame of the justice and democratizing movements of the 20th century with the powerful light of the emerging movements of the present time, reflected in the Occupy Wall Street initiatives.

As veterans of the Civil Rights, Women's, Peace, Environmental, LGBTQ, Immigrant Justice, labor rights and other movements of the last 60 years, we are convinced that Occupy Wall Street is a continuation, a deepening and expansion of the determination of the diverse peoples of our nation to transform our country into a more democratic, just and compassionate society – a more perfect union. We believe that the rapidly expanding and racialized impoverishment of our population, the rise of mass incarceration, the celebration of the culture of war and violence, all create the bitter divisions among the peoples of our nation and throughout the world. Indeed, we believe such developments among us ultimately diminish the quality of life for all humanity, beginning with our own children who watch as we lower the priority for their care and education.

We applaud the miraculous extent to which the Occupy initiative has been nonviolent and democratic, especially in light of the weight of violence under which the great majority of people are forced to live, including joblessness, foreclosures, unemployment, poverty, inadequate healthcare, etc. Among the Council of Elders, we place the highest value on the role of compassion and nonviolent action in our personal and organizational lives. From that hard-won grounding in the humanizing movements of the 20th century we seek to support and join with Occupy Wall Street in contributing to the dreams and visions of many in this nation for a beloved community, a multi-generational, multi-racial, compassionate, democratic society with equality, liberty and justice for all – always searching for partners in the creation of a more peaceful, sustainable world, a world with living, loving and growing space for all of our children. ◆

Council of Elders Organizing Committee
Rev James Lawson, Jr, Los Angeles, CA
Dr Vincent G Harding, Denver, CO
Rev Phillip Lawson, San Francisco, CA
Dolores Huerta, Bakersfield, CA
Dr Bernice Johnson Reagon, Washington, DC
Dr Grace Lee Boggs, Detroit, MI
Dr Gwendolyn Zoharah Simmons, Gainesville, FL
Sister Joan Chittister, OSB, Erie, PA
Marian Wright Edelman, Washington, DC
Rabbi Arthur Waskow, Philadelphia, PA
Rev Dr George (Tink) Tinker, Denver, CO
Rev John Fife, Tucson, AZ
Dr Mel White, Lynchburg, VA
Rev Nelson Johnson, Greensboro, NC
Joyce Hobson Johnson, Greensboro, NC

nationalcouncilofelders.com/statement.html

UAW Local 2865 Resolution in Support of Occupy Oakland General Strike

31 October 2011

Whereas UAW 2865 witnesses firsthand how the 1% (in the form of UC (University of California) Regents and top UC executives) conspire to steal ever more from students and workers through repeated tuition hikes, reduced services, layoffs, increased workloads, outsourcing and other austerity measures; and

Whereas we stand for the rights of all people to living wage jobs with affordable healthcare, quality education, a voice on the job, fair housing and a well-funded public sector, and

WHEREAS: Unemployment is the highest it has been since the Great Depression, and people are staying unemployed longer now than in the Great Depression, a third of California homes are underwater, a fifth of the foreclosures nationwide are in California, and San Franciscans alone have lost almost $6 billion in home value, costing their city over $74 million, and

WHEREAS: Occupy Wall Street is a people-powered movement that began on 17 September 2011 in Manhattan's Financial District, and has spread to over 100 cities in the United States and actions in over 1,500 cities globally. The movement is inspired by popular uprisings in Egypt and Tunisia, and the Wisconsin protests earlier this year, and aims to expose how the richest 1% of people are writing the rules of an unfair global economy that is foreclosing on our future, and

WHEREAS: Occupy Wall Street has galvanized public sentiment and a broad-based movement protesting the corrosive power of major banks and multinational corporations over the democratic process, and the role of Wall Street in creating an economic collapse that has caused the greatest recession in generations, and

WHEREAS: The National AFL-CIO and Change to Win coalitions have endorsed Occupy Wall Street, a growing number of trade union activists have joined this movement, both as individual workers, and as part of an increasing number of International and Local union contingents connecting their own fights to the larger demands of the movement for economic justice and fairness, and

WHEREAS: Union and Community organizations together have been working in coalition since the crash of the economy to force Banks to pay for public services and to renegotiate predatory loans with home owners, governments and non-profit agencies, and

WHEREAS: Public safety officers have used excessive force against peaceful protesters at Oscar Grant (Frank Ogawa) Plaza and violated their first amendment rights when more than 500 public safety officers with firearms aimed at the occupiers, tore down their tents in a predawn raid on 25 October; and

WHEREAS: Public safety officers on the evening of 25 October again used excessive force injuring and endangering the lives of demonstrators when they marched to protest the violence against the occupiers that morning;

THEREFORE BE IT RESOLVED that this union will encourage its members and allies to act in support of 2 November actions and honors as a 'Sanctioned Union Strike Line' Occupy Oakland and Occupy Wall Street, encourages union members and Local unions to participate in the movement, will actively support any unionized or non-unionized worker who refuses to break up, 'raid', or confiscate the belongings of protesters, and calls on unions representing DPW[1] workers to not participate in such activity, and

BE IT FURTHER RESOLVED that this union and its allies stand with our sisters and brothers of Occupy Wall Street, Occupy Oakland, and cities and towns across the country who are fed up with an unfair economy that works for 1% of Americans while the vast majority of people struggle to pay the bills, get an education, and raise their families, and

BE IT FURTHER RESOLVED that UAW 2865 recognizes that protest movements, like strike lines and organizing campaigns, do not have curfews, are not 9-5 activities, and in doing so UAW 2865 recognizes and will work to protect the right for Occupy Oakland to protest 24 hours a day, on-site and with proper protection including food, medical supplies, water, and tents, and

BE IT FURTHER RESOLVED that UAW 2865 has endorsed and will continue to endorse and turn out members to Occupy Oakland rallies and events, to provide in-kind donations like tents and food, and

BE IT FINALLY RESOLVED that UAW 2865 joins its sister unions in the UC Berkeley Labor Coalition in forwarding this resolution for adoption to other local unions and central labor bodies. ◆

uaw2865.org/?page_id=3964

1 Department of Public Works.

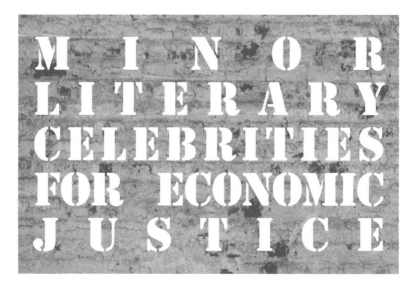

Occupy Wall Street Library Resolution

American Library Association
1 December 2011

American Library Association President Molly Raphael released the following statement regarding the destruction of the People's Library:

'The dissolution of a library is unacceptable. Libraries serve as the cornerstone of our democracy and must be safeguarded. An informed public constitutes the very foundation of a democracy, and libraries ensure that everyone has free access to information.

'The very existence of the People's Library demonstrates that libraries are an organic part of all communities. Libraries serve the needs of community members and preserve the record of community history. In the case of the People's Library, this included irreplaceable records and material related to the occupation movement and the temporary community that it represented.

'We support the librarians and volunteers of the Library Working Group as they re-establish the People's Library.'

Resolution in Support of the People's Library

Whereas; Libraries serve as a cornerstone of our democracy and must be safeguarded. An informed public constitutes the very foundation of a democracy, and public, academic, government, special, and particularly unofficially constituted or 'guerrilla' libraries ensure that every citizen has free access to a wide range of information.

Whereas; The Occupy Wall Street (OWS) People's Library in New York City's Zuccotti Park served as an example of a 'guerrilla' library as well as a reminder that libraries are an organic part of all communities, not just those that are officially sanctioned by larger institutions such as governments or businesses.

Whereas; Libraries serve the needs of community members and preserve the record of community history.

Whereas; In the case of the People's Library, this includes irreplaceable records and archival material related to the OWS movement and the temporary community that it represents. Every library collection is entitled to exist and be protected regardless of supporters or detractors.

Whereas; We support the librarians and volunteers of the OWS movement Library Working Group as they re-establish the People's Library.

Be it resolved; The American Library Association deplores the destruction of the OWS movement People's Library, all libraries, all library collections and property, and the disruption of the educational purpose by that act, whether it be done by governments or governmental agencies, individuals or groups of individuals and whether it be in the name of honest dissent, the desire to control or limit thought or ideas, or for any other purpose. ◆

connect.ala.org/node/160826

Solidarity Statement
We walk by asking, we reclaim by Occupying

jóvenes en resistencia alternativa
13 November 2011

Comrades,

A few days ago, we sent out this letter inviting comrades in Mexico to join our campaign in solidarity with the Occupy Oakland movement, in California, USA. On 20 November, the Oakland Commune celebrated its one-month birthday, and in the past few weeks this movement has emerged as an important site of autonomous resistance and organization, in a city emblematic with a strong legacy of militancy and anti-capitalist activism. After the first attempt by the police to evict the camp on 25 October, thousands took to the streets marching in protest and the police responded with brutal repression, using 'chemical weapons' against the protesters. On 26 October, following a second march, at the General Assembly of Occupy Oakland, 3,000 people approved a call for a General Strike on 2 November. The Oakland General Strike on 2 November (the first in the city since 1946) was an overwhelming success, blockading the Port of Oakland, with more than 50,000 people participating. Since then, the Occupy Oakland movement continues to resist, alongside related movements throughout the world, and we are very concerned by the possibility of another eviction attempt and more repression in the coming days. For these reasons, we feel it is extremely important to send this message of solidarity to our comrades on the Other Side of the border, to show our support.

Saludos rebeldes,
jóvenes en resistencia alternativa

To the Peoples of the World
To the Occupy Movement
To the Oakland Commune
To Our Sisters and Brothers in Struggle on the Other Side of the Border

We don't need to remind you of the deep connections between Wall Street, Gringo Capitalism and our Mexican misery. From Imperialist wars to the initial experiments in agrobiotechnology, Mexico has been the principal landscape for offensives by northern capital. We have participated and continue to, in the uprising of the Zapatistas against the neoliberal attack of NAFTA.[1] The uprising which set the spark for the movement against neoliberalism. We met each other at the summits of Seattle, Prague, Genoa, Miami and Cancún. We met each other through a great global conversation.

It's been a long time since we fought together in the movement against neoliberalism and the world has changed since those times. Today the narco war is devastating our society. As two sides of the same coin, on one side we have the narco and on the other the militarization of the country. These two faces are crushing us from both sides. Although it seems like they fight, they are both at the service of capital and in the modern world local capital is connected in a strong fashion to global capital. In the last few months we have learned these connections between Wall Street and narco money. According to one analysis, narco money was the liquid capital necessary to rescue the banking sector from the initial hits of the financial crisis in 2008.[2]

Further, the huge quantity of drug profits needs a laundromat just as large. Although we don't have a detailed balance, we know that Wall Street facilitates this laundering. For example, according to the US justice department, one bank, Wachovia, laundered $378 billion narco dollars from Mexico between only 2004 and 2007. This bank fell and ironically was acquired by Wells Fargo, the same bank which still has the salaries of our fathers and grandfathers who worked in the *bracero* program. The same bank which funds detention centers for immigrants where our brothers and sisters die only trying to provide for their families.

But in Mexico there isn't only the cultivation of misery. Here we drew one of the first lines of struggle against global capitalism in our laboratory of resistance. With humility in front of you, our comrades, we would like to tell of our experience. Encampments and occupations are common in Mexico and comrades joke about the lack of space to put up more encampments. But this isn't by chance and was won through struggle.

One recent example: in 2006, in the state of Oaxaca, the local teachers' union set up an encampment in the center of Oaxaca City during their annual collective bargaining. One morning, on 14 June, the state police tried to take down the camp of the teachers and the city rose up, they not only retook the plaza but kicked the police out of the city. The Commune of Oaxaca was born on this day and the following six months transformed Oaxaca and the participants in the uprising.

Like you, they also had problems of repression and representation. Against the repression they put up thousands of barricades each night to protect the population from the murderous paramilitaries of Governor Ulises Ruiz, who they struggled to kick out. Against the lying representation of the media, they took over their television and radio studios, collectivized the resources and began to have conversations that had never been had by those means.

We are following closely everything that is happening in Oakland. The police kill youth like Oscar Grant and gravely injure anti-war veterans such as Scott Olsen. The media lies about the popular participation in the movement and they propagate superficial divisions. The self-defense and self-representation of our movements are essential to our collective struggle. We invite you to learn from our experiences and we hope to learn from yours. Together and in concert we are toppling this miserable system.

In our stories you will see your story.
We Walk by Asking, We Reclaim by Occupying.
From Mexico with total support for Occupy Oakland. ◆

SIGNED:
jóvenes en resistencia alternativa
Universidad de la Tierra en Oaxaca, AC
Colectivo Radio Zapatista
Regeneración Radio
Colectivo Cordyceps
Colectivo Noticias de la Rebelion
Amig@s de Mumia de Mexico
Furia de las Calles
El Centro Cultural La Piramide
Marea Creciente México (Capítulo del red internacional por justícia climática Rising Tide)
Konvergencia Gráfica
Sublevarte Collective
Hacklab Autónomo
El Enemigo Común
Centro Social Okupado 'Casa Naranja'
Gustavo Esteva, Oaxaca, México
Bocafloja, DF, México

Patricia Westendarp, Querétaro, México
Alejandro Reyes Arias, Chiapas, México
José Rabasa, México
Cristian Guerrero, México

elenemigocomun.net/2011/11/mexican-solidarity-occupy-oakland/

1 North American Free Trade Area. 2 See the article by James Petrus at
saboteamos.info/2011/05/26/imperialismo-banqueros-guerra-de-la-droga-y-genoc

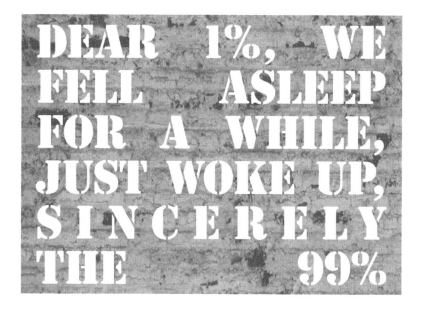

Message of Solidarity to Occupy Wall Street

Organization of Women's Freedom in Iraq
3 November 2011

Dear Occupy Wall Street,

The people of the world are watching you, following your news and hoping that – rather than just vent your anger and frustration – you achieve all of your dreams.

While democracy should guarantee all people an equal say in the decisions that affect their lives, you find yourselves forced to take to the streets, as politicians and bankers make decisions behind closed doors and hire an army of police to send you back home with nothing.

While a wealthy 1% ravages your jobs, health, and very lives, their focus is always on their banks and not on the welfare and future of innocent, unsuspecting millions of people. In times of growth, those banks are sustained by your labor, resulting in extravagant luxuries for the 1%; while their economic failures and crises deny you basic resources and economic rights.

This is the same 1% that pursued the war on Iraq without hearing the millions who marched – in the United States and around the world – expressing their opposition. While claiming democracy, the 1% builds vast armies to be launched not just against people all over the world, but also within their own borders.

A second wave of global revolutions has begun as the 99% (that is, the global working class) rejects the tyranny, marginalization and poverty which capitalist authoritarian governments force onto billions of us. Despite all claims of representation, capitalist states make the people pay the price of the economic failures of their political systems with unemployment and government cuts, while the banks get bailed out by the same resources that people's toil has created. Avoiding the poverty and starvation of billions is never the concern of these so-called democracies as much as the stability of their own political rule. Moreover, that same 1% recreates the same failing model of 'democratic' capitalist political structures in newly invaded countries around the globe.

The so-called democracy of Iraq, created by the Western capitalist states, divides Iraqi oil reserves between the 1% politicians and a massive, newly built army, which is now well trained to crush Iraq's Tahrir Square demonstrations (active since 25 February), with live ammunition, torture and beatings. While the 99% of Iraqis seethe with anger, waiting for the right conditions to claim what is theirs, they eagerly follow your progress in occupying Wall Street, as our enemy is one whether they are American or Iraqi. That enemy is the 1% of ruthless exploiters.

Although plans of US withdrawal from Iraq have been publicized worldwide, we are certain that US bases will remain around our cities and villages in one form or another, fully ready to attack and crush any popular uprising, whenever deemed necessary. Although the US administration has already installed Iraqis to maintain systems of inequality and suppression in Iraq, they will continue to keep their military arsenals on full guard for a worst-case scenario. This is what our newly installed democracy grants us: poverty, inequality, suppression of dissent and a lack of civil liberties for the vast majority of the people, especially women.

People of the world have come to refuse a culture of wars and also the 'democracy' of the rich. It is time for a political system of equal wealth for all, in other words, a socialist system, where free-market rules cannot starve billions while filling the pockets of a few. Connecting such a movement globally was beyond even the wildest dreams of most visionaries, but has proven to be within reach in 2011. And your #Occupy movement has played a leading role in igniting it.

While hunger and wars are planned and organized by a ruthless 1%, it is the responsibility of the 99% to create a better world, built on values of humanity, equality and prosperity for all. In this world, decision-making will not be taken by World Banks, capitalists, and their representative statesmen, but by the immediate representatives of the working class.

Putting demands to the 1% is not the solution, as they have failed repeatedly and can only proceed with their methods of starving working people and bringing on more economic failures.

The time has come for a second step. After occupying the street, it is time to break into the castles and palaces of the 1%, and claim what is rightfully yours, to start a new era based on global peace, equal division of wealth, and humanity.

We stand behind you and carry on our continuous resistance to the rule of the 1% in Iraq, Syria, Egypt, Tunisia, Yemen and the entire world.

Long live the struggles of the 99%, and down with the 1%! ◆

Yannar Mohammad
Organization of Women's Freedom in Iraq

jadaliyya.com/pages/index/3048/message-of-solidarity-to-occupy-wall-street-from-t

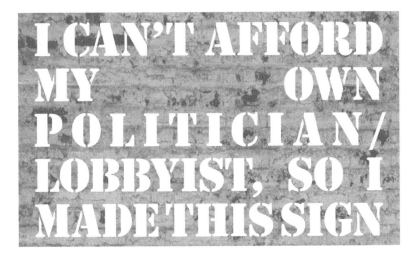

Response to OWS Egypt Delegation Proposal

Comrades from Cairo
13 November 2011

Note from the editors of In Front and Center: On 10 November, the General Assembly of Occupy Wall Street passed a proposal (see the minutes here[1]) allocating $29,000 to send an OWS solidarity delegation to Egypt on 25 November to monitor the upcoming elections. Each working group was then contacted and asked to nominate two representatives to go on this trip. Many urgent and important questions and concerns have since been raised. We are republishing a letter from activists in Cairo expressing their deep concern with this decision the GA made.

To our kindred occupiers in Zuccotti Park.

When we called out to you, requesting you join us on 12 November in defending our revolution and in our campaign against the military trial of civilians in Egypt, your solidarity – pictures from marches, videos, and statements of support – added to our strength.

However, we recently received news that your General Assembly passed a proposal authorizing $29,000 to send 20 of your number to Egypt as election monitors. Truth be told, the news rather shocked us; we spent the better part of the day simply trying to figure out who could have asked for such assistance on our behalf.

We have some concerns with the idea, and we wanted to join your conversation.

It seems to us that you have taken to the streets and occupied your parks and cities out of a dissatisfaction with the false promises of the game of electoral politics, and so did our comrades in Spain, Greece and Britain. Regardless of how one stands on the efficacy of elections or elected representatives, the Occupy movement seems outside the scope of this; your choice to occupy is, if nothing else, bigger than any election. Why then, should our elections be any cause for celebration, when even in the best of all possible worlds they will be just another supposedly 'representative' body ruling in the interest of the 1%

over the remaining 99% of us? This new Egyptian parliament will have effectively no powers whatsoever, and – as many of us see it – its election is just a means of legitimating the ruling junta's seizure of the revolutionary process. Is this something you wish to monitor?

We have, all of us around the world, been learning new ways to represent ourselves, to speak, to live our politics directly and immediately, and in Egypt we did not set out to the streets in revolution simply to gain a parliament. Our struggle – which we think we share with you – is greater and grander than a neatly functioning parliamentary democracy; we demanded the fall of the regime, we demanded dignity, freedom and social justice, and we are still fighting for these goals. We do not see elections of a puppet parliament as the means to achieve them.

But even though the idea of election monitoring doesn't really do it for us, we want your solidarity, we want your support and your visits. We want to know you, talk with you, learn one another's lessons, compare strategies and share plans for the future. We think that activists or as people committed to serious change in the systems we live in, there is so much more that we can do together than legitimizing electoral processes (leave that boring job to the Carter Foundation) that seem so impoverished next to the new forms of democracy and social life we are building. It should be neither our job nor our desire to play the game of elections; we are occupying and we should build our spaces and our networks because they themselves are the basis on which we will build the new. Let us deepen our lines of communication and process and discover out what these new ways of working together and supporting one another could be.

Any time you do want to come over, we've got plenty of comfy couches available. It won't be fancy, but it will be fun. ◆

Yours, as always, in solidarity,
Comrades from Cairo

infrontandcenter.wordpress.com/2011/11/14/comrades-from-cairo-respond-to-ows-egypt-delegation/

1 http://nin.tl/HerBod

Library

Bound together by their impressionistic, casual tone, these accounts of Occupy sites report on conversations taking place around the country, on what people thought about their local Occupy movements – on the 'sonic structure of belonging'.

As **Barbara Kingsolver**'s 'Another American Way' makes clear, in Johnson City, Tennessee, as in many small cities across the US, local political traditions and regional culture shape and strengthen the Occupy movement, and give 'the 99%' a particular resonance. While media accounts of the early days of OWS puzzled endlessly over the relationship between movement participants and 'the public', **Angus Johnston**'s account of conversations at a deli near the Liberty Plaza encampment suggests that, as much as anything else, Occupy provides a vocabulary for already existing views. As **Adrienne Maree Brown**'s blog posts explain, the Occupy/ Decolonize movement has grown through extended interaction between sites as individuals travel from place to place, metaphors circulate and compelling actions inspire emulation. Writing to Detroit from New York City and Oakland, and then from Detroit after returning home, Brown follows what has become a standard narrative trajectory for participant writers on Occupy, from initial skepticism to partial reassurance, to excitement and lingering concern for the movement's future. The collective letter to the first General Assembly of Occupy Detroit, which she presents, reiterates that skepticism and hope, drawing on Detroit's powerful history as a 'Movement City' and its recent experience of 'life AFTER capitalism'. **Keguro Macharia**'s description of Occupy DC, by contrast, is punctuated with allusions to Kibera, an unauthorized urban settlement in Nairobi whose impoverished population is often used to stand in for ideas of African overpopulation and underdevelopment. His notes on 'voice and space' capture the harmonies and dissonances of Occupy and the potential for a 'sonic structure of belonging'. Oakland-based **Jaime Omar Yassin** has provided some of the most continuous reportage and analysis of a single Occupy site. On Day Four at Frank Ogawa/Oscar Grant Park in Oakland, two questions are on his mind: the racial and class composition of the encampment and the danger of co-optation by organizations committed to liberal electoral politics.

Another American Way

Barbara Kingsolver
18 November 2011

When I went looking for Occupy Johnson City, Tennessee, the spiky profile of pickets and placards struck my eye first, and then the people underneath them, but it did not look like a global uprising *per se*, just an orderly crowd in a parking lot. But a crowd, there's a sight, in a town where people mostly drive-thru or drive on. I saw some American flags and a sign that said 'God Hates Banks' and figured this had to be it. From across the street I heard one person say a few words at a time, repeated by the crowd in the unmistakable 'from this day forward…' cadence of a wedding or a swearing-in, and again I wasn't sure I was in the right place. As it turned out, the call and response was the people's microphone, famously re-invented in New York to subvert the ban on amplifiers. Here in Tennessee it sounds like people taking vows. Repeat as one: men in UMW[1] jackets, farmers in their town clothes, college kids, retired schoolteachers, young couples pushing strollers, the wilderness guide in a kilt, the homeless man with the sign in Latin. Really the temptation was to ask any given person, what is the story? Because there is one.

This is Appalachia, home of the forested Cumberland and Wildwood Flower and NASCAR and 18 per cent unemployment and bless your heart. Home of mountaintop removal, wherein coal companies find it profitable to tear the earth's own flesh from its bones and leave the stunned, uprooted living to contemplate drinking poison, in the literal sense. Birthplace of the Blair Mountain rebellion, where underpaid labor ran up against big capital in an insurrection unlike any other this country has known. That was in 1921, and by many accounts the approval rating of big capital here has not improved. Just this month, a dispassionate Wall Street analysis ranked us the fifth-poorest region in the land. The people's microphone in this context sounds like a tent revival. It took twice as long to say anything, but induced full participation, which is also very southern, come to think of it.

At length we agreed to march ourselves down State of Franklin Street, and as we stretched across block after block of stopped traffic, people in their pickups and dinged-up station wagons and gas-conscious sedans honked and cheered to see our 'tax greed' signs, and did not advise us to get a job or a haircut. The orthodox objections have grown ridiculous. Every system on earth has its limits. We have never been here before, not right here exactly, you and me together in the golden and gritty places all at once, on deadline, no fooling around this time, no longer walking politely around the dire colossus, the so-called American Way of consecrated corporate profits and crushed public compassion. There is another American way. This is the right place, we found it. On State of Franklin we yelled until our throats hurt that we were the 99% because that's just it. We are. ◆

occupywriters.com/works/by-barbara-kingsolver

1 United Mine Workers

What I Saw at #OccupyWallStreet Last Night, and What I Saw When I Left

Angus Johnston
29 September 2011

So last night I wandered down to Occupy Wall Street for the second time. I'd visited the night before, and been impressed – impressed by the richness of the space, impressed by the process and enthusiasm of the general assembly. I wasn't (and I'm still not) sure what it all adds up to, but I found it invigorating and compelling. So I went back.

I spent some time strolling around, talking to people and checking out what was happening. I ate some free food. I sat in on a workshop on building democratic structures in progressive organizations. I compared notes with a couple of friends who were there.

And then the general assembly got started. The evening GA is a decision-making meeting, but it's also a place where lots of announcements get made – OWS has a lot of working groups on issues ranging from first aid to legal support to action planning, and the GA is where they all check in. I'd sat through all those announcements the previous night, and been mostly fascinated, but it was less compelling the second time through and the pavement was cold and hard, so after a while I figured I'd stretch my legs a bit and circle back in time for the meat of the meeting.

So I took a stroll through the neighborhood, and wound up at a deli that was open and had comfortable seating in the front. I bought a beer for a couple of bucks and sat down to check my email and read a few pages of the book I'd brought.

There was a young woman at the register, paying for a soda and chatting with the counter guy about the Occupy Wall Street protests – she worked in the neighborhood and was on her way to check them out for the first time. I didn't catch much of what she said, but when the counter guy made a comment about Eisenhower, I listened... and tweeted:

@studentactivism: Counterman at a deli 3 blocks from #OccupyWallStreet just quoted Ike's warning on the military industrial complex.

'And Eisenhower was a general.' I remember the guy saying. 'A general.'

A few minutes later I tweeted this:
@studentactivism: 'The government has become the puppet of the big corporations.' – The same deli guy. #OccupyWallStreet

And this:
@studentactivism: #OccupyWallStreet. It's not just for dirty hippies anymore.

And this:
@studentactivism: 'Ordinary folks are getting dicked.' – Same deli guy #OccupyWallStreet

I was tweeting all this, by the way, not because it struck me as strange, but because it struck me as so ordinary – while at the same time so at odds with dominant narratives of the Occupy Wall Street protests. (And not just those in the big media, those in the look-down-your-nose left, too.) New York City is a left-liberal city. It's a city that went for Obama over McCain by an 85-15 margin. It's a city whose majority white districts went for Obama 2-to-1. It's a city where what passes for reactionary is Staten Island, where Obama took 47 per cent of the vote. To hear this middle-aged white guy saying this stuff didn't surprise me at all.
But I kept listening.

@studentactivism: 'I buy you a beer today, you buy me a beer tomorrow. That's the only way it's gonna work.' – The OTHER deli guy #OccupyWallStreet

The other guy behind the counter was younger, and black. The woman who'd started the conversation had long since moved on, but a couple of regulars had taken up positions with their own beers at a table in front and the discussion was rolling on.

@studentactivism: Now the black deli guy is holding forth on the need for cross-racial class solidarity. #OccupyWallStreet #NotJoking

I wish I'd transcribed more of this, but by the time I thought to try to write down what I hadn't tweeted, most of it was gone. I do remember him saying 'some guys are all "The niggers! The spics!" But niggers contribute to the economy too. Faggots too.'

He repeated the bit about faggots for emphasis, looking around, kind of hoping that someone would say something he could correct. But by now the four of them were all enthusiastically agreeing to everything, egging each other on.

@studentactivism: Black deli guy: 'Everybody said "Obama's gonna get shot". Nah. He plays the game.' #OccupyWallStreet

This was, I think, in response to the white deli guy saying that no American president in half a century had ever taken the interests of ordinary people seriously.

I'd bought a second beer at some point along the way, but by now it was kicked. As I was about to head out, I piped up for the first time. 'You guys are killing me,' I said. The white counter guy grinned. 'I thought the meeting was up there,' I said, pointing in the vague direction of the plaza.

@studentactivism: Me: 'I thought the meeting was up there.' Deli guy: 'We've been saying this for 30 years.' #OccupyWallStreet

We talked for a few minutes more. None of the four of them had been up to the protest, it sounded like, at least not to do more than walk by and check it out on the fly, so I shared some of my impressions. We did the enthusiastically-agreeing-with-each-other bonding thing for a few minutes. We all agreed that the protest was a lovely development. Then one of the guys sitting at the front table said 'But what's their plan?'

I said I'd gotten the impression that people there had a lot of different ideas about what needed to be done, and that I wasn't sure they were all going to agree on an agenda for change any time soon. Then I said that I wasn't sure that was a bad thing.

I said it seemed like pretty much everyone there basically agreed on certain basic principles – that something was seriously broken in the American economy, that something was seriously broken in American politics, and that an accelerating concentration of wealth and power in the hands of a small minority was at the root of most of that brokenness. People differed on how to address that problem, I said, but they all pretty much agreed about what the problem was, that it needed to be tackled, and that it wasn't really being tackled now.

I was struck by the 'what's their plan' question in a few ways. First, because it was the first even vaguely critical comment about OWS I'd heard in the whole discussion – for half an hour these guys had been been talking about and around the protests, and everything they'd said was emphatically positive. Second, because it wasn't asked in a spirit of attack but a spirit of curiosity, and maybe gentle prodding – a central premise of the conversation I'd snooped on was that there's no obvious fix for what's gone wrong. For many on the chattering left 'what's their plan' is the rhetorical lead-up to a dismissal, as if it's the job of 500 strangers in a park to come up with a concrete step-by-step proposal for reforming (or overthrowing) global capitalism. But here it wasn't that. Here it was a real question: 'What can be done?'

If Occupy Wall Street is as marginal as its liberal-left critics assume, then no answer to the guy at the table's question would make any sense at all. Five hundred strangers in a park will never themselves be the engines of any profound societal transformation. But if what I saw last night is real, if OWS is offering a critique that resonates in content – if not necessarily in form – with a broader and more eclectic swath of the country, then maybe those 500 strangers are pounding on a door that's a bit less well-armored than it looks.

Maybe what they have to offer isn't a plan so much as an opportunity to have a bigger conversation, or even just an invitation to continue and expand a conversation that's been going on in small ways in small places for a long time.

And that's a conversation I'm really eager to see continue. ◆

studentactivism.net/2011/09/29/what-i-saw-at-occupywallstreet-last-night/

from liberty plaza; let it breathe

Adrienne Maree Brown
9 October 2011

yesterday I got to liberty plaza, finally.

since it came to my attention I have been making my way towards it, wanting to see it and feel it myself, though with some trepidation. I tend to roll with a critical crowd, and I have to work hard sometimes to keep my heart open when there are lots of critical questions sitting there for me to ask:

is it a bunch of privileged white kids?
is it stinky dropouts?
is it a mash-up of wingnut messaging?
is it our tame tahrir square?
or…
is it the decentralized movement we have been awaiting?
is it safe for queer people, people of color, for me?
is it rooted with existing movements for economic justice?
I had to know.

so I went. getting off the train at wall street there is immediately a little hand-written taped-up piece of paper pointing towards zuccotti park. first I walked around the perimeter, lined with people facing outward with signs, taking in the love, admiration, disrespect, insults and ignorance of the passers-by with a generally curious and calm presence.

I wound my way through the inner park, taking in all the systems and offerings and community there, as well as hundreds of others like myself, come to see and feel this massive cultural happening. I saw a few folks I knew, but they were also there seeing how to plug in. that excited me.

what I felt there was a resounding yes, yes to all of my questions, and many more.

more precisely, what I felt was the surge of energy I used to get at a march, realizing that there were so many people wanting change, people who had walked completely different pathways to reach the same conclusion that they were willing to give their precious life-force to changing the systems of our time.

this has the potential to be deeper, because it feels less fleeting, less temporary, less spectacle. marches have left me feeling so unheard for so long.

here, I noticed the wingnut messaging, and the whiteness... and yet I felt close to tears a few times, seeing unexpected diversity in the crowd, seeing the self-organized systems emerging for creation of art, sharing of information, health and wellness. there was even a table of 'coaches' to help people figure out what their role in the movement could be.

no one is special, and everyone is needed.

to speak to the whiteness of the crowd, I actually felt moved to see so many white people, very normal-looking white people, standing around the edges of this park looking liberated themselves, holding up signs that criticize capitalism.

some were speaking from their privilege, and others from their own economic struggles. but to have masses of white people in the streets talking about the economy with a progressive decentralized grassroots perspective, and have it not be the tea party, is a tipping-point signal.

the crises are becoming clear even to those not being directly oppressed, or those directly organizing. and people are ready to stand up and dream of something different.

and yes of course it would be amazing to see even more people of color there.

my sense was that we need only show up, in whatever capacity we can, and there we will be. there is also a case to be made for white privileged folks sleeping in the park to hold space for people of color and poor folks who may not have the luxury to drop work and do so, but are in alignment. solidarity can look so many different ways.

it's movement.

I have been in movement spaces for a long time, and we have a way of doing things which is so steeped in critique that I have often wondered if we would strangle movement before it could blossom. sometimes I think we put up the critiques to excuse ourselves from getting involved, and sometimes I think we do it to protect our hearts from getting broken if it doesn't work out. critique, alone, can keep us from having to pick up the responsibility of figuring out solutions. sometimes I think we need to liberate ourselves from critique, both internal and external, to truly give change a chance.

the major critique I have heard of this effort is the lack of demands, and multitude of messages.

my thought so far is, humans have a multitude of cares, of passions… trying to lockstep us into one predictable way of being is the essential desire of corporations, because if you can predict what people will want and do, then you can profit off of coming up with appropriate products and activities for them. this movement is instead making it as easy as possible to enter, no matter what passion brought you to the square.

and in terms of the demands, it seems the central demand is to build and expand a conversation that is long overdue in this country, a conversation which doesn't have simple cut and dry demands. we are realizing that we must become the systems we need – no government, political party or corporation is going to care for us, so we have to remember how to care for each other.

and that will take time, and commitment, a willingness to step outside of the comfort of the current and lean into the unknown, together. to listen to each other across all real and perceived divides.

I have heard stories of folks having issues, bringing them to general assembly, and being able to shift the process, even as newcomers. I have seen random people call for the people's microphone, and others – including myself – jump in to spread the message, regardless of the message.

the whole thing seems so utterly not produced, not micromanaged, and not acting from a place of crisis which excuses top down elitist decision-making processes – not rushing itself.

I see this as a natural evolution from conversations and gatherings and organizing that has been building for years, call and response across time from the battle in Seattle, the street forums that take analysis beyond the choir.

it's taken a long time to get to this place. now it's time to let the fruit burst on our tongues and savor the flavor of something tangible that we grew with our courage to hold the line against the inhumanity of corporate greed. let's spend less time on the imperfection of the process, and more time articulating and crystallizing our lessons.

liberty square is important. the call to occupy wall street is important.

and like any anti-Zionist American with an analysis of imperialism here at home and abroad, I am not a fan of the proliferation of events that are naming themselves 'occupy "insert city"'. I get it. we are going to occupy America with justice, to take up the space of being in this country, in these cities and in these banks, be vocal occupants of this place, reshaping it to something that yields solidarity in place of shame.

I love the other options I am hearing: 'decolonize "insert city"', 'occupy within' and 'foreclose "insert institution"'.

it feels spacious. it feels like something you can do, no matter where you are, by authentically applying yourself to the changes you wish to see. at liberty plaza it is a physical occupation. in Detroit it may be a massive redistribution of food and shelter resources heading into the winter. tomorrow I will get to see what it looks like in Oakland.

don't sit this out. it has room for you. find out, start, or help shape what is happening in your town.[1]

11 October 2011

moved to write more…

just home from occupy Oakland, and hearing reports from the first general assembly meeting in Detroit. last night I heard from folks who had gone to check out occupy SF, and I am following the budding of several cities in their parallel efforts.

in each instance there are various levels of excitement and disappointment.
there is such urgency in the multitude of crises we face, it can make it hard to remember that in fact it is urgency thinking (urgent constant unsustainable growth) that got us to this point, and that our potential success lies in doing deep, slow, intentional work.
we need to go beyond having a critique/counter analysis/alternate systemic plan for society – we have to actually DO everything differently, aligned with a different set of core principles for existence[…]

occupy wall street didn't start off as big as it is now, it started small and built community, cultural norms and communication… and it's still building.

the challenge in other cities is that we are all starting off with a lot more people at the table with ideas and directions and agendas to push.

that means time spent on getting a clear decision-making process in place will be worth every second in the long run.

that means facilitators skilled in consensus and synthesis have an important role to play.
that means that individuals and organized bodies with all variety of experiences are showing up, and we have to humble ourselves to value all contributions, from the newest people to the most organized professionalized folks.

that means our socialized practices to control each other and compete are going to emerge, and we have to be attentive and accountable as we try to open ourselves to something larger than our particular formation or analysis.

that means we can do, be, and create whatever we want to see, knowing ours is one effort in the midst of many, and the multitude is where our power lies[…]

another lesson I observed from the people's mic experience at occupy wall street: if someone called for the mic, they were granted it. but if people weren't feeling the statement, eventually they stopped repeating it.

I shared that observation with Jenny Lee from allied media, and she observed that, in a way, twitter has prepped us for this succinct and self-selected rebroadcasting of each other.

and just like with the people's mic, and our social media efforts, what we pay attention to grows. let's cultivate the movement we want, and leave space for others to do the same.
there's room. let it breathe. ◆

adriennemareebrown.net/blog/2011/10/09/from-liberty-plaza/

adriennemareebrown.net/blog/2011/10/11/let-it-breathe/

1 See at occupytogether.org

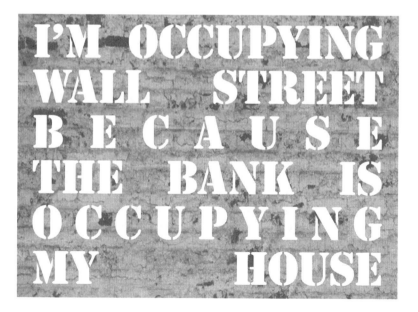

One Step in Building the 'Occupy/Unify' Movement in Detroit

Adrienne Maree Brown, Jenny Lee, Yusef Shakur, et al.
18 October 2011

as detroit began having conversations around what occupy efforts could look like here, it sparked conversations and self-reflection about our distinctions of movement and community. this letter was drafted on a pirate pad and collectively edited and signed onto by tons of detroiters – it is a living document which continues to be tweaked.

as the process continues to unfold, and unity continues to develop in the movement here, i feel that this is a powerful touchstone of the values being cultivated in detroit, and could potentially be a useful model for folks working to articulate their unique iteration of this international phenomenon, rooting it in history and current events at the most local level. thanks to yusef shakur and jenny lee for taking the first steps on this!

To the first General Assembly of Occupy Detroit,

We are inspired by the actions of Occupy Wall Street and the opportunity it has given so many people to stand up and get involved in shaping the fate of this country.

We are inspired by the protocol of consensus decision-making and inclusivity being used on Wall Street, where anyone who shows up is asked: 'What can you contribute to this movement?' In return, participants are supported to bring their best selves to the work of creating a new world. We propose that Detroit embrace that same protocol.

In the spirit of bringing our best selves to this process, we offer this background knowledge, which anyone attempting to organize in Detroit must first understand before taking any action that aims to speak for Detroit. We all have a lot to learn from each other. Nothing said here should be taken as a claim to 'know more' or 'better' than anyone else. As just mentioned, it's about all of us bringing our best selves to this historic uprising, and doing it creatively, nonviolently and together.

Detroit is a Movement City. Detroiters have been organizing resistance to corporate greed, violence and oppression for nearly a century; from the birth of the labor movement here in the 1920s to the radical black workers' movements of the '60s to the current poor people campaigns against utility shutoffs that allow dozens of people to die each year. We have organized resistance to racism, sexism, homophobia, Islamophobia, ableism and the criminalization of youth, to the systematic destruction of the environment in poor communities of color, to the dehumanization of people with disabilities, and so many other injustices – as they manifest in our daily lives and are reflected in practices that dictate access and distribution of resources, as well as policies at the local, state and national levels.

Detroit is moving beyond just protest. Because we have survived the most thorough disinvestment of capital that any major US city has ever seen; because we have survived 'white flight' and 'middle-class flight,' state takeovers, corruption and the dismantling of our public institutions; because the people who remained in Detroit are resilient and ingenious, Detroiters have redefined what 'revolution' looks like.

Detroit is modeling life AFTER capitalism. In Detroit, 'revolution' means 'putting the neighbor back in the hood' through direct actions that restore community. It means maintaining public welfare programs for residents who are without income which protect said low-income families from facing utility shutoffs and homelessness. It means outlawing poverty in any form since the resources to prevent such a condition remain abundantly available to this state. It means Peace Zones for Life that help us solve conflict in our neighborhoods without the use of police, reducing opportunities for police violence. It means food justice and digital justice networks across the city supporting self-determination and community empowerment. It means youth leadership programs and paradigm-shifting education models that transform the stale debate between charter schools and public schools. It means 'eviction reversals' that put people back in their homes and community safety networks that prevent people being snatched up by border patrol. It means artists who facilitate processes of community visioning and transformation, and organizers who approach social change as a work of art. In Detroit, the meaning of 'revolution' continues to evolve and grow.

Detroit will not be 'occupied' in the same sense as Wall Street. The language of 'occupation' makes sense for the occupation of the privately owned Zuccotti Park on Wall Street. But this language of 'occupation' will not inspire participation in Detroit and does not make sense for Detroit. From the original theft of Detroit's land by French settlers from Indigenous nations, to the connotations of 'occupation' for Detroit's Arab communities, to the current gentrification of Detroit neighborhoods and its related violence – 'Occupation' is not what we need more of. We will, however, participate in creating anew out of what remains in Detroit today.

Detroit's participation in the 'Occupy Together' actions must grow out of Detroit's own rich soil. It cannot be transplanted from another city's context. We recognize that 'Occupy Detroit' has attracted the participation of people from across the state of Michigan. This is a good thing, IF people take the time to understand the unique history and current work of Detroit's social movements. This letter aims to be a starting-point in that process. The reimagined work of activists is to confront and take down systems of oppressive power, on the one hand, while building a new and just world on the other. Let's do it. Together. Now. ◆

adriennemareebrown.net/blog/2011/10/18/one-step-in-building-the-occupyunify-movement-in-detroit/

Also published in *My Soul Looks Back: Life After Incarceration*, by Yusef Shakur

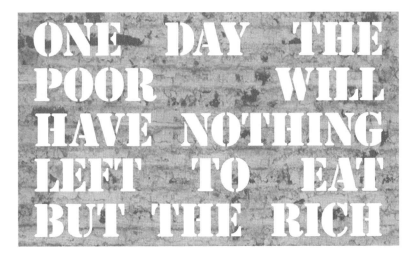

Occupy DC (Hasty Notes)

Keguro Macharia
16 October 2011

I walk to McPherson Square, one of the main arteries of Occupy DC. On a first pass, I am reluctant to walk through the park. A few earnest people are talking to some of the DC homeless who stay around the park. I recognize a certain 'I have come to help Kibera[1]' look. And feel ashamed for thinking this. A few cellphones are out, documenting occupation, documenting the homeless. DC is a tourist town. The Kibera-ness of it will not leave me. It is the first time I have felt so close to Kibera while in the States. A man is yelling about Jesus – later in the day, he will yell, 'Mitt Romney will not save us, Rick Perry will not save us.' He never says Barack Obama will not save us.

* * *

I return to McPherson Square with a friend who is bold enough to walk through the park. My friend, who lives close to the park, tells me that the tents have mushroomed, grown from a few to more. McPherson is not particularly big, so each additional tent makes a difference. It is relatively quiet, reminds me a little of the people I would encounter as I jogged through Seattle's Volunteer Park a thousand years ago. A few people cluster around a man who expounds on something in the vein of a street preacher, a man happy to have an audience. He is familiar, a blend of Hyde Park exhibitionism with Nairobi evangelism. What he says seems unimportant – too familiar, something already known – but the making too-familiar of others' narratives is ideological and material violence at its most quotidian.

Listening matters. Seeing matters.

'I speak for the bush' flashes through my mind. Perhaps the quotidian violence it maps might become less quotidian, less a part of urban modernity.

Kibera-ness still nags.

* * *

I tell my friend I am feeling ungenerous. This is why I see Kibera-ness. But this might not be quite right. Still. I like to pay attention to these moments of unease.

We make our way to the Lincoln Memorial, from where a march will ensue to the newly constructed MLK memorial.

* * *

On our way there, we encounter several joggers – DC is a jogging city – almost all white, almost all male, with a certain busy-ness to them. We pass by two white men, one of whom says, 'too many people, there are too many people'. His jogging has been rendered difficult, it seems.

DC always has 'too many people' over the weekends. It is a tourist town. The crowds mass and swell and pulsate. Those who can, visit monuments and museums during the week to avoid the crowds. Perhaps some of us like 'too many people'. Like Helga Crane, we might enjoy being swallowed into crowds.

'Too many people' takes on greater significance as we approach the crowds massing around the Lincoln Memorial – mostly black, many with union t-shirts, others sporting t-shirts featuring MLK, Jr.

'Too many people.' Kibera-ness beckons.

There's a sense of kinship in the air – groups cluster, families come out together, one seeks inter-generational cohorts. I have been reading Christina Sharpe on Corregidora, about the work of 'making generations'. I am thinking, now, of the generation-making work taking place through a shared commitment to labor.

'Workers' Rights are Human Rights.'

* * *

Kibera-ness recedes, as does the US, for a moment, and I think about the courageous Kenyans who occupied the Ministry of Education.[2]

My frames kaleidoscope: Egypt, Wisconsin, Nairobi, Wangari Maathai.

More joggers.

* * *

Along the march trail, I hear 'We Will Overcome', briefly. I wonder about the kind of memory work taking place in this group of multi-generational marchers and activists, many of whom are training their children how to think about and practice belonging, how to occupy the spaces created by history and how to create history by occupying and extending spaces.

I wonder about the promise that sustains a note, extends it into a melody, sends the melody around the world – I first heard 'We Will Overcome' in 1985, in my mother's reedy voice as she attended the 1985 women's conference in Nairobi – and returns the melody with newly visioned bodies.

Making Generations.

* * *

Voice and space come together in complex ways in DC.

In a recent essay, Gayle Wald discusses Marian Anderson's 'historic 1939 concert on the National Mall', to 'think about sound as a tool in struggles over space, including spaces that symbolize the nation'. Going beyond a focus on the word-content of music, Wald directs us to consider 'vibrations,' the palpable – if inchoate – feelings created by music in our 'bodies'. Wald's attention to 'vibrations' enables her to consider Anderson's performance as sounding together, that is, binding, a sonic structure of belonging.[3]

Anderson's singing voice filled space. Acoustically speaking, her vibrations spread infinitely outward, touching even people unable to hear them. Wald's argument strikes a chord as I think-feel 'We Will Overcome' as a vibration through time, a sonic legacy that makes generations, perhaps especially in DC.

* * *

Much of the coverage around Occupy Everywhere has focused on rhetoric – what is being said, how it's being said, what's not being said, what should be said, who should be saying it. Even as there is 'nothing new' about much or any of the rhetoric, simply, and powerfully, an aggregation of it and listening and hearing. Coverage has also paid attention to the seeing of occupation – photographs abound.

I find myself wondering about the sound of occupation – Migritude[4] is still on my mind. What vibrations are being created?[5] How are they resonating through bodies? What forms of collectivity emerge and are affirmed through such soundings? Not, in this instance, the meaning of words and songs, so much as their presence.

* * *

While the tone of 'too many people' grated earlier today, a mark of a jogger's impatience with inefficiency, it can vibrate differently: too many people are unemployed and underemployed, too many people are part of the 99% and the 53% (as one placard read today), too many people hold on to the sonic promise of 'We Will Overcome'.

In resonating bodies, 'too many' turns into 'so many': a syntax of action unfurls. ◆

gukira.wordpress.com/2011/10/16/occupy-dc-hasty-notes/

1 Kibera is the largest informal settlement in Nairobi, Kenya, and home to many of the country's poorest people. **2** Link to video of the action: http://nin.tl/GKvbcq **3** Gayle Wald, 'Soul Vibrations: Black Music and Black Freedom in Sound and Space' in *American Quarterly* 63.3 (2011), 675 and 680. **4** Shailja Patel, *Migritude*, Kaya Press, 2010. **5** Link to an article about the OWS 'human microphone': http://nin.tl/GPQeF8

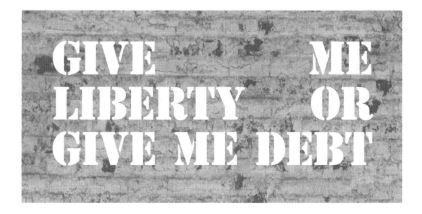

Occupy Oakland Day Four:

Wherein I speak to some folks and the General Assembly debates Move On's move in

Jaime Omar Yassin
14 October 2011

Part 1: Talking to people doesn't really make things clearer, but it is interesting

Occupy Oakland on Thursday Afternoon, Day Four

From about half a dozen tents set up on Monday night, the grassy area of Frank Ogawa Center is now completely covered in tents, too many to accurately count. I was astonished, actually, at how quickly the community had grown. There was a fully functioning mess hall and kitchen, which I'm told serves food round the clock, an information desk and porta-potties courtesy of a donation by some local unions, and a children's tent.

The kitchen: a minor miracle of human engineering at Occupy.

I'd had some initial prejudices about Occupy Oakland. I saw the first day as a re-run of the regular demonstrations I had been a part of in this very square for years now, with similar organizations represented; people from what can almost be described as a caste of political activists, and a lack of substantive class and race representation. At the same time, I thought that the open structure of Occupy lends itself to a snowballing kind of diversity, with no real safeguards against a majority representation of working class and people of color from the neighborhoods surrounding Ogawa.

Since my hopefulness for the budding movement was based on rapid change and a complete replacement of the matrix of the organization – from relatively privileged political organizers to members of Oakland communities – I wanted to see if my initial perception was still holding. Since one of the things that's bothered me about Occupy coverage, both mainstream and alt, has been the attempt to assign either diversity or hippie/loser status on the basis of a few interviews, I'll state right here that the people I talked to aren't representative of anyone but themselves – they've given me no insight into the composition of the community at Ogawa in general.

I did want to interview people of color and people out of their twenties, and so those are the people I sought out for the most part. I will say that it's obvious that the space has drawn the area's surrounding homeless population and that during waking hours, attracts a great number of curious local people and passers-by. Some haven't even heard about Occupy before they happened upon Ogawa by chance.

The Occupy events were only a faint buzzing in the background for Oscar, an unemployed construction worker in his late thirties who I found sitting enjoying the warm day on the steps of the plaza in front of the city hall building. He'd heard of them, but tuned them out and admitted he didn't really pay attention to news. Hungry and a bit drunk, he'd walked by at two in the morning, surprised to see the kitchen open and a cook making flapjacks. Oscar is living with friends, so the idea of escaping a full house and staying with the Ogawa community for the night was appealing. Though he didn't think that there were very many people there in the same position as he, he did feel very welcome and at home.

Oscar had been out of work since the housing crisis began three years ago. Though he considered Occupy Oakland a good start, he was skeptical about whether the system could be changed at all. He wasn't sure if he would stay another night, though I did see him there later after sunset setting up a tent.

The space had attracted some homeless people as well who seemed to have a mixture of practical and political reasons for being there. Kali, who was in his late thirties, boasted that he'd been the first person at Occupy Oakland; he'd been sleeping on a park bench on Broadway in front of the park on Sunday night anyway. He told me that he was homeless by choice, as a reaction to having spent most of his adult life in prison. This echoed a comment by another person I spoke to, who went by the name of Truth, who also claimed his homelessness was a personal choice.

To a certain extent, I saw this as political bravado, of a kind no different than any activist explaining the philosophical basis of their lifestyle. But one issue kept bubbling up from various people I spoke to, especially those who were out of work or homeless: and this was the idea that even having a job was not a solution to the problems facing our society. Kali had come to feel that the pursuit of money was at the foundation of life's problems – greed and accumulation were inherently negative, and were bound to result in a dysfunctional society.

As Truth put it, he had made his choice on a subconscious level by the time he was old enough to do simple addition, watching his mother work, sometimes at two jobs, to keep her family above water at the Acorn projects in West Oakland. He'd tried holding down a job and a place to live, but realized, looking at a paycheck that was a little over 200 dollars a week, that the struggle to stay above water would be constant. He also found the hierarchies and competition of the workplace to be ultimately negating.

Demarco, a young man from East Oakland who'd recently lost his job as a security guard, echoed these feelings as well. He'd been fired from his job of four years, he said, because his employer did not want him accumulating pension time and other benefits – the employer had been seeking a pretext, and eventually constructed one. He felt that his union, SEIU, had let him down, giving him a run-around of 800 numbers and unanswered calls, and leaving him alone to defend himself against his employer in arbitration. He saw this as a betrayal of what the union had told him it was there to do, and the reason that he paid his dues.

Even so, Demarco felt that his precarious position might not be worth fighting for anyway. It seemed that he would always be fighting for a job he was bound to lose, falling behind, and then spending another few years catching up, only to repeat the cycle. There was a problem in society of solidarity, according to Demarco. People hoped to escape the worst situations, and so focused on their own well-being. It was an illusion, he thought, since everyone would eventually find themselves in those circumstances.

Demarco had only been at Ogawa for a few hours. He was curious about the Occupy movement, and felt that it embodied some of his feelings about economic and political problems he was experiencing. He was already excited, and considering the next step, which would be to spend the night.

When I asked Demarco if he felt that his race and class experience was represented at Ogawa, his answer was equivocal. Though he'd seen many black people at the event and had been talking to people who were unemployed and/or homeless, he responded that there still weren't enough black people at Ogawa, but that in his mind race and class were artificial separations.

The issue of representation was also a consideration for Jack Bryson, though he was careful in dealing with it. Foremost, he was excited and positive about Ogawa and felt that only good things could come of it; he rejected some criticism as being a 'crab in the bucket'. Bryson had become politicized when his sons witnessed the killing of their friend Oscar Grant at the hands of police at a BART station. Before that, he said, he'd been asleep, engrossed in work and other issues, and unconcerned with politics.

After his experience with organizers and activists in the Justice for Oscar Grant activism, he felt that all political movements were connected. Bryson had been active at the prisoner strike at Pelican Bay prison when Occupy Oakland had been organized; but he had heard about it from some of the people that he'd been involved with in the Oscar Grant organizing, who were also involved in Occupy.

Bryson had joined the POC group which had formed through the General Assembly to address issues of people of color. For many people of color, Bryson said, there was a concern about losing their own representation and having white people speaking for them. Though he had a lot of respect for the white organizers he'd met over the years, he said it was clear that different experiences create different priorities and concerns. Many middle-class whites had only become concerned about the economy when their own economic well-being became as precarious as it had already been for communities of color for years – he called this, 'the shackle being on the other foot'.

White people were also sometimes oblivious to the dangers faced by people of color who entered the justice system as a result of activism – what could mean a citation for a young white person, could mean jail time or expensive bond for a non-white activist.

Regardless, he still felt as if Ogawa would ultimately become a watershed moment, and that it had inspired a new sense of political activism not just in the US, but around the world.

As I said, my conversations don't tell us much about the composition of the group. There are apparently over one hundred tents by now – people were struggling to find an unclaimed spot to set up as night fell on Thursday. There's just too many people at Ogawa, interacting in too free-form a way to understand the social dynamics, at least in the short term.

But the question remains of whether diversity of participation is actually being felt in the decision-making process at the General Assemblies. From what I could tell, I would say that the answer to that is not very encouraging. Kali, for example, told me that he'd been listening in on some of the GAs. He told me that he'd gotten an ironic laugh out of discussions he'd overheard at a prison-writing workshop at Ogawa. When I asked him why he didn't speak up so that people could learn from his experience – that is, really know what a prisoner might want to get out of an exchange – he dismissed the idea.

I think this is indicative that the political process, as it's presented by activists, can be intimidating and seem like 'something they do', and not for the non-activist.

While I was at the GA that night, I saw some disturbing signs of where that kind of feeling may emerge from as well. There was a system set up for communication amongst the group to foster participation which I thought was quite ambitious and laudable – it was meant, especially, to avoid heckling and other kinds of negative reactions which can stifle emerging voices. But there was heckling coming from the upper rows of the amphitheater around city hall, anyway, and it was 100 per cent white, young and male. It seemed pretty typical of what I'd heard for many years now, based on ideas not being perfect enough, or informed enough – not down enough with the revolution. At one point the facilitator had to ask people to stop heckling and booing, but these people ignored the request. I stress they were a tiny fraction. But they made their presence felt enough so that people who were still getting their political sea legs would think twice about sharing their opinion or representing their group at the mike.

While there was substantial representation of the groups by people of color at the mike after the break-out groups, I don't think that that representation was indicative of the general participation at the GA, from what I saw. The GA was overwhelmingly white and young, and seemed by hook or by crook to have weeded out the kinds of people I had spoken to earlier. That's for many reasons I'm sure, but something that the GA should be considering with great seriousness.

Part 2: The General Assembly deals with Move On's move in
That's not to say that the GA functioned poorly. In fact, it was quite heartening to behold the meeting. As I said, I'm still not sure of the protocols, but it did seem dedicated to consensus and toward building it, even if it was frustrating or time-consuming.

In a previous post[1], I mentioned the danger of co-optation from groups like Move On, and Van Jones' Rebuild the Dream organization. As I wrote, shortly after arriving at Ogawa on Monday, I was handed a flier for a march from Laney to Ogawa put on by those organizations and several other community groups and unions that was scheduled for Saturday 15 October. This was also of great concern to many at the GA, who felt various emotions from deep ambivalence to outright hostility to the groups. Many expressed concern about the danger of being co-opted, or of being used as a prop by politicians and organizational management. A lot of this antagonism was based on the Ogawa group's rejection of electoral politics – that was a somewhat unanimous feeling if the crowd's reactions were any gauge. To be clear, it turns out that Move On planned the event over a month ago, long before the Occupys had started.

To the Move On coalition's credit, it sent out two representatives to explain the coalition's view, their needs and to try to come to some accommodation with the Occupy group, which they claimed to support. An older African-American organizer explained that many rank and file union members and activists were representing their own organizing efforts, and not necessarily those of the organizations. She stressed that the Ogawa group and such organizers had goals and methods in common. This was echoed by a speaker from Occupy, who stressed that the members of the groups and the union did not necessarily line up behind the national-level organizations or their hierarchy and that Occupy was meant to represent the rank and file of organizations, not exclude them.

The resolutions before the group were primarily concerned about how to give access to Move On without undermining the independence of the Ogawa group, and whether or not to allow politicians and other speakers unfettered access to the mike. There was a wide range of responses by spokespeople of the break-out groups, who took to the mike after discussion to express the GA's views. Some were entirely antagonistic to Move On and unions, and wanted to lay down the law to them. Others felt similarly, but explained that the only way for the group to enforce its will would be aggression, which would end up in physical violence. It was also noted that in such a situation, the only way to stop individuals from Move On from doing as they saw fit, would be through intimidation and violence, and that therefore it was important to come to an accommodation.

I was impressed by the GA's commitment to hammering out the situation fairly and in a representative way. Though it obviously was not smooth; the resolutions before the group concerning Move On had to be constantly re-explained, and sometimes confusion reigned, followed by annoying heckling and cat-calling. In the end, the group decided to accede to the Move On coalition's event, but to apply the standards of communication to speakers as if they were individuals in the group – no longer than two minutes on the mike, be they Danny Glover, Union representative or politician.

One of the speakers representing Move On, Charles Davidson, was someone I had interviewed in April at the US Uncut tax day demonstration.[2] I remembered that at that time he expressed frustration at the national Move On organization, and was dissatisfied with some of their capitulations and their retreat on US wars and occupations.

I asked him via email if he had a statement about the issue. Davidson wrote that the march was focused on budget cuts on healthcare, social programs and infrastructure, and on pressuring Congress to create jobs and address the housing crisis. Davidson also stressed that he did not trust the Democratic Party, and that he didn't support Move On's alliances with the party in general, but that he did support certain progressive Democrats such as Barbara Lee and Dennis Kucinich. He also stressed that there were many Move On members who'd been involved in political activism for years, and that the Occupy movement should try to embrace, rather than alienate, them and the union members that would be involved in the event.

That being said, he did echo Move On's line, shared for the most part by the organizations and unions involved, that the fight was mainly focused on Republicans in the House. This is the main bone of contention with a majority of Occupy, in that it wants to remain free of any kind of party affiliation or electoral participation.

The GA finally decided to allow speakers from the event to only speak for two minutes, and that there would be rebuttal from the Occupy group. We'll see how this works out on Saturday. ◆

hyphenatedrepublic.wordpress.com/2011/10/14/occupy-oakland-day-four-wherein-i-speak-to-some-folks-and-the-general-assembly-debates-move-ons-move-in/

1 In an earlier post on Occupy Oakland: http://nin.tl/GKyErs 2 http://nin.tl/GJlCF7

Facilitation

The importance of 'process' has been a recurrent theme in discussions of Occupy/Decolonize. This section addresses both the theory and the practice of participation.

Anne Tagonist, locating the power of OWS in the power of affiliation: 'We Are Us... We Are Not You Any More,' expounds the pleasures and fears that accompany a step out of 'politics as Americans understand politics' – and thus out of America. A multi-racial, multi-generational collective of organizers and activists, DeColonize LA withdrew from Occupy LA early in the existence of the encampment at LA City Hall and shifted their energies to supporting both new and existing popular assemblies throughout the city. Larisa Mann describes the centrality of 'feminine' skills – care-giving, maintenance, teaching, communicating, feeding each other – to Occupy/Decolonize's resistance. Answering those who hope to 'win' the 'occupation', she argues that the creation of a visible space for living, talking, caring – things increasingly privatized or hidden – is Occupy's most radical act. Hannah Chadeyane Appel, expounding the rituals of a decision-making process that insists that 'logistics *are* politics', casts an ethnographic eye over the OWS General Assembly. Looking closely at who is experienced as 'disruptive' in OWS Spokes Council meetings and General Assemblies, Appel argues for the value to radical politics of disruption, messiness and inefficiency. Sonny Singh sees the impulse towards efficiency in process pitted against the need for 'radical, transformative justice' in the workings of the OWS Spokes Council.

Heirs to
the Autonomen

Anne Tagonist
16 November 2011

I am probably the last person in the world who thinks Occupy Wall Street was doing everything right. The vague agenda, the leaderless organization, the odd ritualistic decision-making that so many commentators found so vexing, I loved. I've spent the last two months terrified that they would abase themselves with a manifesto or an internet petition, and I'm entirely charmed that my fears have not come to pass. As I write, a judge has forbidden OWS from re-establishing their encampment, and it isn't clear whether the folks will fight that or simply surrender and move to another park. The American left has spent the last century forgetting that it isn't enough to be right – you also have to win – but even if they do keep moving meekly on, I think OWS has come closer to succeeding as a result of their apparent absurdity.

Look, everybody knows how you change the law, even financial regulatory law: incorporate as a PAC, line up interested parties as financial support, establish a set of principles, hire a consultant or a think tank to draft model legislation, and deploy lobbyists and campaign donors strategically to get your change attached to some can't-fail bill in both houses. It isn't foolproof, but it works, and that's what everybody who wants to make a political change does. OWS knows this as well as anyone – better, maybe. Chanting and waving signs doesn't accomplish anything; at best it fits in as a 'third wing' next to those lobbyists and campaign donors, a pressure tactic to embarrass or terrorize reluctant lawmakers. This is what the Koch brothers did in Wisconsin, and what their media lackeys accused unions of doing with OWS – except that this wasn't the story at all.

Nobody went to Zuccotti Park, or their local affiliate park, because of a shrewd political calculation. Occupy Wall Street wasn't the best tactic available to reach a political goal. The Occupy movement succeeded because several thousand people decided, for their own personal emotional reasons, that they really wanted to be one of those guys.

I'm not alone in this analysis. Two fairly important thinkers, anthropologist David Graeber and author Daniel Quinn, came to this conclusion independently and wrote about it online. Occupy Wall Street wasn't a political formation, it was an affiliation narrative, a metastory that structured the world so that people who associated themselves with it – identified with its protagonists, to be literary about things – were part of a great and just collective, with noble aims and brave methods. It was a hero tale, about you, and all your new awesome friends. All you had to do was show up and join in.

And what a thing to join it was! Social psychologists would have to work very hard to come up with a better set of practices to consolidate group identity! The initiation rite was a collective violation of a mass-culture taboo – sleeping out in the city – for which the daring were rewarded with a warm welcome into a deeply interwoven community. It would be an act of hubris to suggest something like The People's Mike in fiction – chanting, in unison, about Big Ideas is one of the strongest social consolidation mechanisms known, up there with marching and singing, and OWS did a lot of those together as well. Behind all the signs, under all the slogans, ran a refrain stronger than words – We Are Us, We Are Us, We See Each Other, We Acknowledge Each Other, We Value Each Other, We Are Us.

When these sorts of organizing techniques are imposed from above, we call them brainwashing. When they are voluntarily constructed by participants, we call them something else: religion, from re-ligare, to re-connect. What OWS was doing wasn't politics as Americans understand politics – OWS was forming a tribe.

Oh don't look at me like that. We're a tribal species. If you think that only applies to people with strange tattoos and exposed bosoms, you're just being an exceptionalist. We structure our understanding of the world on tribal lines – what does an environmentalist look like? What does a Mormon look like? Why do you have ready answers for those questions? You know some Mormons are black… but you get my point. All great movements have had tribal aspects – communism, back when communism mattered, was intensely tribal. There were communist hospitals, communist restaurants, communist marriages, and that great cliché, the red diaper baby, to carry the tribe forward a generation. When environmentalists were actually a threat (think Earth First! or No M11) they were so tribal that the majority of participants in a campaign may not even have been able to articulate the issues at stake, but were still able to contribute mightily to the effort.

In fact, No M11 spawned an actual tribe – the Dongas, who I encourage you to read up on. They're still out there, raising their Donga children. My point is, we long for affiliative narratives, and when we share them with people, we tend to share our lives as well – our productive activities, our play, we even tend to be endogamous within our narrative affiliations. Carry it forward a generation, and 'tribe' is as good a word as any. No matter how silly the actual origin of OWS (or the Dongas, or the Mormons) may be, after a few generations any pidgin becomes a creole. All you have to do is keep telling the stories and having babies.

I doubt OWS made these decisions consciously; I think something larger is happening. I think OWS, and all the Occupy movements around the world, and the Arab Spring for that matter, considered the affiliative narratives available in our global culture and rejected them all. There is no good progressive movement. There is no good nationalist movement. There is no good socialist, or Islamist, or any other movement whose precepts are really attractive right now, and the global mass culture narrative is truly awful. One corollary of We Are Us is pretty obvious – We Are Not You Any More. OWS is a rejection of consensus America, just as the Tea Party was, just as the TNC (Transitional National Council) rejected 'Libya'.

Is this dangerous? Of course. Bleeding Kansas was tribal too – by Osawatomie, it didn't matter what the Bible said any more, you were either one of us or you were agin us, whoever us might have been. To stretch the analogy further, that decade was probably also the nadir for the concept of 'America' as an affiliation narrative – evidenced by the bruises on Senator Sumner's face. That tribal war killed two per cent of the entire population before it quieted down. It also put the last nail in the coffin of human slavery in America, and I have a hard time imagining how else that could have happened.

Tribalism is frightening, if you believe it can be avoided without losing all the stakes. Right now, to use OWS' own cosmology, you'd have to be in the 1% to feel confident with that Other Method of political change. We do ourselves no favors – and do OWS no honor – if we pretend that forming a strong tribe that believes what OWS believes is somehow less important than giving $100 to that Glass Steagall reform PAC which doesn't exist. Does it further fracture the union? Yep. Is it better than losing everything, claiming to stand for compromise, bipartisanship, and rational deliberative process, and standing powerless in the middle of what is already a tribal war? You tell me. What's an aquifer or an ice cap worth to you? How lonely are you willing to be? ◆

huntgathermedicine.com/2011/11/16/heirs-to-the-autonomen/

Statement

DeColonize LA
16 October 2011

On October first, hundreds of people from around Los Angeles answered the call from Occupy Wall Street to start claiming public spaces to meet and decide together what to do to build an economy that meets the needs of the people in the place of capitalism. As the day progressed, a group of people with previous working relationships as organizers in various communities in Los Angeles and trusted allies gathered to collectively share thoughts and ideas about what we were witnessing and taking part in. Our first impression was that the 'occupation' resembled a carnival and that it was disorganized. What we eventually realized, however, was that the 'occupation' was, in fact, very carefully organized, but for objectives we did not anticipate. Crouched under the banner of 'leaderlessness' was a small circle of organizers unaware of and unapologetic for their own privileges, and fiercely intent on maintaining their grasp on power and ownership over Occupy LA.

On the first day, we convened discussion circles which dozens of people gradually joined. We called for these circles because we felt we needed to hear from each other, as attendees of the Occupation, prior to the General Assembly. Coming from an anti-authoritarian, horizontal perspective and practice, we understood that building relationships with the other participants and hearing ideas and concerns would be the basic building blocks to form a collective understanding of why we were at the Occupation in the first place and how we could participate. A 300-person General Assembly meeting cannot provide the space or opportunity for all of the participants to develop trusting relationships: this happens over time by discussing experiences and working on projects together. While we have shared our experiences from our organizing in direct action movements and our ideas for moving forward, we have also learned a lot from other participants. This is the beauty of occupations and similar actions; it is difficult not to come together as a community. But as we have pointed out, throughout the duration of the Occupation, many people have felt excluded, especially those comprising the most disadvantaged segments of the '99%'.

During the General Assemblies on the first and second day of occupation, we witnessed fundamental breakdowns in the consensus process, resulting in undemocratic decision-making. This was complemented by deception, coercion, and fear-mongering by the leadership to get their way. We were troubled by actions of those in leadership positions and/or facilitators of various committees who sought to control the direction of the Occupation through non-democratic decision-making regarding the relationship with the Los Angeles Police Department. Any discussions or proposals at the GA criticizing or objecting to collaboration with the police are immediately shouted down by the leadership. By obstructing any discussion of the relationship between the Occupation and the police we have been prevented from making plans for strategic responses to police aggression like arrests or brutality, which potentially endangers people who have issues related to criminal records, immigration status, race or gender identity. Occupy LA has excluded the concerns of people that have long experience with the police in their neighborhoods and also in protests, and by doing this they also exclude people who could participate but feel unsafe and disrespected because of a lack of recognition by Occupy LA of their concerns.

We made several attempts to present proposals, workshops and discussions at the General Assembly, in small groups and in one-on-one conversations. Although the overall Occupation movement nationally aspires to use participatory democracy and the consensus process to be inclusive of the people, the efforts by the leadership to maintain informal control have prevented discussion or recognition of patriarchy, white supremacy, classism, heteronormativity and other layers of oppression that exist in the broader society, which continue to be perpetuated within this 'occupation'. Women of color in particular have been silenced. Many of us are tired of futilely trying to explain to middle-class white activists that they really aren't experiencing the same levels of oppression as people of color or the working class or underclass. The constant rhetoric of the '99%' and calls for blind 'unity' have the effect of hiding inequalities and very real systems of oppression that exist beyond the '1%-99%' dichotomy and rendering invisible the struggles of a majority of the people in this city.

But the final straw for us was that a participant in Occupy LA distributed fliers[1] at the 4 October General Assembly with the names and photos of 25 individuals associated with the Committee to End Police Brutality and accusing these participants (some of whom are part of our affinity group) of trying to hijack and destroy the movement and provoking the police. If this individual isn't actively working for the police, he has definitely helped them through his actions. One of these fliers most likely landed in the hands of a police officer, undercover agent, or informant, and passing them out had the effect of breaking the solidarity among the participants in the Occupation and sows fear and distrust in the movement. The leadership does not understand that we are not 'offended' by the fliers, but feel threatened and unsafe now that this list has been circulated. We have also been hearing reports from occupations in other cities about issues similar to the ones at Occupy LA: lying, accusations of being provocateurs or cops, exclusion and harassment. These dynamics could cause the movement to stray away from social revolution and place the occupations dangerously close to electoral recuperation by one or more political parties.

Most people who remain at the encampment are aware of some of these issues. We have felt an incredible amount of support from them as we have cried and yelled and stormed off in response to some of the incidents that have occurred over the first two weeks of the 'occupation'. The more we have talked with our friends who are occupying other cities, the more we have realized that the problems we are experiencing are common across the movement. Race, class, and gender privilege should be recognized, discussed, and countered through proactive steps to create practices that spread responsibility and power among the participants like rotating facilitation of meetings of committees and General Assemblies. We must foster a culture of taking ownership of privilege by recognizing it and committing to the other participants that we will all accept the concerns of others and allow ourselves to be held accountable by each other to the principles we profess. This is how we can start to take concrete actions to dismantle the formal and informal roles where privilege can accumulate, which allows some participants to avoid accountability.

We all want to be participants in this movement. We want to share our knowledge and experience with other participants who may have never been to a protest before so that we can help them feel empowered and safe. We want to be in the streets challenging Capitalism and the government that supports it, rebuilding our communities through struggle. We don't want to be excluded for being who we are. We don't want to be attacked or endangered for raising concerns about transparency and strategy. We don't want to have to be responsible for checking privileged activists on their racism, sexism, classism and heteronormativity. This is why we, as a collective, have opted to shift our energy from Occupy LA and focus on building popular assemblies throughout the City, in order to acknowledge the organizing and community initiatives by the most marginalized communities to survive and confront this economic crisis and those who continue to demand justice but are not heard at City Hall.

We don't want our presence to detract from the still unclear goals and strategy of the Occupation. We don't intend for this to be divisive, rather we believe that the movement needs to spread and reach more people across LA in innovative and effective ways. We are not asking anyone to pack up their tent and join us, but we believe in the autonomy of individuals to act in the ways they believe to be most strategic and effective in our communities. ◆

In solidarity,
DeColonize LA!

unpermittedla.wordpress.com/2011/10/16/statement-from-decolonize-la/

1 See a photo of the flier at http://nin.tl/H6rMBI

On Occupy Wall Street

Larisa Mann
10 October 2011

Having just returned from Occupy Boston on what may prove to be a decisive night, if rumors are correct, I'm pleased to say that I am still seeing what I thought I was seeing and hearing from people actually at these burgeoning events. It's impressive, and important, and exciting almost beyond belief.

I'm not even going to engage with the 'but what do they waaaaaant' crowd, or the 'they're so inarticulate' crowd, because so many folks have answered these concerns clearly enough. But I thought I'd share some of my thoughts on why these occupations are important.

I was initially repelled by the analysis, especially from leftists, and I have to say especially (though not entirely) from leftist men, which sounded like a lot of armchair quarterbacking about how to 'win' the 'occupation'. This contrasted pretty dramatically with what I found interesting and inspiring about the occupations on Wall Street and beyond. The occupations, by focusing on creating spaces for living and for having dialogue, highlight how little space we have in our lives for either of those things. The society we live in parcels out living space and space to talk and think, based on money first and foremost. Caregetting/giving, learning, reading, talking, getting/giving food, communicating – all are privatized more and more. People assume they are supposed to happen in our homes, but fewer people can actually afford to do them at home, or can't afford the home itself. We are supposed to hire people or services to provide them, if we can afford it, and ration our participation in all of these most human and humanizing activities based on their cost.

So the most radical thing the occupations have done is made visible a lot of that work, and made it accessible. They show it is possible for people to self-organize things like food, like medical care, childcare, a library, media centers, internet, etc.

There has been commentary, especially from, I would say, a more macho side of the left, about how camping isn't real protest. These people are just camping, they are not, so to speak, sticking it to the Man. Well, the most effective way the man keeps everyone in line is through our dependence on expensive infrastructure which we don't control and can barely afford.

In the camps, people are providing it for themselves and each other. So rather than saving up money, inheriting it, borrowing it, abandoning one's responsibilities, or simply not having any yet, in order to stick it to the Man without fear of losing your healthcare or childcare or whatever... these people in these camps are demonstrating how you can do without the Man. And the skills that come from that are indeed transferable.

And as I keep suggesting, these skills are also unglamorous. Often seen as 'feminine'. The caregiving, organizational, maintaining skills. But they are the skills that make things accessible to more people, especially to people more at the margins. They are also the skills of people who are not dependent on the system, they make it easier to resist selling out or buying in.

And then there are the skills and practices of decision-making and discussion. People are learning what a general assembly can be – they are seeing people who care about whether decision-making is done in a non-hierarchical way – about whether voices are heard. People are not only noticing whether too many similar people have spoken, but are saying 'I think someone else from a different gender/ background should speak instead of me, because a lot of people like me have already spoken'. Just demonstrating that it's worthwhile to consider these things, that it makes for better decisions. And one of the nicer moments of that was learning that Occupy Boston rather quickly made itself aware that the term 'occupation' is rather a loaded and non-liberatory one for many indigenous/native peoples on this land as well as elsewhere. Especially as the day approached which celebrates the invasion of native people's lands by Columbus. And although the work of decolonization is undoubtedly still to be done, the fact that this was acknowledged and space left to discuss and move forward on native people's concerns in relation to occupation as well as Wall Street shows, already, a better and more inclusive (in the right way) movement than I have seen. Overall I have been impressed with the gracious and generous participation and analysis of many Native people[1] to these various camps, as well as several important critiques[2] which show the way towards better moves in the future.

So yeah, add in the diversity I saw at Occupy Boston. Yes, in Boston. As I walked around, I heard multiple languages and a good smattering of solid working-class Boston accents. I saw asian, arab, latino, black, white, native, and all kinds of folks, in clusters, twos and larger groups. I saw folks from 16 to 60, at least. I saw queer, cis, trans and straight folk in every style and scene and age, crusty-punk kids in layers of dingy denim and patches, college kids in t-shirts, union members in their union gear, medics in home-made uniforms with goggles and bandannas. While linking with the medic tent, I met an EMT who came to offer her time, and a former military medic checking out the piles of donated supplies (including two huge tubs from the nurses' union). I chatted with the father and mother from Braintree (south shore!) who had brought their four children to see the camp. 'I work in Boston,' he said. 'I drove by this every day, watching it grow. I think it's just great. It's so great what you're doing here. I wanted to bring my kids so they could see people standing up for something, doing things for themselves.'

I also overheard conversations, among groups of people, on subjects ranging from critiquing the gender binary to McChesney's analysis of media propaganda. There were hundreds of people there when I arrived, and more were streaming back after what had sounded like a truly huge students' march (Boston is a college town after all). I saw guitars and saxophones and the inevitable drum circle. But overall what I saw was excitement, and hope, and people connecting across their differences – not by erasing them, but because we saw that we are on the same side anyway whether we like it or not, and we've got a lot of work to do.

From the early days now: two good reports and the first decent analysis.[3] Although by now even the *New York Times* editorial staff has wised up and basically admitted that their first hatchet/hack job by Gina whatever is a pile of crap.

And Mike has been doing a great series of posts; especially strong for me is the way he lays out a lot of background very clearly as he is wont to do.[4]

And of course Zunguzungu is always a treasure, of thought and of further links.[5] Just read everything.

And lest you think this is totally unrelated to other stuff I do – I'll just say that my dissertation is about 'exilic spaces' which are spaces in which people's interactions and relationships are not determined by colonial capitalist power. People's identities are not defined only by their oppressors and exploiters, but instead are lived out in relation to a life outside, in resistance to, and predating global capitalism.

I came to this through focusing on creative practices that embody and reinforce **exilic spaces** of discourse. This term comes from

Jamaican scholar Obika Gray, whose work I am eternally indebted to Erin for introducing me to. In this case 'spaces' are physical spaces, but are also partly a metaphor for a way of speaking/communicating in which communication – including music – is not commodified. So, riddims, sampling, answer tunes, call-and-response, fan fiction, all aspects of dynamic, social interactions with creative works – they create around themselves kind of exilic space in which you are not, traditionally, expected to ask permission in order to participate. But they are not only metaphorical! Exilic discursive spaces need exilic physical spaces – where actions are not controlled or monitored (and don't require permission), in order to flourish. My work investigates, among other things, how copyright freezes communication/music into commodifiable chunks that are attached to particular entities ('owners'). If spaces of creativity track and enforce this, through, say, software that monitors your social activity, it can kill the essence of living dialogue/ musicking. I'm not entirely sure how much the occupations are exilic spaces, or simply the willful carving out of a different society in the cracks and fissures in commodified space made by our inability to live fully within it. Well, it makes me think anyway. ◆

djripley.blogspot.com/2011/10/on-occupy-wall-street.html

1 Links to an article on indigenous interventions on the framing of Occupy, and an image of indigenous participation in Occupy Oakland: http://nin.tl/H3293u and http://twitpic.com/6ykfwz 2 See, for example, Jessica Yee's article at http://nin.tl/H2BVl8 3 http://thesis.jrbaldwin.com/ occupywallstreet# http://nin.tl/H2zQCV http://nin.tl/H2C8ok 4 http://rortybomb.wordpress.com 5 http://zunguzungu.wordpress.com 6 http://soundclash.wordpress.com

The Bureaucracies of Anarchy
Part 1: The Rituals of General Assembly

Hannah Chadeyane Appel
30 October 2011

If you have spent any time with Occupiers, you have seen people (sometimes by the thousands) hold their hands above their heads and wiggle their fingers. Jazz hands? Cult sign? Known as 'twinkling' when it expresses a positive sentiment, the hand signals[1] are perhaps the most visibly and phenomenologically ritualistic part of Occupy Wall Street's General Assembly process, a protracted exercise in mass participatory decision making.

At a minimum, the phrase 'General Assembly' has two meanings in the Occupy Wall Street/Occupy Together movement (see General Assembly Guide[2]). On the one hand, it is used to refer to the collective Occupy participants in and beyond Liberty Park (as in, we are all part of the General Assembly). On the other hand, and more specifically, it refers to the nightly, open meetings held in the park and across the country at 7pm. That these rituals of contemporary anarchist activism have made their way quite seriously into the pages of *Bloomberg Businessweek* magazine[3] tells us something about the destabilizations of our present moment.

A 'general assembly' means something specific and special to an anarchist. In a way, it's the central concept of contemporary anarchist activism, which is premised on the idea that revolutionary movements relying on coercion of any kind only result in repressive societies. A 'GA' is a carefully facilitated group discussion through which decisions are made – not by a few leaders, or even by majority rule, but by consensus. Unresolved questions are referred to working groups within the assembly, but eventually everyone has to agree, even in assemblies that swell into the thousands. It can be an arduous process. One of the things Occupy Wall Street has done is introduce the GA to a wider audience, along with the distinctive sign language participants use to raise questions or express support, disapproval or outright opposition.

Since 17 September 2011, General Assembly (GA) in the second sense has been held nightly in Liberty Park. After the GA on Sunday evening, 30 October, however, this will no longer be the case. What was this nightly ritual? What is taking its place? In offering partial answers to these questions, this two-part Dispatch attempts a brief ethnographic meditation on the bureaucracies of anarchy and the spaces of politics.

Every night, the GA meeting at Liberty Park starts with members of the facilitation working group (WG) introducing themselves over the people's mic to those assembled. All are welcome at these meetings, and downtown's after-work crowd often fills in the twilight square, with others lingering around the edges. Meeting facilitators change every evening, and anyone can facilitate a GA after attending a facilitation training, held every afternoon at 5pm. In general GAs are co-facilitated, and meetings begin with the two facilitators introducing themselves, followed by introductions from those filling the other facilitation-team roles: stack-taker, stack-greeter, time-keeper, and minute-keeper. There is clearly an increasing effort to keep this nightly team diversified by gender, ethnicity, nationality, and sexuality, though less so by age. 'Stack' refers to the list of people who would like to speak in any of the GA's four phases: agenda items/proposals, working group report-backs, announcements and soap box. As each phase of the meeting begins, the stack-taker compiles the names of those who wish to speak. GAs follow 'progressive stack' and 'step-up, step-back' guidelines, described at the beginning of every meeting as twin processes in which those whose voices are traditionally marginalized will be prioritized, and those who speak often are asked to step back so that others can step up. Lovely, in theory; unsurprisingly complicated in practice.

After the facilitation team introduces themselves and defines stack, the ritual of GA proceeds to descriptions and demonstrations of the hand signals. One of the facilitators narrates and demonstrates, and she is echoed on the people's mic: 'Hands up, fingers waving means *"I feel good! I like this!"'* Hands in the GA shoot up, twinkling, and the group responds **'Hands up, fingers waving means *I feel good! I like this!'*** The facilitator continues: 'Hands flat, fingers waving means *I'm on the fence. I'm not so sure.'* (The echo of voice and gesture). 'Hands down, fingers waving means *I don't feel so good. I don't like this.'* (Echo, gesture.) The narrator continues to explain and demonstrate the hand signals for Point of Process, Point of Information, Clarifying Question or Comment, Wrap It Up (to be used with compassion, it is always specified) and, finally, a Block: arms crossed in an x in front of your chest. 'A block is very serious,' the facilitator always explains. (**A block is very serious**, we all repeat.) 'A block means you have ethical or safety issues with the proposal on the table, and you are willing to leave the movement if it passes. If you present a block, you will be asked to explain your block in front of the whole GA.'

Once the ritual of explanation and demonstration of the hand signals is over, GA proceeds to agenda items and proposals, always the first and generally most important issues covered at nightly meetings. Proposals are ideas that require consensus in order to proceed – various forms of direct action, spending OWS money in excess of $100, endorsing a particular march or event as 'OWS', or a new form of bureaucratic procedure. Proposals can only be brought by or through already-existing working groups (WGs) though anyone can join any WG at any time, and suggest a proposal. Proposal content spans the sublime to the ridiculous, but the rituals and rigor of the consensus process makes them all seem hyper-bureaucratic and arduous. A few examples:

As of mid-October, OWS was receiving 500 packages *per day* of donated goods, all of which were delivered to a PO box at a family-owned UPS franchise store near Wall Street, for which OWS was paying $40/month. The Shipping, Inventory, and Storage Working Group (which operates out of a space donated by the local Teachers' Union) proposed that, after negotiating with the business owners, the movement begin to pay $500/month for an ironically named 'corporate account', given that the mass volume of goods received far exceeds the business' stated maximum volume for PO box accounts. After a series of clarifying questions and friendly amendments from the GA about the precise relationship between this franchise and UPS corporate, and the relative merits of changing our account to a USPS account, their proposal reached consensus.

The Stop Stop & Frisk Working Group proposed that OWS officially endorse their action in Harlem (at which Cornel West and Communist Party spokesperson Carl Dix were both subsequently arrested, *see video*[4]). The GA agreed overwhelmingly and consensus was reached without clarifying questions or friendly amendments.

The Legal Working Group introduced a recent proposal by explaining that, 'so far, we have been focusing our energies on getting you out of jail and applying for permits'. Going forward, they proposed that no individual person or WG apply for permits, injunctions or file a lawsuit through the city in the name of Occupy Wall Street without first consulting with Legal. 'If you're taking legal action that will affect this occupation as a whole, or if you're taking legal action *in the name* of this occupation... we propose that you consult us before you do so.' This was a controversial proposal, and though it eventually reached consensus, many present were worried that they were being asked to abdicate their individual legal rights and volitions to a team of 'experts'. Only when the Legal WG clarified that all were still welcome to file lawsuits and permits as individuals did the proposal pass.

Each of these and many other proposals I've seen – from Media asking for $25,000 to upgrade their IT equipment to the conciliatory proposal finally brought by the Pulse Working Group (the drummers) in conjunction with Community Relations and Direct Action – were in their own ways contentious and arduous. Moreover, those just passing through the movement's symbolic center on their way home to dinner, often hoping for clarity or even a brief shot of economic justice talk, were often sorely disappointed that GA is overwhelmingly taken up by questions of bureaucracy: how much do we pay UPS? how long can the drummers drum? do I have to consult Legal before filing for a permit?

This brings us toward questions about the spaces of politics, which I take up in part two of this dispatch. What is the relationship between the making and maintenance of Liberty Park in Lower Manhattan (its mail, its legal procedures, its noise statutes) with the making and maintenance of the broader ideas and actions of a growing movement that exists as much in the media and social networking as it does in disobedient reclamations of the commons? For a month and a half, it has been an almost-sacred tenet of OWS that the medium is the message, that the reclamation of privatized public space not only for engaged citizenship, but also for free food, shelter, clothing, healthcare, libraries, education, wifi and more, is OWS politics. Logistics, the claim goes, are politics. And yet even to those most dedicated to that position, it rarely feels like enough. Bureaucracy rarely feels transcendent.

In the latest developments of the bureaucracies of anarchy in OWS, these contentions over the spaces of politics have been brought to the fore in the single most controversial GA proposal in the movement's young life: to change the very process of consensus itself, and to move from a nightly General Assembly to a Spokes Council Model. What is at stake? If logistics are politics, as many in the movement have strongly claimed, then this move looks to signal Bakunin's warning about the hierarchy of the bureaucrats. If, on the other hand, as the movement has grown, GA has become so hyper-bureaucratic that it has effectively stalled effective organization, the Spokes Council model claims to remedy that by giving those who determine where and how we eat or receive mail a separate decision-making structure through which to work, enabling the rest to use GA to consider 'larger' ideas, for instance, the constitutional amendment abolishing corporate personhood and overthrowing Citizens United. Regardless, on Friday 28 October a 9/10ths *vote* (note: *not* consensus) passed the Spokes Council Model, and there will no longer be nightly GAs at 7pm in Liberty Park.

The Bureaucracies of Anarchy
Part 2: People Before Process

14 December 2011

Some time in early October I showed up to an OWS organizers' meeting at 16 Beaver Street. 16 Beaver, like 56 Walker or Charlotte's Place, is one of these magically anachronistic spaces in lower Manhattan that feel like something out of Patti Smith's *Just Kids* – free space for art, activism and organizing, embedded in some of the most expensive real estate in the world. Of course, to label these spaces 'anachronistic' is to cede to capital its totalizing power. With a nod to J Fabian, this would deny the coevalness of diverse forms and uses of urban space within contemporary capitalism. So let's invoke

both Fabian and radical feminist geographers JK Gibson-Graham, and rejoice that there *are* such spaces in lower Manhattan today.

But I digress. Walking into the expansive, exposed-brick third floor of 16 Beaver that October evening, there was an Arabic class going on in the back and, in another corner, roughly 20 OWS open-source folks having an animated meeting. Roughly 30 of us there for the organizers' meeting made a third circle of chairs in the middle of the space.

As with nearly all OWS meetings I've attended, this one had an over-full agenda, and it *started* at 10pm. 'Process' is the way facilitators handle these time-crunches. Described in Part I of this post, process refers to the combination of hand signals, stack-taking and facilitated meeting organization used in OWS, and consensus process more broadly. Process intends to allow everyone's voices to be heard, while also speeding along the often-onerous meetings. If someone goes 'off-process' – say by offering a proposal during the report-back section of the meeting, or offering a verbose and unrelated opinion when participants are busy trying to figure out a logistical problem – there is a hand signal ('point of process') intended to bring the meeting back on course.

That night at 16 Beaver was one of the first indoor meetings I attended. The four walls and overhead lights enclosed and intensified the space in a way that I hadn't experienced at General Assemblies (GAs) in the park, rendering starker some of the human dynamics of process. In particular, the ways in which this 'horizontal' and 'radically democratic' process can marginalize people was radically spotlighted.

* * *

Race came up in one of the early agenda items, and 'Hector' (a young Chicano man in his early twenties) passionately declared that race was an imposed construct to be intentionally rejected. 'Sarah', an African American woman in her later twenties, at the meeting as a representative of the OWS People of Color Caucus (POC), vehemently objected to Hector's characterization of race. She suggested that he ask the people most vulnerable to racist 'stop & frisk' policing tactics in Harlem if race was something one could choose to reject on an individual, intentional basis.

As their debate blossomed and drew others in, hand signals for 'point of process' began to go up around the circle, as some participants expressed their opinion that this conversation was not part of the meeting's agenda. The facilitator acknowledged the points of process, and suggested that we move on. Sarah was deeply upset, explaining that the space did not feel safe to her if there wasn't room to talk openly about race. Others felt not that they were foreclosing a conversation about race, but rather that they were 'staying on process', and hoping to get home at a reasonable hour. These divergent experiences of the evening did not divide neatly along racial lines. There were different people on different sides of the issue, though the facilitator's white male identity was not helpful. The meeting eventually moved on, and Sarah stood up to leave the meeting, frustrated. Several participants intercepted her and had an intense, supportive, side conversation on process and privilege.

The bureaucracies of anarchy, in other words, are rife with signals of oppression. Today, two months and one eviction after this long-ago October meeting, questions of how an ostensibly inclusive and horizontal process can marginalize people remain at the center of the tensions (productive tensions, in my opinion) in OWS.

These tensions manifest most spectacularly in Spokes Council meetings, held Mondays, Wednesdays, and Fridays at an indoor venue (often 56 Walker) in lower Manhattan. At a Spokes Council meeting in early December, a visitor from Occupy Detroit got up to speak. She noted that in Detroit, people come to Occupy meetings to speak their minds and to hear others speak, but when they try to participate, people more familiar with the movement's rituals wave strange hand signals in their faces, telling them that their most passionately held beliefs are not 'on process'. *This marginalizes people,* she said. *It makes them feel like the Occupy movement is not for them or their concerns.*

Others objected to her that the hand signals and process guidelines are introduced before every meeting, and there is no way to hold meetings in the absence of some agreed-upon structure. They insisted that the process is, by design, open to everyone, and that it contains its own mechanisms for critique and redress. Some insisted further that those who refuse to use the process are being 'disruptive' in so far as meetings get 'sidetracked' in these conversations. You can read the minutes of the Spokes Council, disruptions and all, here[5] (free registration may be required).

*   *   *

As is so often the case, the label 'disruptive' is most often applied across categories of difference. Those people often considered disruptive in OWS processes have different educational backgrounds, class backgrounds, home statuses (often the chronically homeless) and certainly different psychological habitations of the world. In other words, while race is clearly one category across which 'process' marginalizes, it is not the only one. OWS also deals with the serious issues of how to include and empower the homeless, those with substance-abuse issues, those with mental health issues.

These debates have derailed two-thirds of all spokes council meetings since the model went live at the beginning of November. For some, this has turned the meetings into an exercise in futility, and increased their resolve toward autonomous action within their working groups. Others bemoan the negative media attention that these gaping wounds in the skin of 'solidarity' will surely beckon. But then there are others of us, and I include myself in this category, for whom these 'disruptions' have become some of the most valuable time OWS can spend. They show that ideologies of solidarity, horizontality or radical democracy always already contain their own privilege, their own insides and outsides. True radicalism is much messier, much slower, much more *disruptive* than any smoothly functioning process can handle.

General Assemblies still happen in the cold dark of Liberty Plaza Tuesdays, Thursdays and Saturdays. At this past Saturday's GA (10 December) the first proposal on the agenda was from RAHKA – the Radical Activist Homeless Kicking Ass working group, many members of which had been routinely characterized as 'disruptors'. Their representative asked the GA to approve funds that would allow members of their group to spend the night in the 24-hour McDonald's across the street from the plaza – $2 per person per 12-hour period, to buy the coffee or other menu item that allows them to occupy the space legally. She explained that members of her group are not welcome in the church shelters OWS is using – they are pregnant, have psych disabilities, are trans, have been abused in or kicked out of church shelters; hence the need for another option. As their proposal was debated (through OWS process of clarifying questions, points of information, etc) it came up that they had been offered office space at 52 Broadway. Why didn't they just take that, as the Accounting working group had, rather than support McDonald's? Their representative answered that RAHKA sought to be a beacon of radicalism and transparency in the movement, and because that office space had not been offered to everyone, they refused to occupy it.

RAHKA's proposal passed and the group's many members present were jubilant. They hugged and invited everyone to join them for a coffee in McDonald's between 10pm and 5am. Using the process effectively, RAHKA also subverted its attendant privileges in multiple ways – by refusing the 'insider status' that office space would've conferred upon them, by allowing one man who routinely disrupted their presentation with drunken outbursts his time to speak. In short, RAHKA's proposal, and this post, is a call for the productivity of disruption in the face of persistent privilege. People before process, not only profits. ◆

socialtextjournal.org/blog/2011/10/the-rituals-of-general-assembly-and-the-bureaucracies-of-anarchy.php

socialtextjournal.org/blog/2011/12/people-before-process-the-bureaucracies-of-anarchy-part-ii.php

1 See video of OWS hand signals at http://nin.tl/H2AfVZ 2 http://www.nycga.net/resources/general-assembly-guide/ 3 http://nin.tl/H2CiMD 4 http://nin.tl/H2AoJ7 5 http://www.nycga.net/category/assemblies/minutes-sc/

Occupying Process, Processing Occupy
Spokes Council musings by one POC

Sonny Singh
1 February 2012

What follows does not reflect or represent the views of the People of Color Caucus at Occupy Wall Street but only the views of the author himself.

At the notorious Occupy Wall Street spokes council meetings, the People of Color (POC) Caucus[1], of which I am a member, often finds itself in the role of whistle-blowing and bringing a critical perspective to the discussion. I have gotten the sense that most people at spokes – sometimes including the facilitators – just want to 'get through' the agenda with little to no drama or disruptions. While I can relate, given that these meetings are long and often frustrating, this approach doesn't create a culture that fosters critical thinking or the voicing of dissent. So, often when the POC Caucus voices concerns about a proposal being made or something happening in the room, I sense a lot of hostility towards us.

Last week, the issue of banning 'violent people' from Occupy Wall Street came up at a spokes council meeting I attended. Those of us in the POC shared the deep concern of the majority in the room that certain individuals have made others feel unsafe by committing physically aggressive or violent acts towards others. Many at the meeting were getting understandably worked up about it and insisted on a zero-tolerance type policy when it comes to violence and thus banning so-called violent people for life from OWS.

When it was finally our turn to speak on stack, I raised a question about the meaning of the word 'violent' and how we wanted to make sure people are specific about the actions of a person being deemed 'violent'. Violence means different things to different people. Violence can be verbal, physical, sexual, institutional or state-sanctioned. Pushing someone could be seen as violent. Yelling could be seen as violent. Damaging property could be seen as violent. Raising your voice and calling out racism or sexism in a meeting could be seen as violent (no, this is not a hypothetical scenario).

So, we were concerned about three 'violent' people (all who happened to be people of color themselves) being permanently banned from OWS and kicked out of the church they were living in without being clear and on the same page about what constitutes violence. We have not had this conversation at Occupy. Many assumptions are made when people talk about someone being violent, and to raise the question is apparently taboo.

As soon as I opened my mouth with our concern, dozens were down-twinkling with looks of disgust on their face, muttering sarcastically to each other, and even shouting out loud, shocked and appalled that I would even ask such a question. The sense in the room was, 'There goes POC again causing trouble and holding us up from moving forward'. People assumed we were condoning the actions of the 'violent' people in question simply because we raised a question about what violence means.

I was pissed. No one was listening to what I was saying. I'm a very calm and collected person. I use my words carefully and deliberately. I was not being the slightest bit antagonistic. But even for someone as calm as me, I could barely finish expressing my concern because of the backlash that was unleashed as soon as I opened my mouth.

One of my POC Caucus comrades eventually couldn't take it any more and spoke out of 'process' to explain that raising these sorts of concerns is exactly why we exist as a caucus at spokes council. Because communities of color have suffered violence for generations – the violence of white supremacy, the violence of the police, the violence of mass incarceration, the violence of poverty. Again, no one listened to what she was saying but only put up their 'point of process' hand signs and rolled their eyes.

I was talking about it with another friend from the POC Caucus on the phone the next day, and he felt like we have lost all good faith in the spokes council. We have no credibility whatsoever any more.

Honestly, it's been a tough couple of months of figuring out how to engage with this movement. A lot of people who I consider comrades, friends, and fellow travelers have gotten fed up with the dynamics at spokes council as well as other meetings and have understandably stopped showing up. It's been hard. Sometimes I feel like my role is far too focused on process, and I'd rather be focusing on something that feels more concrete, something that has tangible results, something that feels more like action.

But what I always come back to is that if we can't figure out these kinds of process questions, what are we really building? Most of us can agree that Occupy Wall Street is not only about confronting big banks, corporations and the state, but also about creating alternatives to this oppressive system. How we in this movement interact with each other, hold ourselves and each other accountable, and sustain our community are questions just as important as what our message is and what our next direct action is.

I remember when I first got involved in OWS in late September I would always tell people that the 'how' is just as important as the 'what' when it comes to this movement. And that's what makes it so different from other mass movements, and that's what I'm so excited and inspired by.

I'm less than inspired right now by the 'how' of OWS, but continue to believe that we must figure it out if we intend to be a lasting force. We have to create the processes to deal with ugly and, yes, violent situations, and these processes must reflect our values, not the values of the status quo.

When I raised the question about what violence means at the spokes council meeting last week, one person defensively responded that the person in question was 'dragged out by the police', and has had the cops called on them several times. From what I could tell, this was compelling evidence to the majority of the room that this person was clearly a pathological violent disruptor who must be kicked out of the movement for life. Clearly if a cop drags someone out of a meeting, there is no question that the person being dragged away 1) deserves it and 2) is without a question a violent aggressor who must be thrown out indefinitely.

The irony was too much for me. The NYPD are now champions of keeping us safe? Well, if we are using police intervention as our barometer of whether someone is violent or not, then maybe the next step, as a friend jokingly suggested, will be to create a Jail and Prison Working Group and then a Solitary Confinement Working Group to keep the disruptors in check. Maybe we can recruit some of our cop friends to facilitate those meetings. They are, after all, the 99%, aren't they?

What can I say – things have gotten out of control.

I have a feeling that many in OWS would agree with Audre Lorde's statement, 'The master's tools will never dismantle the master's house'. But are we willing to make the leap that is necessary to embody this as individuals and as a movement? Are we willing to stop reacting impulsively and aggressively to difficult situations (and difficult people) and start listening for change? Are we willing to create new tools that may not already exist?

These process questions that many of us have been grappling with may very well make or break OWS. The good folks in the Safer Spaces Working Group[2], along with many others, have been working hard to come up with community agreements and an accountability process rooted in anti-oppression and transformative justice. But we have such a long way to go to get the buy-in of the 'average' person at OWS.

On the one hand I'm tired of this conversation, I'm tired of being down-twinkled at, I'm tired of the POC Caucus not being taken seriously, I'm tired. But if we can make it through this together and adopt radical, transformative justice[3] approaches to accountability, violence, and harm in our community, perhaps we will in turn be well on our way to creating viable alternatives to this system we all abhor. ◆

infrontandcenter.wordpress.com/2012/02/01/occupying-process-processing-occupy/

1 https://www.facebook.com/POCcupy 2 http://nin.tl/H2Cr2A 3 http://www.generationfive.org/tj.php

Safer Spaces

Central to the successes of Occupy/Decolonize has been the affective environment it has fostered. Through formal working groups and informal interventions, movement participants have reminded their comrades that solidarity is not sameness.

Jaime Omar Yassin's description of a day with Occupy Oakland – salsa class; children's tent; labor movement workshop; conflict resolution; suicide prevention – evokes both the utopian and the decidedly ordinary. In one of many feminist interventions in Occupy's development, the **Occupy Boston Women's Caucus** recalls their comrades to the importance of women in social-justice movements, and calls out the movement for reproducing traditional gendered behaviors and attitudes. Occupy/Decolonize is one of the first large-scale movements to emerge in the US since the recent surge to visibility of organizing among trans and gender-non-conforming people. This statement, in particular, reflects the efforts of '**a bunch of trans women occupiers**' to assert the necessity of moving from rhetorical gestures at inclusivity to actual practices of solidarity. **Aaron Bady** has consistently offered insights about the specifically urban settings of Occupy ever since Occupy Oakland established its downtown encampment. Here, he discusses the trope that merges political disruption and social contagion: the problem of 'vermin'. The response – and lack of response – of radical communities to sexual violence has been a recurrent issue in US social-justice movements. The **OWS Safer Spaces Working Group** describes the general problem, and, by recounting their own approach to a particular sexual assault, offers a model to others.

Occupy Oakland: Hugs Are Also an Option

Jaime Omar Yassin
24 October 2011

On a warm Sunday afternoon in Ogawa Plaza, there's a salsa class going on. Just a few feet away, a labor organizer is giving a workshop on the Occupy movements and the labor rank and file. Little kids are given space to play and express themselves creatively in the children's tent. Across the camp by the kitchen, people are eating, talking, smiling. Conversations break out spontaneously between strangers who are happy to take advantage of the camp's loosened social rules. Oakland residents have come looking for ways to volunteer, to be a part of this weird bloom of activity and existence that goes far beyond the original idea of 'Occupy'.

In all, it's clear that Ogawa Plaza is used by more people in the community, in more diverse ways, than ever before.

There are problems, as right-wing pundits point out. While in a rational world, it would only necessitate pointing out that these critics are the very people who regularly advocate bombing and destroying other countries for merely looking at the US the wrong way, their criticism is paralleled in mainstream media headlines that emphasize the idea that people who take drugs, have criminal records or are otherwise unsavory are not denied entry into the camp, so long as they are willing to peacefully co-exist.

The people who reject that agreement can create problems and they usually emerge at night. But these problems always existed in downtown Oakland. If anything, the Occupy space has provided a space where others can mediate the conflicts that arise, and where ideas of how to de-escalate conflict can be broached and improved upon.

Last night, for instance, the camp faced multiple conflicts. All involved hurt feelings or perceived crossed lines but none were substantive and, most importantly, none required jail, violence or the threat of violence for resolution. What I find most valuable about even these admittedly frustrating burps of conflict is that they involve people in the issues that affect their lives and they give people a chance to ask questions about how they handle aggression, and what the goal of stopping such problems is, or should be.

One example: a man obviously jacked up on stimulants, and perhaps also mentally ill, wandered into the camp. At first, people hoped that he would simply wander off the same way he came in, but he lingered, spouting neologisms and emitting hyper-active anxiety. A few campers decided that they would escort him out but, in doing so, I think, prolonged the problem by being overly aggressive about it and making it personal.

I had a brief but contentious conversation with one of these campers about how the issue had been resolved. He genuinely thought that his was the best way and, given the slowness to respond by myself and others, I can't blame him for thinking that. It's not clear whether simply talking to the man would have made him leave.

After the camper I was talking to left, the hyper one returned into the plaza. But just as he was making his way back to the steps from the entrance, he was intercepted by another camper. At first, we simply thought that this was one of the handful of homeless people who sleep in the plaza, but outside the community. But as we watched and prepared to deal with the hyper-man again, a curious thing happened. The two hugged, and the hyper-man turned and abruptly left.

The other camper came over to our group and, when I asked him what had happened, he simply said, ' I just listened to him'.

There are problems at the camp; there's misogyny, homophobia, racism, aggression. In short, everything that existed around Ogawa is still there today – it's not yet a utopia. But the difference is that now people have the opportunity to confront problems head on and innovate on ways to deal with them.

Note: At some point in the night, as well, a man was prevented from committing suicide by Occupy Oakland campers/protesters.[1] As I keep saying, OO has solved far more problems in the area than it's caused. ◆

hyphenatedrepublic.wordpress.com/2011/10/24/occupy-oakland-hugs-are-also-an-option/

1 See video at http://nin.tl/HxSTUP

Statement

Occupy Boston Women's Caucus
18 November 2011

The following statement was read by Elizabeth Dake and Zena, members of the Occupy Boston Women's Caucus, during the General Assembly on Saturday, 18 November 2011.

We, the women of Occupy Boston, are here to tell you that two months is far too long to have occupied without a feminist perspective.

Downwardly mobile middle-class white men are finally realizing what women and people of color have known for too long. Capitalism is destructive. Capitalism oppresses and exploits. If you're not talking about sexism and racism, you're not talking about economic justice.

'A few bad apples' can't exist without a community that condones their attitudes and behaviors. Oppressive language and behavior are an effort to limit our participation and silence our voice.

We chose to disrupt the GA because those with privilege have avoided spaces devoted to anti-oppression, when they are the ones who most need to hear this.

As the 99%, we must actively break down the systems which divide us.

Women have historically been the spine of social justice. We are the 52%: without us, revolution is impossible. ◆

occupyboston.org/2011/11/20/womyns-statement/

OWS Must Resist Cis-Supremacy and Trans-Misogyny

A Bunch of Trans Women Occupiers
18 November 2011

As feminists, we enthusiastically support women's groups and women-designated safer spaces, but, as trans women and allies, we oppose (and will categorically block) any group or space that excludes trans women [see Note 1], as well as any standard that functionally asserts authority over our self-determined gender identities [2]. Most immediately, all of us – transgender and cisgender alike – must stand together to block the trans-excluding affinity groups 'Women Occupying Nations' and 'Strong Women' from Spokes Council participation.

By denying the existence of cisgender privilege and furthering the disempowerment of trans women, trans-excluding groups and spaces violate both the letter and spirit of our Principles of Solidarity [3]. The elimination of systemic oppression against marginalized people is a core goal of the Occupy movement, but self-identified 'womyn-born-womyn' [4] do not constitute a marginalized group relative to other types of women. Throughout the world, trans women are among the people most marginalized by systemic oppression. In the US, trans women face extreme violence (a 1-in-12 chance of dying from a violent crime), poverty (50-per-cent unemployment rate) and criminalization (trans women, especially trans women of color, are routinely subject to police profiling) [5].

To fight this systemic oppression – including transphobia, cis-centrism, cis-supremacy and trans-misogyny – it is essential we support the self-determination of all people oppressed by coercive, non-consensual gender assignments.

Allowing any group or space to define gender by cis-centric standards is intrinsically at odds with gender liberation and trans people's right to autonomous self-determination. It is a fundamental affront to solidarity.

For decades – from the Stonewall Rebellion to Occupy Wall Street

– trans women have stood at the forefront of social justice movements, often at great personal risk. But even within these movements, trans women have been excluded, silenced, shamed and abandoned as political liabilities. Since mid-July, trans women have played a critical role in OWS, including the creation and operation of OccupyWallSt. org, the *de facto* voice of the global Occupy movement.[1] Nonetheless, we are prepared to leave the New York General Assembly and its empowered Spokes Council en masse if trans-excluding groups, spaces, and individuals continue to be tolerated by this body.

Over 50 groups have already signed on to a trans-inclusive safer spaces policy[2] (and any group which has not is encouraged to join!), but for Occupy Wall Street to hold true to its Principles of Solidarity, we must take the additional step of ensuring that trans people's identities are respected, and that trans women are safe and welcome in all women's spaces.

Block Or We Walk.

About This Statement

I am a homeless trans woman and sex worker from DC who has organized in trans communities for years. I am also a trauma survivor and a person with psychiatric disabilities. Since arriving in New York, I have been elated to find support from other trans women in the movement. Overall, trans people are embraced by the 99% movement. However, we have also been disturbed to see spaces within the occupation, including spaces designed for survivors of assault, that are hostile to or excluding trans women. We have also encountered blatantly transphobic ideas from particular individuals on several occasions. As a feminist and rape survivor, and given the fact that trans women are more likely to be victims of sexual assault than cis women, I am shocked to see a culture of transphobia attempting to co-opt OWS. For these reasons, I have partnered with members of the NYCGA queer, women's and people of color caucuses (as well as trans and trans-allied supporters of the Occupy movement more broadly) to author this statement.

Notes

1. For the purposes of this document, we use trans women broadly to refer to all male-assigned and intersex, non-male-identifed, people who feel they have a place in women's spaces. For definitions and background, see this Trans 101 Glossary at The Distant Panic: thedistantpanic.com/glossary

2. This would include any policy that defines gender by individuals coercively – assigned sex at birth, current or former body type, assumed socialization or adherence to medical standards. Even if such a group or policy were to include certain types of trans people but exclude others based on arbitrary distinctions, it is still transphobic and oppressive. For example, some people, including segments of the trans community itself, allow trans women who have had genital reconstruction surgeries to enter women-only spaces, but continue to endorse the exclusion of trans women who have not had such procedures. Even when supported by a trans woman, such ideologies violate trans people's self-determination and are contrary to the goals of trans liberation. Many trans women elect not to have such surgeries, while others simply cannot have them for health reasons. Additionally, the exclusion of non/pre-operative trans women is classist, as such procedures are extremely expensive. Most importantly, a central tenet of feminism asserts that a person should not be defined by their (past, present, or future) biological bodies. Sex and gender are socially constructed categories; there is nothing inherently male about any type of body, and possessing certain genitalia does not make a person more likely to be violent.

For more on the myth that trans women experience male socializations see Tobi Hill-Meyer's article ' Language, Reality, and My Trans Girlhood'.[3]

3. 'Recognizing individuals' inherent privilege and the influence it has on all interactions' and 'empowering one another against all forms of oppression' are foundational Principles of Solidarity, consensed upon by the Liberty Square General Assembly on 23 September.[4]

4. The very idea of womyn-born-womyn spaces is connected to tangible histories of exclusion and transphobic violence. The concept originated during the cis-supremacist witch-hunts which sought to systematically remove trans women from feminist organizations during the 1970s. Such policies have resulted in physical violence against trans women and other gender non-conforming people, ranging from the denial of life-saving services and safer spaces for women who are survivors of rape and sexual assault to the physical expulsion of trans women from feminist music festivals. See Trans Women Belong Here (a group of women protesting trans-exclusion at Michigan Womyns Music Festival)[5] and The Curvatures blog post about Vancouver Rape Relief.[6]

5. See the DC Trans Coalition's Reports and Research or Campaigns pages for more facts about trans oppression.[7] ◆

infrontandcenter.wordpress.com/2011/11/11/ows-must-resist-cis-supremacy-and-trans-misogyny/

A slightly different version is posted at:
occupywallst.org/media/pdf/trans-statement.pdf

1 See Gina Quattrochi's interview with Justine and Zoë, two of the four trans women among the five creators of the occupywallstreet.org website and the @occupywallstreet Twitter feed: http://nin.tl/HmWpWn **2** http://nin.tl/GZTQnS **3** http://nin.tl/Hx8zcp **4** http://nycga.net/resources/principles-of-solidarity/ **5** http://transwomenbelonghere.blogspot.co.uk **6** http://nin.tl/HoN75Y **7** http://dctranscoalition.org

Society Must Be Defended From Rats

Aaron Bady
20 October 2011

Occupy Oakland is 10 days old now, and is beginning to attract a very predictable and more or less uniform kind of media attention. Or shall I say uniformed? The fact that the camp at Frank Ogawa Plaza has constructed and effectively runs an around-the-clock kitchen which is efficiently distributing food to any who want it – including Oakland's large transient population – will not be mentioned, or at least not treated seriously. Instead we will read about rats, fights, drugs, and dirt. This article headlined 'Rats and drugs mar Occupy Oakland tent city, officials say', for example, is a classic example of stenography journalism:

> OAKLAND – City officials said Tuesday they may have to shut down the Occupy Oakland tent city in coming days because it is attracting rats, alcohol and illegal drug use. A pre-existing rat problem around Frank H Ogawa Plaza, which public works employees are normally able to keep under control, has been exacerbated by the demonstrators' presence, said city administrator spokeswoman Karen Boyd. The problem 'has gotten worse with all the food and people and couches', Boyd said. Because the protest has people cycling in and out, she added, the city is having to repeat the message about how to store food and keep the area safe. Boyd said she wasn't sure how to describe the extent of the growing rat problem, but that it's been reported in complaints by local businesses, workers and even the demonstrators themselves. This comes on the heels of increasing reports of illegal drug and alcohol abuse, fighting and sexual harassment in and around the camp of about 100 tents, Boyd said.

The fact that the journalist 'reporting' the story simply repeats, at length, what a single city spokeswoman tells him should be seen as the gift from the newspaper to City Hall that it is. I've underlined the main verbs in the first six sentences to make that as clear as possible; that story is almost literally nothing but variations on 'what City Hall told us [about the people protesting against it]'. And so, the 'objective' reporting just happens to repeat exactly the narrative that City Hall wants to tell – things were under control before, but now the demonstrators are 'attracting rats, alcohol and illegal drug use' — and imagine out of existence any possible counter-narratives which might be told.[1]

But the story that City Hall wants to tell is preposterous. There *are* rats there at night because there are *always* rats there at night. I'm sure the smell of food does attract more vermin than usual – even as the presence of people also repels them – but the bottom line should still be obvious to anyone with a brain: you don't normally have a rat 'problem' in the park at night because you don't normally have *any people there* (or at least not any people the city cares to notice). Even during the day, the only people that use this (quite unused) park are on their lunch break, eating their sandwiches or whatever, and then at night the rats eat their leavings. And no one cares. But now that there are *people* there – people creating a political headache for City Hall – now, suddenly, the rats are an *important problem*. Suddenly, coincidentally, the city is very concerned about 'rats'.

I invite you, by the way, to take a stroll through any part of the adjacent downtown Oakland at two in the morning and observe the rats which have been living off Oakland's messy humans for many decades, and who will for many more. They're not hidden, or even particularly shy; you're just not there to see them and have your sensibilities offended by their presence. But that entire area is a filthy fast-food ridden stretch of a typical dirty downtown, well and truly 'marred' by the fact that day-time humans leave their waste everywhere for the night janitors to feast on, and who are the real causes of whatever vermin problem it has. It would be truer, in fact, to say that Oakland's rats are invading the Occupation's camp.

But rats are not bothersome when no one important is bothered. Because the issue isn't who *brought* the rats, it's the fact that they are now *visible*, them and the dirty messiness for which they are being made into a lazy symbol. The City was *fine* with that park when no one was there, when rats scuttled across it at night while drug dealers sold drugs and homeless people slept and urinated in the shadow of City Hall. Oakland simply did what any self-respecting city does with such disfiguring blots on its honor: it occasionally sends the police out to chase them away and then it ignores them when they come back.

And it longed for that plaza to be clean and picturesque in the way a good plaza should be: empty of people.

But hey, did you see what I did there? I was talking about rats, and then suddenly I was talking about human beings. Did you notice it when you were reading it? Did you feel any cognitive dissonance? What kind of cognitive dissonance did you feel?

If you didn't, it's probably because 'rats' and 'vermin' is a common way of talking and thinking about this country's underclass, the human beings who, because they sell drugs or don't have a stable home, don't quite seem like the sort of people we have to care about. They seem dirty. We might even let ourselves get stupid enough to imagine them as *parasites* (as if we ever gave them anything). And it's this tropological confusion that City Hall wants to encourage, and which the entire *Oakland Tribune* article is built around reinforcing: you start with the rats, and then suddenly you're talking about human beings. You don't have to actually *say* that the people camping there are messy, dirty, undesirable parasites. But the message gets across as clearly as a wink between friends. When an anonymous Oakland police officer describes 'the scene in tent city as akin to a scene from *Lord of the Flies*,[2] you don't even need to have read *Lord of the Flies* to understand what he's really saying: without civilization, we have only the dirty jungle of matter out of place. Clean that up. We certainly don't want 'Homeless people, ex-convicts, at least one registered sex offender, students, unemployed hotel workers, anarchists and reform-minded activists [to] freely mingle together in what amounts to a democracy free-for-all'.[3]

What in the hell is a 'democracy free-for-all?' Is Occupy Oakland a socialist experiment in communal living or is it what Hobbes called the 'war of everyone against everyone' that occurs in a state of nature? Because those are actually two completely different things. And that *Tribune* article wants you to think of the second, to shudder at the thought that all those people might 'freely mingle' and so they make it, peculiarly, into a 'free-for-all'. The free association of unlike types is a battle, you see. And we will bring peace back to that 'free-for-all' when they're all arrested.

But it's even more important to look at the larger narrative frame being presumed: if you think of what's happening through a public-health perspective – if the problem is 'how do we keep this space *clean*?' – it will seem rather obvious that the presence of the campers is a problem. And so it will seem intuitive that they should be cleaned up, tolerated for a while at most, but certainly not allowed to be permanent. Yet, good gracious me, why stop there? Dozens of homeless people camp out in a four-block radius of City Hall every night. *Think* of the mess they make. Wait, did I say 'dozens'? I meant hundreds. They should be cleaned up. They should all be cleaned up. And the drugs and alcohol, and the people that use them, oh my. We should probably clean them up, too. Plus, you know what the biggest mess-makers in that area are? Let's get rid of all those fast-food restaurants and drug stores and institute an overnight curfew while we're at it and also ban pedestrians and human occupation. That'll clean the place up and get rid of the rats.

What if, instead, we think about how the occupation is changing the area, rather than blaming it for all the symptoms of social dysfunction that long preceded it, and which the people in it are actually trying to address? We might see, for example, something like what Omar saw:[4]

'One thing I did want to write about was the revolutionary power of the kitchen at Occupy Oakland. At some point, the idea of having a place where people could grab some food while they occupied, developed into the idea of a permanent and round-the-clock food-creating infrastructure, which would hydrate and feed all who came up, regardless of their affiliation with the camp. The camp participants I spoke to remarked in wonder how organic the process had been, and that the idea had not come from any one person or strategy. In my view, that's what's created the incredible diversity of the camp, which now houses a large homeless population, and draws in a large number of local residents – hungry, peckish or simply curious – who then interact with each other and with the activists there. The resulting meeting of minds has been a real joy to witness. I hope I'm not overstating the case, but I truly believe that if Oakland Occupy – and more broadly most of the Occupy Movements – has any value at all it's in this capacity of creating a place where the previously apolitical or politically unsophisticated can learn from each other and others, and become politicized without the confines of an ideology/goal or institution.'

But, of course, he's been spending hours at a time in the camp, talking to people and participating and thinking. He's just some blogger. And even if the author of that *Tribune* article spent more than the hour or so that most journalists spend, in order to get their pictures and move on, he doesn't seem to have noticed much while he was there; the only thing he heard or saw appeared to have come to him on City of Oakland stationery. So he doesn't let you see that the net effect of removing the camp from Ogawa Plaza, if they do 'clean it up', will be to make it back into a pristine-looking and unused park, at the expense of shutting down 'a permanent and round-the-clock food-creating infrastructure, which would hydrate and feed all who came', and this can only seem like a *loss* if we remember that all of those people down there being all homeless and undesirable – all those 'rats' and 'flies' that we don't have to *explicitly* call them – will still be out there no matter what. We just won't have to see them, or even know about the people who are actually down there feeding them and being fed by them. Frank Ogawa Plaza might now be the least segregated and most economically diverse neighborhood in Oakland but, if we can get rid of it, we can go back to being blandly assured by City Hall officials that Oakland's economically devastated human infrastructure is under control, well and adequately policed by nice men in nice clean police uniforms. And we won't have to know otherwise. ◆

Update: Also, please read Omar's follow-up: 'Occupy Oakland, Day 10: On Rejecting the City's Request to Return to Invisibility'[5]

zunguzungu.wordpress.com/2011/10/20/society-must-be-defended-from-rats/

---

1 The closest thing to actually talking to any of the occupiers that the reporter does is this bit of boilerplate: 'Participants have named numerous complaints, most of them having to do with economic disparities and with corporate influence over government.' **2** http://nin.tl/H8jUQP **3** http://nin.tl/H3020m **4** http://nin.tl/HrWJRj **5** http://nin.tl/HsRWOf

Transforming Harm & Building Safety

Confronting sexual violence at Occupy Wall Street and beyond

Occupy Wall Street Safer Spaces Working Group
4 November 2011

We are writing this statement to inform our fellow Occupiers about an incident of sexual assault at Occupy Wall Street (OWS) and the response to it. We are also writing this statement to respond to media accounts that blame the survivor, and that attempt to use this horrific incident to attack OWS. We write this statement as supporters of OWS, as fellow survivors, and as allies.

On the morning of 29 October, a woman participating in OWS was sexually assaulted at Liberty Plaza. The person whom she identified as having assaulted her was arrested on 1 November for a previous assault. He has since been released on bail.

On the morning of the assault, the survivor was accompanied to the hospital by a group of women from OWS, including a social worker, to support her and act as advocates. From the moment the incident was discovered to the present time, the survivor has been surrounded by a network of allies and trained advocates offering resources to provide emotional, medical and legal support. At every step of the process, and in line with the core principles of survivor support, her wishes as to how she wanted to proceed have been honored, and information from a range of sources has been provided to her about her options. The survivor knew immediately that she wanted to make sure that the person who assaulted her did not harm anyone else at OWS. Community members honored this demand by asking that this person stay off site and, when he refused, monitored his activity, ejected him from the space and escorted him to police custody.

These efforts provided the survivor with the time and space to carefully review the options available to her. Following two days of discussion with family, friends, supporters and anti-violence advocates, the survivor decided to make a report to the police and to push for a criminal investigation and prosecution. Supporters from OWS accompanied her to the police station and will continue to support her throughout the legal process.

We have been saddened and angered to observe some members of the media and the public blame the survivor for the assault. A survivor is never at fault. It is unacceptable to criticize a survivor for the course of action they chose to take or their community for supporting them in that choice. Additionally, we were troubled at the time of her report that responding police officers appeared to be more concerned by her political involvement in OWS than her need for assistance after a traumatic incident of sexual violence. A survivor is not at fault for being assaulted while peacefully participating in a public protest to express their political opinions. We are aware that this is one of several known cases of sexual assault that have occurred at OWS. We are dismayed by these appalling acts and distressed by the fear among many Occupiers that they have caused, as well as their negative impact on our ability to safely participate in public protests. We have the right to participate in peaceful protests without fear of violence.

We are also concerned that segments of the media have attempted to use this incident as another way to disingenuously attack and discredit OWS. It is reprehensible to manipulate and capitalize on a tragedy like this to discredit a peaceful political movement. OWS exists within a broader culture where sexual assault is egregiously common: someone in the US is sexually assaulted every two minutes, most assaults are never reported, and most rapists are never held to account. We live in a culture of violence in which sexual assault is often ignored, condoned, excused and even encouraged. We note that it is particularly difficult for survivors of assault at OWS to feel confident in reporting crimes to the NYPD – the NYPD's unjustifiably aggressive and abusive policing of OWS has undermined trust in the police force amongst protesters.

As individuals and as a community, we have the responsibility and the opportunity to create an alternative to this culture of violence. Advocates, some of whom are survivors themselves, have worked for decades to address sexual violence generally. We are working for an OWS and a world in which survivors are respected and supported unconditionally, where they are supported to come forward, and where every community member takes responsibility for preventing and responding to harm. We are redoubling our efforts to raise awareness about sexual violence. This includes taking preventative measures such as encouraging healthy relationship dynamics and consent practices that can help to limit harm.

We are creating and sharing strategies that educate and transform our community into a culture of consent, safety and well-being. At OWS, these strategies currently include support circles, counseling, consent trainings, safer sleeping spaces, self-defense trainings, community watch, awareness campaigns and other evolving community-based processes to address harm. We encourage survivors to connect with support and advocates, and to access medical, legal, and social services, as well as available community-based options. We stand together as a community to work towards the prevention of sexual violence and harassment, and to provide unwavering support for anyone who has been assaulted. We commit to creating a culture of visibility, support and advocacy for survivors, and of accountability for people who have committed harm. ◆

With hope and solidarity,
Members of the survivor's support team at Occupy Wall Street

occupywallst.org/article/transforming-harm-building-safety/

People of Color

Although discussions of race and Occupy have been complex and fraught, they have also made clear the stakes different communities of color have in the movement – in both its effects and its development.

While arguing that Occupy's initial success was tied to its initial whiteness, **Bruce A Dixon** proposes the specific values of participation in the movement by Black and Brown people. Acknowledging that the movement would have looked very different had it been less white, Dixon looks to Atlanta for ways to claim it for people of color. **Rinku Sen**, casting her eye over a variety of US Occupy sites, calls for weaving a racial analysis that goes beyond questions of demography and representation into the very fabric of the movement, in which she sees both dangers and promise. A number of Occupy/Decolonize sites have adopted statements on the rights of indigenous peoples – some largely symbolic, others addressing the concrete political agendas of indigenous movements in the Americas. **The American Indian Movement of Colorado**'s platform proposal – adopted by Occupy Denver – with its specific demands and its critique of the term 'Occupy', is representative, though more detailed, than many, and echoes the statements of solidarity made by other indigenous organizations.

    Manissa McCleave Maharawal's 'So Real It Hurts' documents a crucial intervention in the drafting of OWS' 'Declaration of the Occupation of New York City'. Perhaps more than any other, this widely circulated account, which first appeared on Maharawal's Facebook page, has shaped discussions of race, process and Occupy/Decolonize. The effect of the 'block' that she and other members of South Asians for Justice undertook, and her account of its emotional cost, has been no less influential. Navigating the space between critiques of Occupy by African-American radicals and the sometimes naïvely voluntaristic rhetoric of outside supporters of OWS, **Tammy Kim** proposes that New York City can learn something from Oakland. Drawing on her experience as part of the Immigrant Workers' Rights Solidarity working group at OWS, she considers the meanings of and possibilities for different kinds of participation by people of color in the movement. Writing from Vancouver, where spirited opposition to the 2010 Winter Olympics brought indigenous justice issues to the fore, **Harsha Walia** calls on Occupy/ Decolonize not to 'underestimate the difficult terrain ahead'. Seeing Occupy as 'brilliantly transitional', she underlines the importance of internal struggles to the struggle against those in power. East Bay blogger **low end theory**'s vigorous response to Ishmael Reed's stern criticism of Occupy Oakland highlights the importance both of class divisions within communities of color and of the broader racialization of class to understanding the opportunities and difficulties the movement presents. Without losing sight of the complexity of either dynamic, he keeps his focus on the need to avoid 'political quietism'.

Occupy Where? What's In It For Black and Brown People?

Bruce A Dixon
2 November 2011

Those that initiated the early occupations in most cities were white. They have re-established the long-lost right of the poor to congregate in public and express their discontent. If this is not to be a right which only whites enjoy, it's time for us to step up too. There will be race and class tensions, with the increased participation of black and brown people in the occupation movement. But these are growing pains, and necessary. It's time, as Glen Ford has said, to claim our place in the 99% and spell out what that looks like.

Occupation Where? What's In It For Black and Brown People?
The answer is plenty, and we need to hurry up and claim it.

The tactic of 'occupation' has reclaimed the right of poor and jobless, even homeless, people to congregate, to assemble and to be discontented in public. That's no small thing, and it's surely not a thing that could have been accomplished if the first occupiers had been young, jobless and black or brown instead of white.

If the first occupiers in Zuccotti Park had been young and black, they'd instantly have been branded a street gang and arrested en masse, with or without violence, but certainly with little media play or sympathy. If the first occupiers were black, and blathering about the ravages of finance capital and how neither of the two parties were worth a damn, they certainly would not have been endorsed by what passes for the preacher-infested local leadership of black communities. Tied as they are to corporate philanthropy, corporate financing, the corporate-run Democratic party and its corporate-friendly trickle-down black president, our black misleadership class would have run, not walked, away from black occupiers who failed to identify as staunch pro-Obama Democrats.

What if the occupiers had been brown? Here's a clue. In the last few years, hundreds of thousands of immigrants at a time have stayed away from work in near general-strike proportions to march on May Day, no less, for their human rights. The anecdotal evidence is that ICE[1] agents raided many workplaces in California, Texas, New York, Arizona, Illinois and elsewhere, and that without much notice in the corporate media, a wave of retaliatory harassment, jailings and deportations ensued. Certainly, the Obama administration is on track to deport a record 400,000 immigrants for the third year in a row, already far outstripping Bush's eight-year total. There are in fact, gang injunction-type laws in many states which make it a criminal offense for young people in designated (black and brown) neighborhoods to assemble in groups in public places for any reason.

Make no mistake about it, reclaiming the right of the poor, jobless and discontented to peaceably assemble, while politically paralyzing mayors and police forces used to cracking heads and dispersing malcontents is a project only white protesters could have accomplished without police violence and massive arrests.

Forty-eight years ago black organizers registering people to vote, organizing farm co-operatives, freedom schools and sharecroppers' unions in Mississippi were being maimed and murdered with impunity. SNCC's[2] James Foreman had the vision to recruit young white college students to Mississippi's Freedom Summer to take some of those arrests and blows. He knew that the spectacle of nonviolent white youth being viciously attacked would drive media coverage and public sympathy for the Freedom Movement in a way that the murder and jailing of black activists would not. Things do change, but some things change less than we'd like.

The second thing the wave of occupations has done is inject a note of reality into the nation's political discourse. The plain truth is that Democrats don't rule. Republicans don't rule. Corporations reign. Plutocrats decide. Finance capital rules. Capitalism works for the 1% and against the other 99%, and is therefore fundamentally illegitimate. Discredited are the nonsense phrases about how 'government has to live within its means', and 'the rich are the job-creators'. 'We are the 99%' may not be deep analysis of political economy, but it's a promising start, an open door, an invitation to investigate and explain how inequality and injustice are not bugs in the system, but have always been its basic features. These were utterances which six months ago were deemed outside and beyond sensible political discourse. Now they are admitted as the plain truth by millions. The occupiers are more popular than either of the political parties, driving Republicans to denounce them, and Democrats to walk the fine line of claiming them while also collecting a billion in Wall Street contributions for the 2012 presidential race alone.

The third thing the occupations have done is provided a standing place to go for people wanting to take part in something meaningful, something that challenges the established order. By being visible and using their bodies to occupy space day after day in hundreds of cities and towns, occupiers are magnets for people to come, to connect and compare their lives and expectations with those of neighbors. This is exactly the sort of thing corporate marketing and the corporate domination of the cable and broadcast airwaves are calculated to prevent.

Corporate media are something akin to the matrix in the movie by the same name, in that they provide a round-the-clock universe to immerse oneself into. Maintaining these occupations as sites where people can unplug themselves and connect with whatever real-time and meat-space (as opposed to cyberspace) political activity and movement exists near them is a vital public service.

So what's in it for us, and how do we claim it?

The occupation, both as tactic and as movement, has opened a door that we need to stick our foot in before it closes. As Glen Ford said, black and brown people have to step up and claim our place in the 99%. There's bound to be resistance on the part of some. I've met occupiers who claimed the concerns of immigrants and black people had no place in the Occupy movement because they were 'divisive'. They said this to me in an Atlanta park that the occupiers shared with a hundred homeless black men.

A caucus of the occupation in Atlanta aims to broaden the occupation to the long-term and everyday concerns of black Atlanta by putting forth an 'occupy the BeltLine' strategy. Atlanta's BeltLine project is a greenwashed gentrification project, a massive publicly financed real-estate scam that steals 10-figure property-tax revenues from schools and city services over the next 20 years to build upscale yuppie residences and shopping, and pay corporate welfare to favored banksters and lawyers.

Atlanta also has a mass transit system that is forced to pay its own way with no help from the state. Although mostly black Fulton and DeKalb counties paid for its multibillion-dollar infrastructure over a generation, its further development is being dictated by business interests openly hostile to the transit needs of Atlanta's working poor. Gentrification isn't just the scourge of black urban communities nationwide. It's the core 'economic development' model for urban America.

If occupying public spaces with human bodies is a tactic that works for white hipsters in the middle of town, why can't it work elsewhere, with them AND with us? Why can't it work with the abandoned and foreclosed properties in our neighborhoods? Why can't it work with our public transit system? These are the questions that black activists in Atlanta and elsewhere are asking. ◆

blackagendareport.com/content/occupy-where-whats-it-black-and-brown-people

1 Immigration and Customs Enforcement. 2 Student Nonviolent Coordinating Committee.

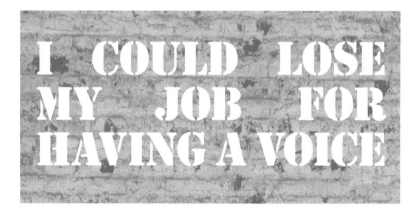

Forget Diversity, It's About 'Occupying' Racial Inequity

Rinku Sen
1 November 2011

The incident is well known now. When civil-rights hero Representative John Lewis asked to address Occupy Atlanta, the activists' consensus process produced a decision not to let him speak. For many, the denial was a damning answer to a question that had arisen since the earliest, overwhelmingly white occupiers first took over Zuccotti Park: Is Occupy Wall Street diverse enough?

'Diverse enough for what?' is the query that leaps to mind. Diversity alone will not ensure that OWS advances an economic change agenda that is racially equitable.

The notion of taking over Wall Street clearly resonates with communities of color. Malik Rhassan and Ife Johari Uhuru, black activists from Queens, New York and Detroit, respectively, started Occupy the Hood to encourage and make space for people of color to join the movement. On 19 October, a different group, Occupy Harlem, put out 'a call to Blacks, Latinos and immigrants to occupy their communities against predatory investors, displacement, privatization and state repression.'

Such interventions have been necessary. The original OWS organizers didn't consciously reach out to communities of color at the beginning; as a result, many people of color felt alienated. But local movements seem able to self-correct – and some newer occupations have been racially conscious from the start.

In Atlanta, the Lewis decision was followed by renaming Woodruff Park, the local occupation site, Troy Davis Park. In Albuquerque, the General Assembly, after a long and difficult discussion, renamed its movement (Un)Occupy Albuquerque in recognition of the history of indigenous lands. In San Diego, where 10 October was named Indigenous People's Day, speakers have come from members of the Islamic Labor Caucus as well as immigrant and Native American communities.

These are all great symbols of racial solidarity. We must now move from questions of representation to ask, how can a racial analysis, and its consequent agenda, be woven into the fabric of the movement? We need to interrogate not just the symptoms of inequality – the disproportionate loss of jobs, housing, healthcare and more – but, more fundamentally, the systems of inequality, considering how and why corporations create and exploit hierarchies of race, gender and national status to enrich themselves and consolidate their power. As the New Bottom Line campaign has pointed out through a series of actions across the nation launched the same week as OWS, the subprime lending practices of Bank of America, JP Morgan Chase and Wells Fargo have devastated communities of color. A 2009 study found that 85 per cent of those hardest hit by foreclosures have been African-American and Latino homeowners.

If racial exclusion and inequity are at the root of the problem, then inclusion and equity must be built into the solution. OWS has resisted making specific demands, but local groups are taking up campaigns and actions. The challenge and opportunity of this moment is to put these values at the center of their agenda.

The signs are promising. In Boston, Occupiers joined a march that protested gentrification and financial abuse from a racial justice standpoint. In Oakland, the organization Just Cause/Causa Justa has inserted an anti-discrimination agenda, illustrated by a beautiful poster by artist and activist Melanie Cervantes reading, *Somos El 99%*, which is a prominent feature of the encampment there. (The poster exists in multiple other languages too.) New Bottom Line has asked Occupiers to make pointed, tangible demands of regulators and banks. Occupy Los Angeles has taken up actions supporting homeowners in the midst of foreclosure. A hearty response from other cities would go a long way toward legitimizing OWS as a movement that recognizes the fundamental role of racial discrimination in shaping our economy.

As some Occupy cities are demonstrating, addressing race is far easier when there is already a history of white activists and those of color advancing common goals. In Flagstaff, Arizona, a city where activists have worked alongside Native communities for years, the local Occupy website features calls to resist a fake-snow-making scheme on a mountain sacred to Native tribes, as well as a plan by Senator John McCain and Representative Paul Gosar to reinstate uranium mining around the Grand Canyon. At Colorlines.com, which has covered the role of race in the Occupy movement, one commenter offered the example of Occupy Los Angeles – a city with a long history of collaborative economic justice campaigns with a clear race angle – as a model to emulate. 'The LA folks seem to be able to reconcile how to fold race, monetary and social issues all into their messages,' she wrote.

The Occupy movement is clearly unifying. Centralizing racial equity will help to sustain that unity. This won't happen accidentally or automatically. It will require deliberate, smart, structured organizing that challenges segregation, not only that of the 1% from everyone else, but also that which divides the 99% from within. ◆

colorlines.com/archives/2011/11/forget_the_diversity_debate_its_about_ occupying_racial_inequity.html

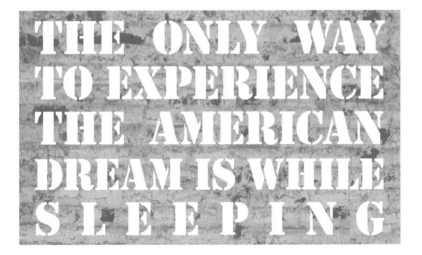

An Indigenous Platform Proposal for 'Occupy Denver'

The American Indian Movement of Colorado
9 October 2011

'Occupy Denver' Adopts Colorado AIM initiative on indigenous peoples' rights! In unanimous consensus, Occupy Denver endorsed the initiative by the American Indian Movement of Colorado on the rights of indigenous peoples (see entire document below). After an hour of discussion, Occupy Denver wholeheartedly supported the proposal at its evening General Assembly. The document was adopted just hours after Boston had accepted a similar, but much less detailed and less specific, proposal.[1]

An Indigenous Platform Proposal for 'Occupy Denver' from Colorado AIM:

> 'Now we put our minds together to see what kind of world we can create for the seventh generation yet to come.'
> – *John Mohawk (1944-2006), Seneca Nation*

As indigenous peoples, we welcome the awakening of those who are relatively new to our homeland. We are thankful, and rejoice, for the emergence of a movement that is mindful of its place in the environment, that seeks economic and social justice, that strives for an end to oppression in all its forms, that demands an adequate standard of food, employment, shelter and healthcare for all, and that calls for envisioning a new, respectful and honorable society. We have been waiting for 519 years for such a movement, ever since that fateful day in October 1492 when a different worldview arrived – one of greed, hierarchy, destruction and genocide.

In observing the 'Occupy Together' expansion, we are reminded that the territories of our indigenous nations have been 'under occupation' for decades, if not centuries. We remind the occupants of this encampment in Denver that they are on the territories of the Cheyenne, Arapaho and Ute peoples. In the US, indigenous nations were the first targets of corporate/government oppression. The landmark case of Johnson v M'Intosh (1823), which institutionalized the 'doctrine of discovery' in US law, and which justified the theft of two billion acres of indigenous territory, established a framework of corrupt political/legal/corporate collusion that continues throughout indigenous America, to the present.

If this movement is serious about confronting the foundational assumptions of the current US system, then it must begin by addressing the original crimes of the US colonizing system against indigenous nations. Without addressing justice for indigenous peoples, there can never be a genuine movement for justice and equality in the United States.

Toward that end, we challenge Occupy Denver to take the lead, and to be the first 'Occupy' city to integrate into its philosophy, a set of values that respects the rights of indigenous peoples, and that recognizes the importance of employing indigenous visions and models in restoring environmental, social, cultural, economic and political health to our homeland.

We call on Occupy Denver to endorse, as a starting point, the following:

1. To repudiate the Doctrine of Christian Discovery, to endorse the repeal of the papal bull Inter Caetera (1493) to work for the reversal of the US Supreme Court case of Johnson v. M'Intosh (1823), and call for a repeal of the Columbus Day holiday as a Colorado and United States holiday.

2. To endorse the right of all indigenous peoples to the international right of self-determination, by virtue of which they freely determine their political status, and freely pursue their economic, social and cultural futures.

3. To demand the recognition, observance and enforcement of all treaties and agreements freely entered into between indigenous nations and the United States. Treaties should be recognized as binding international instruments. Disputes should be recognized as a proper concern of international law, and should be arbitrated by impartial international bodies.

4. To insist that Indigenous people shall never be forcibly relocated from their lands or territories.

5. To acknowledge that Indigenous peoples have the right to practice and teach their spiritual and religious traditions, customs and ceremonies, including in institutions of the State, e.g. prisons, jails and hospitals, and to have access in privacy to their religious and cultural sites, and the right to the repatriation of their human remains and funeral objects.

6. To recognize that Indigenous peoples and nations are entitled to the permanent control and enjoyment of their aboriginal-ancestral territories. This includes surface and subsurface rights, inland and coastal waters, renewable and non-renewable resources, and the economies based on these resources. In advancement of this position, to stand in solidarity with the Cree nations, whose territories are located in occupied northern Alberta, Canada, in their opposition to the Tar Sands development, the largest industrial project on earth. Further, to demand that President Barack Obama deny the permit for the Keystone XL Pipeline, proposed to run from the Tar Sands in Canada into the United States, and that the United States prohibit the use or transportation of Tar Sands oil in the United States.

7. To assert that Indigenous peoples have the right to maintain, control, protect and develop their cultural heritage, traditional knowledge and traditional cultural expressions. They have the right to maintain, control, protect and develop their intellectual property over such cultural heritage, traditional knowledge and traditional cultural expressions. Further, indigenous peoples have the right to the ownership and protection of their human biological and genetic materials, samples, and stewardship of non-human biological and genetic materials found in indigenous territories.

8. To recognize that the settler state boundaries in the Americas are colonial fabrications that should not limit or restrict the ability of indigenous peoples to travel freely, without inhibition or restriction, throughout the Americas. This is especially true for indigenous nations whose people and territories have been separated by the acts of settler states that established international borders without the free, prior and informed consent of the indigenous peoples affected.

9. To demand that the United States shall take no adverse action regarding the territories, lands, resources or people of indigenous nations without the free, prior and informed consent of the indigenous peoples affected.

10. To demand the immediate release of American Indian political prisoner, Leonard Peltier, US Prisoner #89637-132, from US federal custody.

Finally, we also remind Occupy Denver that indigenous histories, political, cultural, environmental, medical, spiritual and economic traditions provide rich examples for frameworks that can offer concrete models of alternatives to the current crises facing the United

States. We request that Occupy Denver actively utilize and integrate indigenous perspectives, teachers and voices in its deliberations and decision-making processes. ◆

unsettlingamerica.wordpress.com/2011/10/11/decolonizetogether/

1 See the Occupy Boston proposal at: http://nin.tl/GRKD52

So Real It Hurts
Notes on Occupy Wall Street

Manissa McCleave Maharawal
13 October 2011

I first went down to Occupy Wall Street last Sunday, almost a week after it had started. I didn't go down before because I, like many of my other brown friends, were wary of what we had heard – or just intuited – that it was mostly a young white male scene. When I asked friends about it they said different things: that it was really white, that it was all people they didn't know, that they weren't sure what was going on. But after hearing about the arrests and police brutality on Saturday and after hearing that thousands of people had turned up for their march I decided I needed to see this thing for myself.

So I went down for the first time on Sunday 25 September with my friend Sam. At first we couldn't even find Occupy Wall Street. We biked over the Brooklyn Bridge around noon on Sunday, dodging the tourists and then the cars on Chambers Street. We ended up at Ground Zero and I felt the deep sense of sadness that that place now gives me: sadness over how, what is now, in essence, just a construction site changed the world so much for the worse. A deep sense of sadness for all the tourists taking pictures around this construction site that is now a testament to capitalism, imperialism, torture, oppression but is also a place where many people died 10 years ago.

Sam and I get off our bikes and walk them. We are looking for Liberty Plaza. We are looking for somewhere less alienating. For a moment we feel lost. We walk past the department store Century 21 and laugh about how discount shopping combined with a major tourist site means that at any moment someone will stop short in front of us and we will bang our bikes against our thighs. A killer combination, that of tourists, discount shopping and the World Trade Center.

The landscape is strange. I notice that. We are in the shadow of half-built buildings. They glitter and twist into the sky. But they also seem so naked: rust-colored steel poking its way out their tops, their sides, their guts spilling out for all to see.

We get to Liberty Plaza and at first it is almost unassuming. We didn't entirely know what to do. We wandered around. We made posters and laid them on the ground (our posters read: 'We are all Troy Davis', 'Whose streets? Our streets!' and 'Tired of Racism, Tired of Capitalism').

And I didn't know anyone down there. Not one person. And there were a lot of young white kids. But there weren't only young white kids. There were older people, there were mothers with kids, and there were a lot more people of color than I expected, something that made me relieved. We sat on the stairs and watched everyone mill around us. There was the normal protest feeling of people moving around in different directions, not sure what to do with themselves, but within this there was also order: a food table, a library, a busy media area. There was order and disorder and organization and confusion. I watched as a man carefully changed each piece of his clothing, folding each piece he took off and folding his shirt, his socks, his pants and placing them carefully under a tarp. I used the bathroom at the McDonald's up Broadway and there were two booths of people from the protest carrying out meetings, eating food from Liberty Plaza, sipping water out of water bottles, their laptops out. They seemed obvious yet also just part of the normal financial district hustle and bustle.

But even though at first I didn't know what to do while I was at Liberty Plaza, I stayed there for a few hours. I was generally impressed and energized by what I saw: people seemed to be taking care of each other. There seemed to be a general feeling of solidarity, good ways of communicating with each other, less disorganization than I expected and everyone was very, very friendly. The whole thing was bizarre, yes, the confused tourists not knowing what was going on, the police officers lining the perimeter, the mixture of young white kids with dreadlocks, anarchist punks, mainstream-looking college kids, but also the awesome black woman who was organizing the food station, the older man who walked around with his peace sign stopping and talking to everyone, a young black man named Chris from New Jersey who told me he had been there all week and he was tired but that he had come not knowing anyone, had made friends and now he didn't want to leave.

And when I left, walking my bike back through the streets of the financial district, fighting the crowds of tourists and men in suits, I felt something pulling me back to that space. It was that it felt like a space of possibility, a space of radical imagination. And it was energizing to feel like such a space existed.

And so I started telling my friends to go down there and check it out. I started telling people that it was a pretty awesome thing, that just having a space to have these conversations mattered, that it was more diverse than I expected. And I went back.

On Wednesday night I attended my first General Assembly. Seeing 300 people using consensus method was powerful. Knowing that a lot of people there had never been part of a consensus process and were learning about it for the first time was powerful. We consensed on using the money that was being donated to the movement for bail for the people who had been arrested. I was impressed that such a large group made a financial decision in a relatively painless way.

After the General Assembly that night there was both a Talent Show ('this is what a talent show looks like!') on one side of the Plaza and an anti-patriarchy working group meeting (which became the safer-spaces working group) on the other. (In some ways the juxtaposition of both these events happening at once feels emblematic of one of the splits going on down there: talent shows across the square from anti-patriarchy meetings, an announcement for a zombie party right after an announcement about the killing of Troy Davis followed by an announcement that someone had lost their phone. Maybe this is how movements need to maintain themselves, through a recognition that political change is also fundamentally about everyday life and that everyday life needs to encompass all of this: there needs to be a space for a talent show, across from anti-patriarchy meetings, there needs to be a food table and medics, a library, everyone needs to stop for a second and look around for someone's phone. That within this we will keep centrally talking about Troy Davis and how everyone is affected by a broken, racist, oppressive system. Maybe, maybe this is the way?)

I went to the anti-patriarchy meeting because even though I was impressed by the General Assembly and its process I also noticed that it was mostly white men who were in charge of the committees and making announcements and that I had only seen one woman of color get up in front of everyone and talk. A lot was said at the anti-patriarchy meeting about in what ways the space of the occupation was a safe space and also not. Women talked about not feeling comfortable in the drum circle because of men dancing up on them and how to change this, about how to feel safe sleeping out in the open with a lot of men that they didn't know, about not assuming gender pronouns and asking people which pronouns they would prefer.

Here is the thing though: I've had these conversations before, I'm sure a lot of us in activist spaces have had these conversations before, the ones that we need to keep having about how to make sure everyone feels comfortable, how to not assume gender pronouns and gender roles. But there were plenty of people in this meeting who didn't know what we were doing when we went around and asked for people's names and preferred gender pronoun. A lot of people who looked taken aback by this. Who stumbled through it, but also who looked interested when we explained what we were doing. Who listened to the discussion and then joined the conversation about what to do to make sure that Occupy Wall Street felt like a space safe for everyone. Who said that they had similar experiences and were glad that we were talking about it.

This is important because I think this is what Occupy Wall Street is right now: less of a movement and more of a space. It is a space in which people who feel a similar frustration with the world as it is and as it has been, are coming together and thinking about ways to recreate this world. For some people this is the first time they have thought about how the world needs to be recreated. But some of us have been thinking about this for a while now. Does this mean that those of us who have been thinking about it for a while now should discredit this movement? No. It just means that there is a lot of learning going on down there and that there is a lot of teaching to be done.

On Thursday night I showed up at Occupy Wall Street with a bunch of other South Asians coming from a South Asians for Justice meeting. Sonny joked that he should have brought his *dhol* so we could enter like it was a *baarat*. When we got there they were passing around and reading a sheet of paper that had the Declaration of the Occupation of Wall Street on it. I had heard the 'Declaration of the Occupation' read at the General Assembly the night before but I didn't realize that it was going to be finalized as THE declaration of the movement right then and there. When I heard it the night before with Sonny we had looked at each other and noted that the line about 'being one race, the human race, formerly divided by race, class…' was a weird line, one that hit me in the stomach with its naiveté and the way it made me feel alienated. But Sonny and I had shrugged it off as the ramblings of one of the many working groups at Occupy Wall Street.

But now we were realizing that this was actually a really important document and that it was going to be sent into the world and read by thousands of people. And that if we let it go into the world written the way it was then it would mean that people like me would shrug this movement off, it would stop people like me and my friends and my community from joining this movement, one that I already felt a part of. So this was urgent. This movement was about to send a document into the world about who and what it was that included a line that erased all power relations and decades of history of oppression. A line that would de-legitimize the movement, this would alienate me and people like me, this would not be able to be something I could get behind. And I was already behind it, this movement, and somehow I didn't want to walk away from this. I couldn't walk away from this.

And that night I was with people who also couldn't walk away. Our amazing, impromptu, radical South Asian contingency, a contingency which stood out in that crowd for sure, did not back down. We did not back down when we were told the first time that Hena spoke[1] that our concerns could be emailed and didn't need to be dealt with then, we didn't back down when we were told that again a second time and we didn't back down when we were told that to 'block' the declaration from going forward was a serious, serious thing to do. When we threatened that this might mean leaving the movement, being willing to walk away. I knew it was a serious action to take, we all knew it was a serious action to take, and that is why we did it.

I have never blocked something before, actually. And the only reason I was able to do so was because there were five of us standing there and because Hena had already put herself out there and started shouting 'mic check' until they paid attention. And the only reason that I could in that moment was because I felt so urgently that this was something that needed to be said. There is something intense about speaking in front of hundreds of people, but there is something even more intense about speaking in front of hundreds of people with whom you feel aligned and you are saying something that they do not want to hear. And then it is even more intense when that crowd is repeating everything you say – which is the way the General Assemblies or any announcements at Occupy Wall Street work. But hearing yourself in an echo chamber means that you make sure your words mean something because they are being said back to you as you say them.

And so when we finally got everyone's attention I carefully said what we felt was the problem: that we wanted a small change in language but that this change represented a larger ethical concern of ours. That to erase a history of oppression in this document was not something that we would be able to let happen. That we knew they had been working on this document for a week, that we appreciated the process and that it was in respect to this process that we wouldn't be silenced. That we demanded a change in the language. And they accepted our change and we withdrew our block as long as the document was published with our change and they said 'find us after and we will go through it' and then it was over and everyone was looking somewhere else. I stepped down from the ledge I was standing on and Sonny looked me in the eye and said 'you did good' and I've never needed to hear that so much as then.

Which is how after the meeting ended we ended up finding the man who had written the document and telling him that he needed to take out the part about us all being 'one race, the human race'. But it's 'scientifically true' he told us. He thought that maybe we were advocating for there being different races? No, we needed to tell him about privilege and racism and oppression and how these things still existed, both in the world and some place like Occupy Wall Street.

Let me tell you what it feels like to stand in front of a white man and explain privilege to him. It hurts. It makes you tired. Sometimes it makes you want to cry. Sometimes it is exhilarating. Every single time it is hard. Every single time I get angry that I have to do this, that this is my job, that this shouldn't be my job. Every single time I am proud of myself that I've been able to say these things because I used to not be able to and because some days I just don't want to.

This all has been said by many, many strong women of color before me but every time, every single time these levels of power are confronted, I think it needs to be written about, talked about, gone through over and over again.

And this is the thing: that there in that circle, on that street corner we did a crash course on racism, white privilege, structural racism, oppression. We did a course on history and the declaration of independence and colonialism and slavery. It was hard. It was real. It hurt. But people listened. We had to fight for it. I'm going to say that again: we had to fight for it. But it felt worth it. It felt worth it to sit down on a street corner in the Financial District at 11.30pm on a Thursday night, after working all day long, and argue for the changing of the first line of Occupy Wall Street's official Declaration of the Occupation of New York City. It felt worth it not only because we got the line changed but also because, while standing in a circle of 20, mostly white, men, and explaining racism in front of them – carefully and slowly spelling out that I as a woman of color experience the world way differently than the author of the Declaration, a white man, that this was not about him being personally racist but about relations of power, that he needed to, he urgently needed to listen and believe me about this – this moment felt like a victory for the movement on its own.

And this is the other thing. It was hard, and it was fucked up that we had to fight for it in the way we did but we did fight for it and we won. The line was changed, they listened, we sat down and rewrote it and it has been published with our rewrite. And when we walked away, I felt like something important had just happened, that we had just pushed a movement a little bit closer to the movement I would like to see – one that takes into account historical and current inequalities, oppressions, racisms, relations of power, one that doesn't just recreate liberal white privilege but confronts it head on. And if I have to fight to make that happen I will. As long as my people are there standing next to me while I do that.

Later that night I biked home over the Brooklyn Bridge and I somehow felt like the world was, just maybe, at least in that moment, mine, as well as everyone dear to me and everyone who needed and wanted more from the world. I somehow felt like maybe the world could be all of ours.

Much love (and rage). ◆

facebook.com/notes/manissa-mccleave-maharawal/so-real-it-hurts-notes-on-occupy-wall-street/10150317498589830

1 Link to Hena Ashraf's account of the intervention: http://nin.tl/GQV4RY

Race-ing Occupy Wall Street

Tammy Kim
8 November 2011

Two weeks ago in *The American Prospect*, Kenyon Farrow wrote of 'Occupy Wall Street's Race Problem'.[1] He attacked what he perceives to be a movement dominated by 'white protesters' as well as the rhetoric used by white progressives, citing a protest sign that read 'DEBT = SLAVERY' as well as a quote by writer-politico Naomi Wolf expressing her anger that she, a well-dressed white woman, could be arrested for simply standing on a street corner.

Farrow was evidently annoyed by the hyperbolic signage and Wolf's lack of self-awareness, but it sounds like he hasn't spent much time with OWS. In the early days of the movement, I might have echoed his easy criticism of privileged white grad students and limousine liberals, or punks and anarchists stinking up a park with bad hygiene and immature politics. But as I've learned through direct involvement, Farrow's critique – that Occupy Wall Street's offensive rhetoric alienates African Americans and other people of color from the movement – draws far too many conclusions from too little evidence.

One hears many such excuses, many distancing memes: *it's too white, those people are so privileged, they don't speak for me.* Even bracketing the illogic of applying 'privilege' to militant activists drenched in rain and freezing temperatures, these are flimsy apologetics. Occupy Wall Street has already inserted itself into every conversation in America, and it's this level of rhetoric – *we are the 99%* – not the odd poster, that should concern us. If you don't agree with the messaging, it's on you to change it. If you feel it's not diverse enough, add your body to the mix. In this consensus-based process, participation is our most valuable critical faculty.

One should also recognize the instability of OWS as observable spectacle. It's an evolving, self-made, messy space whose signs, statements and local demographics change day to day, hour to hour. This is, on the one hand, a beautiful strength, a real chance for imaginative dialogue in what Slavoj Žižek rightly calls[2] a deeply ideological time; on the other hand, as *The New Yorker*'s Hendrik Hertzberg cautions,[3] we have yet to see whether this young, loosely organized movement will bear political or policy fruits. Each trip to Zuccotti Park means a new reveal: one day it's a cacophony of agendas, yet overwhelmingly white; the next, it's single message and as diverse as New York City itself. This was true at dawn on Friday 14 October, when tens of thousands of us gathered in Zuccotti Park to prevent New York City from evicting the occupiers under the guise of 'cleaning'. It has also been true many Fridays since, the park 'occupied' by South Asian activists protesting war and police brutality.[4]

Racial-justice activists will be irritated by white leftists, who still seem to dominate the nightly General Assembly meetings. But all of us will be annoyed and offended by plenty of different people we encounter at OWS. This is inherent to the jagged, sloppy process of horizontal movement-building, and it shouldn't be a dealbreaker. While I believe the space must be diverse to succeed, I also appreciate the white occupiers who, in a brave exercise of genetic prerogative, put themselves at the front lines of interactions with police and the wintry elements. To be sure, Zuccotti Park would have been wiped out a long time ago if the encampment were all brown and black radicals. More people of color need to lay claim to OWS, as do the immigrants' rights and anti-war movements – and here we East Coasters can learn from Occupy Oakland – but it's important to remember the real, disproportionate threat posed by law enforcement to racial minorities and non-US citizens.

Moreover, the story of OWS cannot be told simply through what is seen. Among its many behind-the-curtain committees are a People of Color Working Group and an Immigrant Workers' Rights Solidarity group. Terrific, critical coverage of OWS is readily available at *Racialicious* and the *infrontandcenter* blog, and even the *New York Times* has noted the increased involvement of people of color, namely the critical intervention by South Asians for Justice to force revision of the Declaration of the Occupation of New York City. This rather dramatic episode, first recounted by Manissa Maharawal, meant vocalizing racial-justice concerns to a General Assembly crowd of 400. Thanu Yakupitiyage, who was present that night and is active in several OWS working groups, recalls, 'Learning to articulate the nuances around our politics was really important, particularly in a movement where lots of different people are getting involved. And communities of color need to be involved. You can't talk about the greed of corporations and financiers without talking about, for example, how the financial and housing crises specifically impact communities of color.'[5]

As Rinku Sen has written in *The Nation*, the question is really, 'How can a racial analysis, and its consequent agenda, be woven into the fabric of the movement?' The answer begins with activists of color, whose participation at Zuccotti Park itself, or in the less apparent, tireless gatherings animating OWS, serves as the best retort to Farrow's critique. The Immigrant Workers' Rights Solidarity group, in which I've been active, has met many consecutive Tuesday nights. Our membership and attendance have grown at a rate any community organizer would envy – and with little in the way of centralization. Ten minutes with this group should allay any skepticism about OWS's commitment to issues of difference. It is one of the most diverse, committed coalitions I've ever been a part of, and we are already injecting the movement with the concerns of immigrants and low-wage workers. Despite my cynical resistance to the hand signals sometimes used in consensus-based decision-making (and maligned brilliantly by Steven Colbert[6]), I was enthused enough the other night to twinkle my fingers – both in agreement and protest. ◆

hyphenmagazine.com/blog/archive/2011/11/race-ing-occupy-wall-street

1 http://prospect.org/article/occupy-wall-streets-race-problem 2 http://nin.tl/GRJk6L 3 http://nin.tl/GQlt2D 4 http://nin.tl/H2molI 5 http://nin.tl/GQbpsk 6 http://nin.tl/H54rPU

Letter to Occupy Together Movement

Harsha Walia
14 October 2011

I wish I could start with the ritual 'I love you' which the Occupy Movement is supposed to inspire. To be honest, it has been a space of turmoil. But also, virulent optimism.

What I outline below are not criticisms of the Occupy movement. I am inspired that the dynamic of the movement thus far has been organic, so that all those who choose to participate are collectively responsible for its evolution and development. To all those participating – I offer my deepest gratitude and respect. I am writing today with Grace Lee Boggs on the forefront of my mind: 'The coming struggle is a political struggle to take political power out of the hands of the few and put it into the hands of the many. But in order to get this power into the hands of the many, it will be necessary for the many not only to fight the powerful few but to fight and clash among themselves as well.' This may sound dramatic and counter-productive, but I find it a poignant reminder that, in our state of elation, we cannot underestimate the difficult terrain ahead and I look forward to the processes that will further these conversations.

Occupations on occupied land
One of the broad principles of unity of Occupy Vancouver thus far includes an acknowledgement of unceded Coast Salish territories. There has been some opposition to this as being 'divisive' and as 'focusing too much on First Nations issues'. I would argue that acknowledging Indigenous lands is a necessary and critical starting-point for two primary reasons.

Firstly, the word Occupy has understandably ignited criticism from Indigenous people.[1] While occupations are commonly associated with specific targets (such as occupying a government office or a bank), Occupy Vancouver (or any other city) has a deeply colonialist implication. Despite intentionality, it erases the brutal history of occupation and genocide of Indigenous peoples that settler societies have been built on. This is not simply a rhetorical or fringe point; it is a profound and indisputable matter of fact that this land is in fact already occupied. The province of BC in particular is still largely unceded land, which means that no treaties or agreements have been signed and the title holders of Vancouver are still the Squamish, Tseilwau-tuth, Musqueam people. As my Squamish friend Dustin Rivers joked, 'Okay, so the premier and provincial government acknowledge and give thanks to the host territory, but Occupy Vancouver can't?' If we are to, in fact, represent the 99%, then heeding the voices of Indigenous peoples is critical to an inclusive process. Plus, supporting efforts towards decolonization is not only an Indigenous issue. It is also about us, as non-natives, learning the history of this land and locating ourselves and our responsibilities within the context of colonization. Acknowledging the territory we are on is the first step towards this, and other occupations such as those in Boston and Denver and New York have taken similar steps in deepening an anti-colonial analysis.

Secondly, we must understand that the tentacles of corporate control and the collusion of government and corporations have roots in the processes of colonization and enslavement. As written by the Owe Aku International Justice Project[2]: 'Corporate greed is the driving factor for the global oppression and suffering of Indigenous populations. It is the driving factor for the conquest and continued suffering for the Indigenous peoples on this continent. The effects of greed eventually spill over and negatively impact all peoples, everywhere. Indigenous peoples feel the pain first, but it eventually reaches all people.'

The Hudson's Bay Company in Canada and the East India Trading Company in India, for example, were some of the first corporate entities established on the stock market. Both these companies were granted trading monopolies by the British Crown, and were able to extract resources and amass massive profits as a direct result of the subjugation of local communities through the use of the British Empire's military and police forces. The attendant processes of corporate expansion and colonization continue today, most evident in this country with the Alberta tar sands. In the midst of an economic crisis, corporations' ability to accumulate wealth is dependent on discovering new frontiers from which to extract resources. This disproportionately impacts Indigenous peoples and destroys the land base required to sustain their communities, while creating an ecological crisis for the planet as a whole.

NO BANKS
NO BORDERS
NO BROKEN
TREATIES

OCCUPY TO LIBERATE
DECOLONIZE TORONTO

Systemic oppression connected to economic inequality

They want me to remember
Their memories
And I keep on remembering mine
– Lucille Clifton

In creating a unified space of opposition to the 1%, we must also simultaneously foster critical education to learn about the range of systemic injustices that many of us in the 99% have faced historically and continue to face daily. In the context of the Occupy Together movement, the connection between the nature and structure of the political economy and systemic injustice is clear: the growing disparity in wealth and economic inequality being experienced in this city and across this country is nothing new for low-income racialized communities, particularly single mothers, who face the double brunt of scapegoating during periods of economic recession. This cannot be pejoratively dismissed as a 'reduction to identity politics' or as being 'divisive', which for many reinforces the patterns of silencing and marginalization.[3] The idea of the multitude is powerful; it forces a contestation of any one lived experience binding the 99%. Embracing this plurality and having an open heart to potentially uncomfortable truths about systemic injustice and oppression beyond just the 'evil corporations and greedy banks' will actually strengthen this movement. Ignoring the hierarchies of power between us does not make them magically disappear. It actually does the opposite – it entrenches those inequalities.

If we learn from social movements past, we observe that the struggle to genuinely address issues of race, class, gender, ability, sexuality, age and nationality actually did more, rather than less, to facilitate broader participation. I would argue that it has historically been a mistake to cater movements to the idea of lowest common denominator 'mainstream' politics. To be clear, I do not disagree with needing to reach out to as broad a base – i.e. the 99% – as possible; what I am arguing is that we have to critically examine who constitutes the 'mainstream'. If Indigenous communities, homeless people, immigrants, LGBTs, seniors and others are all considered 'special-interest groups' (despite the fact that they actually constitute an overwhelming demographic majority), then by default that suggests that, as Rinku Sen argues,[4] straight white men are the sole standard of universalism. 'Addressing other systems of oppression, and the people those systems affect, isn't about elevating one group's suffering over that of white men. It's about understanding how the mechanisms of control actually operate. When we understand, we can craft solutions that truly help everybody.' Therefore, this should not be misunderstood as advocating for a pecking order of issues or priorities; it is about understanding that the 99% is not a homogenous group but a web of inter-connected and inter-related communities in struggle.[5] As Syed Hussan writes, 'Understand that to truly be free, to truly include the entire 99%, you have to say today, and say every day: We will leave no one behind.'[6] Just as we challenge the idea of austerity put forward by governments and corporations, we should challenge the idea of scarcity of space in our movements and instead facilitate a more nuanced discourse about economic inequality and the growing disparity in wealth locally and globally.

Learning from history and building on successes
While it is clearly too early to comment on the future of the Occupy movement, I offer a few humble preliminary thoughts based on other people's comments on the Occupy Wall Street occupation and the nature of the organizing of the Occupy Vancouver movement. Those of us who have been activists do not claim any particular authority in this movement; as many others have cautioned, more experienced activists should not claim moral righteousness and demoralize those who are just joining the struggle. But we also cannot claim ignorance either.

The Occupy Together movement is brilliantly transitional. As has already been noted, it has been a moral and strategic success to not have a pre-articulated laundry list of demands within which to confine a nascent social movement. As Peter Marcuse writes, 'Occupy is seen by most of its participants and supporters not as a set of pressures for individual rights, but as a powerful claim for a better world... The whole essence of the movement is to reject the game's rules as it is being played, to produce change that includes each of these demands but goes much further to question the structures that make those demands necessary... Demands, as opposed to claims, implicitly assume a setting within the established order. They call for reforms of the status quo, rather than for rejection, for what Richard Sennett has called 'different shades of capitalisms' rather than alternate methods of structuring a society.'[7] Similarly Vijay Prashad has written that the movement 'must breathe in the many currents of dissatisfaction, and breathe out a new radical imagination.'[8]

The creation of encampments is in itself an act of freedom and liberation. Decentralized gatherings with democratic decision-making processes and autonomous space for people to gather and dialogue based on their interests – such as through reading circles or art zones or guerrilla gardening – create a deep sense of purpose, connectedness and emancipation in a society that otherwise breeds apathy, disenchantment and isolation. This type of pre-figurative politics – a living symbol of refusal[9] – is a significant success that should continue so we can actively come together to create and live the alternatives to this system. I am reminded of the modest (anti) Olympic Tent Village in our own city in the Downtown Eastside last year, which was deemed 'paradise' and a place where 'real freedom lives' by residents of the Village. Even a glimmer of freedom and autonomy turns people to choose living rather than surviving and to fight for justice rather than beg for charity.

One lesson that I can offer is for the Occupy Together movement to learn about police violence and police infiltration. In some cities, Occupy organizers have actively collaborated with police and sought permission from police and local governments to carry forward their activities. There is only one way to say this: the police cannot be trusted. This is not a comment on individual police officers who may be 'ordinary people', but the unfortunate reality is that their job is to protect the 1%. The police have a long history of repression of social movements. Marginalized people, such as those who are homeless, Indigenous, youth of color, non-status, and trans people also routinely experience police abuse and do not feel that the police serve and protect their interests. We must take these concerns seriously in our organizing in order to promote participation from these communities. We must also learn to rely on ourselves, not the police, to keep ourselves safe and to hold ground when they are ordered to clear us out. This sounds like an insurmountable task, but it has been done before and can be done again.

On the heels of the Olympics and G20, another recurring issue is that of diversity of tactics. Despite a history in community-based movement building, based on a post-Olympics debate with an ally whom I respect, there has been unnecessary and misinformed fear-mongering that those of us who support a diversity of tactics 'fundamentally reject peaceful assemblies'. For me, supporting a diversity of tactics has always implied respect for a range of strategies including nonviolent civil disobedience. As G20 defendant Alex Hundert, who has written extensively about diversity of tactics, told me, 'It is important to recognize that a belief in supporting a diversity of tactics means not ruling out intentionally peaceful means. These gatherings have been explicitly nonviolent from the start and in hundreds of cities across the continent. Obviously this is the right tactic for this moment.' It is noteworthy that the Occupy Wall Street movement has not dogmatically rejected a diversity of tactics. It appears that the movement there has understood what diversity of tactics actually means – which is not imposing one strategy or one tactic in any and every context. The Occupy Wall Street Direct Action Working Group has adopted the basic tenet of 'respect diversity of tactics, but be aware of how your actions will affect others'.[10] This is an encouraging development as people work together to learn how to keep each other safe within the encampment, while effectively escalating tactics in autonomous actions.

Finally, over time it would be wise to stop articulating that this is a leaderless movement; it might be more honest to suggest that We Are All Leaders. Denying that leadership exists deflects accountability, obscures potential hierarchies, and absolves us of actively creating structures within which to build collective leadership. Many of the models currently being used, such as the General Assembly and Consensus, are rooted in the practice of anti-authoritarians and community organizers. There are many other critical skills to share to empower and embolden this movement. As much as we wish we can radically transform unjust economic, political and social systems overnight through this movement, the reality is that this is a long-term struggle. And there is always the danger of co-optation. Slavoj Žižek warned Occupy Wall Street that: 'The problem is the system that pushes you to give up. Beware not only of the enemies. But also of false friends who are already working to dilute this process. In the same way you get coffee without caffeine, beer without alcohol, ice cream without fat. They will try to make this into a harmless moral protest.' This means that we will need to find ways to do the painstaking work of making this movement sustainable and rooting it within and alongside existing grassroots movements for social and environmental justice.

With all of you, I remain hopeful. As beautifully articulated by Gloria Anzaldúa: 'We have begun to come out of the shadows; we have begun to break with routines and oppressive customs and to discard taboos; we have commenced to carry with pride the task of thawing hearts and changing consciousness. Women, let's not let the danger of the journey and the vastness of the territory scare us – let's look forward and open paths in these woods. Voyager, there are no bridges; one builds them as one walks.' ◆

rabble.ca/news/2011/10/acknowledgement-occupations-occupied-land-essential

1 For example, John Paul Montano's open letter to OWS: http://nin.tl/H9onBM 2 http://nin.tl/H5tfGi 3 Link to an account of 'unintended marginalization' at OWS: http://nin.tl/GPKS0I 4 http://nin.tl/GQqr17 5 A gallery of OWS participants: http://nin.tl/GTUtlc 6 http://nin.tl/GQqUR6 7 http://pmarcuse.wordpress.com/2011/10/07/97/ 8 http://nin.tl/H64b5L 9 See Earl McCabe's assessment of Occupy: http://nin.tl/GR7gSI 10 The relevant meeting minutes are at http://nin.tl/GPO8cm

the last thing we need

low end theory
10 November 2011

All of this has left Oakland's blacks and Latinos in a difficult position. They rightly criticize the police, but they also criticize the other invading army, the whites from other cities, and even other states, whom they blame for the vandalism that tends to break out whenever there is a heated protest in town: from the riots after the murder of Oscar Grant by a transit police officer in 2009, to the violence of the last two weeks downtown and, most recently, near the port.

Some day we may discern the deeper historical meaning of these latest events. For now, what's striking are the racial optics. How did Asian-Americans respond to the sight of a diminutive Asian-American mayor being hooted off the stage by a largely white crowd at a 27 October rally? And where was the sympathy when, in years past, unarmed blacks and Hispanics were beaten or killed? Why did it take the injury of a white protester to attract attention?

Meanwhile, those hurt most by the protests are local business owners and workers, many of them minorities. Jose Dueñas, the chief executive of the Hispanic Chamber of Commerce of Alameda County, blamed the Occupy movement for stalled economic activity. 'We've got no events planned, people are pulling back,' he told a local newspaper. 'We don't blame them.' The cash-strapped city has spent over $1 million so far in occupation-related costs.

Local activism has been pushed aside as well. Even as Occupy Oakland has occupied the Bay Area headlines, hundreds of black, white and Latino parents met to oppose plans to close five schools in black neighborhoods. The following day there was hardly a single line of newsprint about the meeting.

'Trouble Beside the Bay' by Ishmael Reed[1]

I'm frankly surprised by the attention this op-ed is getting, especially from ostensibly radical folks. It's a *New York Times* op-ed, y'all. With occasional exceptions, *New York Times* op-eds are not where actual complicated and on-the-ground political analyses take place; rather, they are usually the place where certain ruling-class perspectives get concretized and validated. That alone, I think, makes this worth being skeptical about. I should add that, as a black person who lives in Oakland, I am part of the 'invading army' in so far as I was neither born nor raised here, but rather ended up here by virtue of the social mobility that comes with having an elite college education that provided the means possible for me to move across the country and settle in Oakland while I completed graduate school. There are plenty other black folks in Oakland just like me. As a matter of fact, Ishmael Reed, the author of this piece, is one of them, if one of a different generation. Although he taught at Berkeley for some time, he was born in Chattanooga, Tennessee, and raised in Buffalo, New York. He is an outsider and an insider too, unless, of course, you buy into the racially essentialist idea that being black makes you an automatic insider to any black community wherever, as though blackness was some sorta cool secret club with membership cards and the like. However nice and reassuring a thought that is, it's one that paves the way toward some shitty political analysis.

If you take the time to learn anything about the protests that took place after the murder of Oscar Grant (and the effective acquittal of Johannes Mehserle, the cop who shot him), you know that the people taking part in 'vandalism' and 'property destruction' in the protests that followed the shooting were not just white 'outsiders'. That was actually a narrative spun afterward by then Oakland Mayor Ron Dellums and the Oakland Police, with the help of some of the local non-profiteers,[2] who sought to attribute the uprisings as an expression of infiltrating anarchists rather than as a legitimate expression and rebellion by Oakland's black and Latino youth, who were just as prominent as white anarchists in smashing windows, raiding stores, setting fires, etc. I didn't and don't agree with a lot of these tactics. But I also saw the ways in which, for leaders of color, blaming these tactics on white anarchists from outside was a way of pretending that things were all good at home, of painting a tidy and orderly picture in which Oakland's black and Latino communities speak with one voice when it comes to political tactics. By pretending that only white outsiders do these things, members of the black elite like Reed actually rob blacks and Latinos who choose to use violence and vandalism as political tactics, of a voice.

This, of course, is a class strategy. When you pretend that the black and Latino communities speak with one voice, you also put yourself into a position to articulate that voice. I mean, really, think about it – how often do you hear the phrase, 'the white community'? And wouldn't you look kinda side-eyed at someone who claimed to speak for it? Yet Reed can, in the *New York Times*, speak for Oakland's blacks and Latinos with no editorial intervention and people will pass that absurdity off as if it were legitimate.

First of all, if white outsiders are to blame for the riots after Oscar Grant's murder, then how is it possible to blame them for a lack of 'sympathy when, in years past, unarmed blacks and Hispanics were beaten or killed'? Riots aren't an expression of sympathy? Or principles? I mean, the Occupy/Decolonize Oakland encampment did distinguish itself from the start by renaming Frank Ogawa Plaza – the site of the encampment – as Oscar Grant Plaza. And that was days, perhaps even a week, before Scott Olsen's injury. Moreover, most of the coverage of Olsen's teargas-canister inflicted injury focused not on his whiteness, but on the fact that he was a veteran. We might also ask, why did it take the injury of a veteran to attract attention?

Second of all, and related to my previous post,[3] Reed allows the middle- and upper-middle class stratum of Oakland's black and Latino populations stand in for those populations in their entirety. What makes the chief executive of the Hispanic Chamber of Commerce more representative of the Latino community than the hundreds, perhaps even thousands, of Latinos who have participated in Occupy/Decolonize Oakland from the start?

The point is, Reed's perspective is a class perspective that is aligned with the 'small business owners', and people who profit from small business owners, in Oakland's community. It is in these folks' interest to pretend that there are no dissenting black or Latino voices because those voices might contradict their own. In Oakland, many (but not all) of the small business owners of color have been a highly organized force, and collaborators with the Oakland Police, in efforts to *criminalize* youth of color. In other words, it's no surprise that Reed doesn't give any voice to the blacks or Latinos involved in Occupy/Decolonize Oakland; the arguments his op-ed makes, and the class position it expresses, depend upon the silence of those potentially dissenting voices.

I was at a general assembly for Occupy/Decolonize Oakland last night, as I have been a few times in the previous two-and-half weeks, and while there is certainly a prominent core of white activists who are present, there is no shortage of folks of color participating, offering leadership, and directing the conversation. A lot of those folks of color are, like me, upwardly mobile and college-educated. That is a good thing and that is also a *real* problem. Many of us are not the most vulnerable of – to use a formulation that I don't love but can live with for now – the 99%. The perception that this is somehow a white movement not only underestimates the ways in which the movement is actually in flux and shifting from day to day, but also the ways in which it may represent a genuine political opportunity for communities of color more broadly if they/we can find ways to mobilize themselves/ourselves, and to tell black petit bourgeois folks like Ishmael Reed and the folks who believe him that they/we have an alternative political vision and actually don't need to be spoken for, thank you very much. Again, this is an instance where I think that well-worn pessimism may actually have the effect of rationalizing political quietism when that is, in my opinion, the last thing we need.

*   *   *

Not to be a tease, but y'all should see some of the messages getting dropped in my inbox. I guess some people don't dig it when you call the black petit bourgeoisie the black petit bourgeoisie? ◆

lowendtheory.org/post/12599712629/all-of-this-has-left-oaklands-blacks-and-latinos

lowendtheory.org/post/12611242435/not-to-be-a-tease-but-yall-should-see-some-of

1 *New York Times*, 9 Nov 2011. 2 See analysis by the Raider Nation Collective: bringtheruckus.org/?q=node/112 3 http://nin.tl/GQGxGd

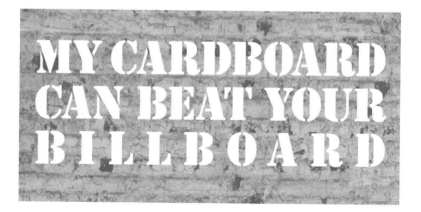

Arts & Culture

The visual culture of Occupy/Decolonize has taken a breathtaking range of forms, both online and off, and an equally striking range of tones.

Some of the sets of images included here, like the infamous photoshopped images of the 'Pepper Spray Cop', are pure products of internet culture. Others, from zombie walks to flying tents, take place in the streets and plazas. Still others, including the 'Octopi Wall Street' meme, rely on verbal play but appear in both electronic and physical form. 'Occupy Sesame Street' and the various uses of Star Wars characters represent the absorption and perversion of popular culture icons by the movement. The migration of online imagery to the streets – the Guy Fawkes masks of Anonymous; lolcats on protest signs – combined with the ironic sensibility that infuses Occupy placards – 'I'm So Angry, I Made a Sign'; 'This Is A Sign' – speak to the importance of bricolage and self-parody to the movement's culture. Beyond the bounds of this section, the texts of protest signs – earnest and sarcastic; insurrectionary and peaceful; classic and innovative – appear throughout this volume.

Writing on the night of the raid that evicted Occupy Oakland from Frank Ogawa/Oscar Grant Plaza, **Jaime Omar Yassin** describes the 'call and response meme' – 'I'm on a Boat!' – that emerged in the encampment's last days as an example of how collective meaning accrues even to the apparently 'senseless'. That the comment thread following this post ultimately drew in the originator of 'the boat', Chris Kendrick, illustrates how the decentralized and immediate ways in which this movement's history is being written change what can be known about Occupy/Decolonize. **Kenji Liu**'s evocative pair of graphics responds to the complexity of Occupy Oakland's renaming of Frank Ogawa Plaza in honor of Oscar Grant. Highlighting the importance of naming as a source of power, he describes his own creative process and demonstrates one way in which different histories can serve as 'a fund of necessary polarities between which our creativity can spark'.

Percentages

Octopi Everywhere

Occupy Los Angeles

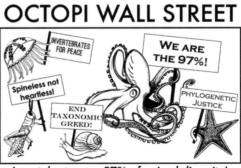

Pepper Spray Cop

Tents

Occupy Cal-Berkeley

Occupy Melbourne

Posters

Alexandra Clotfelter

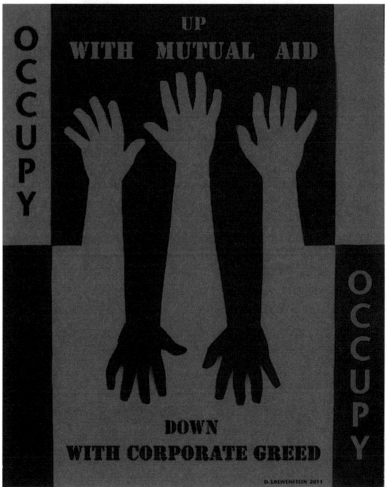

Dave Loewenstein

Eat the Rich

Occupy
Brisbane

Occupy Wall Street

The Empire Strikes Back

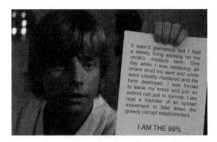

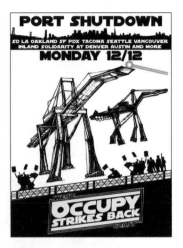

It wasn't glamorous but I had a steady living working on my uncle's moisture farm. One day while I was retrieving an errant droid my aunt and uncle were unjustly murdered and the farm destroyed. I was forced to leave my home and join an extinct cult just to survive. I am now a member of an upstart movement to take down the greedy corrupt establishment. I AM THE 99%

We Are Legion

Occupy
London

Occupy
Philadelphia

Occupy
Dallas

We Are Everywhere

'I'm on a Boat!'

Occupy Oakland navigates in unknown waters (excerpt)

Jaime Omar Yassin (& Chris Kendrick)
17 November 2011

A weird energy enveloped the plaza on the last night of Occupy Oakland 2.0. The infrastructure of the community was quickly deconstructing, for one thing. The kitchen had been partially dismantled to save key components for the future. Largely abandoned, it had stopped serving food. Police foot patrols were symbolically inching their way toward the camp, parking cars on the north side of the plaza, walking a beat in a tight band around the perimeter. More than that, I personally felt a strange disconnect; I described the sensation to someone as a sort of Babel effect. Everyone seemed to be missing each other – though I stress that was just my experience.

Partly to escape the disjointed transformation, I volunteered for a cop-watch run on my bike to see if police were massing anywhere in the vicinity. But when I returned, everyone at the camp already knew that the police were ready to go at the Coliseum – it was being twittered left and right, there was live video of it on youtube. I had wasted my time; in any case, I knew the cops had massed at Coliseum last time and they were likely to again. Really, many of us were sort of milling around for a majority of the late night, not sure what we should be doing, or how we should be thinking about the future of the camp and the movement. Even a party billed as 'Occupocalypse' had fizzled earlier.

I'm on a Boat

But things changed as the night wore on into Monday's early morning. 'I'm on a boat' – the odd call-and-response meme that had emerged a few nights earlier – seems to best characterize the dynamic. There's not too much to the 'I'm on a Boat' phenomenon – every few minutes, like a geyser, someone in the crowd yells out the phrase, and here and there, 10 feet away or around the corner, someone else cries out, 'I'm on a Boat' to the confusion of everyone not in on the joke.

Though admittedly senseless, the term and its dynamic crystallized for me the Occupy Oakland experience. Here, people begin doing things collectively, sometimes those things seem to have one set of meanings and associations, or they don't seem to make any sense at all; little by little, they create their own meanings, ways of looking at things that hadn't existed before. They become important because no one sought to route them into familiar and secure terrain, because they emerged organically. What's created is new, perhaps not immediately recognizable to outsiders to the process – and so that much more powerful[...]

The boat sails

So, as with many evolutions of the last 30 days, though the 'I'm on a Boat' meming may have started out as an act of stress-relieving nonsense, relayed from one participant to another and echoed by bemused onlookers (like me), it has nevertheless become a useful metaphor for the Occupy Oakland movement as it enters its second month of life. Navigating treacherous waters as if the city streets and institutions were an uncharted ocean, OO continues to sail, despite hull-breaches and storms, etching a new social and political map of Oakland and the world along the way.

– and yes, I know that the 'I'm on a Boat' thing is from a Saturday Night Live skit. I still have no idea how it's come to be an echo, bouncing from node to node at the General Assembly and plaza. Anyone is free

*to add its origin in that regard to the historical record in my comments
section[…]*

Chris Kendrick *says:* [23 November 2011 at 5.04pm]
I started the boat! I swear on the occupation. You see it all started
a day before I arrived at the camp, 1 November. I am from SF but
decided to go down to Long Beach to try a new job a couple months
ago. The job was just me and the boss all day, he on the phone talking
to his girlfriend while I built ovens bigger than my old apartment for
the plastic industry. My job before that was as a mover and had my
own moving collective that I made possible with my Sprinter van.
Unfortunately the day I arrived for my new job in Long Beach I got
into an accident on the 405 and my van is only coming out of the shop
here in the next couple days. This accident made me dependent on
the boss as I could not return to my old job until it was fixed. Nor
could I sleep in it while I was down there. Instead I had to sleep on
my boss' sailboat with him. Anyhow, my boss got hella frustrated one
day because he had been fucking around for the last six months and
decided to take it out on me. I told him: 'I don't need to hear this, if
you don't like my job performance then why don't you just fire me.'
He says: 'You wanna be fired, fine, you're fired. Go back to Oakland
and be a dickhead and get the fuck off my boat!' So I grabbed a crazy
kid from Long Beach that had also been fired by my boss a day prior,
and we hopped on the Greyhound with our pay and left for Oakland.
Now the boss is trying to hire me back.

We arrived the day of the General Strike at 5am and stayed at the
music-making section on a bench all day drinking 40s and waving our
big protest sign around. One said 'Fuck You!' and the other said 'hey
fuck this guy!' with an arrow pointing down at anyone under it.

By the second day at the music circle all I could contribute was 'I'm
on a boat'. I screamed this over and over until it caught on. Homies on
the street would come in all evening and rap, usually starting off with
'I'm on a boat motherfucker'. The General Assembly would come over
during the meetings and ask us to keep it down. We would tell them
to fuck off, some people threatened to kick their asses if they asked
again 'cause we were on a motherfucking boat you know. Don't rock
our boat!

Before I knew it everyone staying in the camp was screaming 'I'm
on a boat' and 'boat check!'. The hippies named the new tent town 'the
boat'. The last guy to get arrested during the raid was sleeping in the
boat. The news kept showing this guy being woken up, handcuffed
and dragged through the mud screaming 'I'm on a boat, bitches!'

You might have met me. I was the resident librarian. I eventually rallied a group together and moved the library over to the sidewalk. It was the first place that the cops tore down. I got off that boat just seconds before they tore it down. We still had a joint to smoke so we just hung out till cops raided, then we just drifted around and watched them fuck up our boats.

My name is Chris Kendrick and I started the boat. I also started the response to 'I'm on a boat' with 'I'm on your mom'. My favorite boat was when people would be all serious on the mic at the GA and someone would yell 'I'm on a boat' and I don't know how many times I heard it but the speaker would say every time in mid-sentence 'and I am too also on a boat'.

99% are on the boat, 1% are on the plane. ◆

hyphenatedrepublic.wordpress.com/2011/11/17/im-on-a-boat-occupy-oakland-navigates-in-unknown-waters/

Puppets & Projections

Occupy Wall Street Puppetry Guild

Occupy Portland

Occupy Wall Street

Occupy Austin

Memory is Solidarity
Ogawa-Grant Plaza as Opportunity

Kenji Liu
1 November 2011

'The unity of the 99% must be a complex unity.'
– *Angela Davis, speaking at Occupy Philly*

Historical records tell us Mexico and Spain's names for the Oakland area, but finding out what the Ohlone call it presents difficulty. Obviously, one community's memory, imagination and aspiration has become dominant over others. The ability to name reflects a community's power to leverage that memory into an official story.

In hundreds of cities there are streets and schools named after Dr Martin Luther King, Jr. César Chávez' name is found in fewer places, and Malcolm X's list is shorter still. There are also places renamed informally, such as DeFremery Park in West Oakland, which is often referred to as Lil' Bobby Hutton Park.

It's hard to find a public place named after an Asian American (much less Asian American women). When I first moved to Oakland years ago, I was amazed to find that the plaza in front of City Hall was named after a Japanese American man, Frank H Ogawa. It made me feel like it was okay for me to be here, that I would be acknowledged as real.

Ogawa was the first Japanese American to serve on the Oakland City Council, which he did as a Republican for 28 years until his death in 1994. He was also imprisoned in an internment camp in Topaz, Utah, during World War Two for three and a half years solely on the basis of race. Along with about 120,000 Japanese Americans, other notables interned at Topaz include Black Panther Richard Aoki, civil rights icon Fred Korematsu and artist Mine Okubo.

When the Occupy Oakland encampment changed Frank H Ogawa Plaza to Oscar Grant Plaza, I initially didn't think too much of it. I was more concerned about the term 'occupy', which for me has always had a very strong colonialist and imperialist connotation. (In New Mexico, protesters have renamed their movement (Un)Occupy Albuquerque to connect their fight against corporate greed to the fact that American Indian land has been occupied for centuries.) I felt the plaza's renaming reflected a bridging of the movement to a prominent local issue: police brutality.

But I gradually became aware that many people, not just Asian Americans, felt unsettled about the renaming of Frank H Ogawa Plaza. It was not hard to see the irony of an 'occupy' movement displacing a man of color with another man of color, both targets of different kinds of state violence.

The idea for these images was sparked from a thread on Oakland artist Melanie Cervantes' Facebook wall, where there was an exchange on this issue. It was Melanie who thought of creating some kind of poster addressing the issue, so I want to acknowledge her and her long track record of creating powerful visuals for social justice movements (please see and support Melanie's work at dignidadrebelde.com). It was the work of Melanie and other local artists who supported the Justice for Oscar Grant campaign – as well as the accompanying 'I am Oscar Grant' meme – that largely inspired the posters I created.

I started with the poster featuring Frank H Ogawa against the background of the Topaz War Relocation Center. Then, based on a brilliant suggestion from Jen-Mei Wu (the development process was supported with feedback from many people), I created the reversed poster with Oscar Grant stating 'I am Frank Ogawa'. The latter has become the more popular of the two.

The goal is not to flatten and imply the two men's situations are equivalent. Ogawa and Grant are from different communities and times. However, we can reflect on how a country founded on institutional and structural racism has directly impacted both. This binds the two figures together.

These posters draw arrows between one case of state-sanctioned injustice and another, and try to raise questions about the move to rename the plaza. What do we choose to remember, what do we forget in the process, and why? What are the forces that institutionalize our selective memories?

This isn't unrelated to the anti-capitalism of Occupy Wall Street. The ability to name a place informs what future generations know about it. If few know, for example, that Wall Street was once a real wall dividing the Dutch colony of New Amsterdam from the indigenous Lenape, or that African slaves were once sold nearby, then what connection can anyone make between exploitation of the Americas with exploitation of Americans?

We can have a more complex and nuanced movement for economic and racial justice by honoring both Ogawa and Grant, not as equivalents but in solidarity. This is not just about inclusion, but about having a complex analysis from which to act together. As Audre Lorde has written, 'difference must be not merely tolerated, but seen as a fund of necessary polarities between which our creativity can spark'. We can recognize the different ways capitalism has attacked each of our communities. We can bring this imagination to our aspirations for our places, our movements and our society. ◆

reproductivejusticeblog.org/2011/11/memory-is-solidarity-ogawa-grant-plaza.html

Sustainability

From the beginning, Occupy has dealt with the question of how it will survive and thrive once the initial flurry of interest subsides, grappling with internal contradictions, new conditions for action, and the local and historical contexts that shape future strategies.

Lemony Snicket's aphorisms expose the absurdities of commonplace discourse about economics, politics and OWS, recalling Ambrose Bierce's *Devil's Dictionary* and its combination of political punch and cynical tone. Unpacking the multiple meanings and connotations of the word 'occupy', Dana Spiotta argues that 'everything we need to know' is contained in the movement's name. Vijay Prashad traces the sources and structure of the 'many currents of dissatisfaction' out of which Occupy/Decolonize has emerged. Rejecting multiculturalism and electoral politics as failed strategies, he sees Occupy as the opening to something more radical. Aaron Bady, writing to an audience of social scientists, rejects the idealized account of OWS, insisting instead on the 'resolutely local terms' by which Occupy Oakland – or the Oakland Commune – is best understood and proposes that the abstraction of 'Wall Street' (outside of New York City) makes the concrete aims of local protests appear more radical, objectionable, illegal.

Sarah Jaffe's rebuttal of progressive intellectuals who call for Occupy participants to know their political theory and history raises the largely unaddressed issue of class and access to education. While limiting her attention to formal education as opposed to forms of knowledge acquired in families, churches, union halls, taxicab and barstool conversations, Jaffe establishes that the injuries of class are everywhere to be felt in Occupy and in the liberal responses to it. Emma Rosenthal, reporting on her attempt to visit Occupy LA, describes the ways in which, despite its strategic reliance on the physical presence of bodies in space, Occupy/Decolonize (like other movements) has been insufficiently attentive to the actual bodies in question, to the physical barriers they encounter, to evasions of responsibility for the inaccessibility of the movement's spaces – to the structural exclusion of people with disabilities. Larisa Mann argues that the Occupy movement's growing solidarity with communities targeted by police violence accounts for the brutality of police response to OWS, and locates the radical potential of Occupy precisely in this solidarity. According to novelist **Sara Paretsky**, Occupy radically alters our modes of response to the overwhelming problems of the last half-century, from women's rights to deindustrialization to the fraying social safety net. Its unwillingness to yield to the demand for demands allows it to return not merely to a language of justice and the general welfare but to their achievement.

Thirteen Observations made by Lemony Snicket while watching Occupy Wall Street from a Discreet Distance

Lemony Snicket
17 October 2011

1. If you work hard, and become successful, it does not necessarily mean you are successful because you worked hard, just as if you are tall with long hair it doesn't mean you would be a midget if you were bald.

2. 'Fortune' is a word for having a lot of money and for having a lot of luck, but that does not mean the word has two definitions.

3. Money is like a child – rarely unaccompanied. When it disappears, look to those who were supposed to be keeping an eye on it while you were at the grocery store. You might also look for someone who has a lot of extra children sitting around, with long, suspicious explanations for how they got there.

4. People who say money doesn't matter are like people who say cake doesn't matter – it's probably because they've already had a few slices.

5. There may not be a reason to share your cake. It is, after all, yours. You probably baked it yourself, in an oven of your own construction with ingredients you harvested yourself. It may be possible to keep your entire cake while explaining to any nearby hungry people just how reasonable you are.

6. Nobody wants to fall into a safety net, because it means the structure in which they've been living is in a state of collapse and they have no choice but to tumble downwards. However, it beats the alternative.

7. Someone feeling wronged is like someone feeling thirsty. Don't tell them they aren't. Sit with them and have a drink.

8. Don't ask yourself if something is fair. Ask someone else – a

stranger in the street, for example.

9. People gathering in the streets feeling wronged tend to be loud, as it is difficult to make oneself heard on the other side of an impressive edifice.

10. It is not always the job of people shouting outside impressive buildings to solve problems. It is often the job of the people inside, who have paper, pens, desks and an impressive view.

11. Historically, a story about people inside impressive buildings ignoring or even taunting people standing outside shouting at them turns out to be a story with an unhappy ending.

12. If you have a large crowd shouting outside your building, there might not be room for a safety net if you're the one tumbling down when it collapses.

13. 99% is a very large percentage. For instance, easily 99% of people want a roof over their heads, food on their tables and the occasional slice of cake for dessert. Surely an arrangement can be made with that niggling 1% who disagree. ◆

occupywriters.com/works/by-lemony-snicket

In the Name Itself

Dana Spiotta
27 October 2011

I locate a great deal of the power of Occupy Wall Street in the name itself, Occupy Wall Street, or #OccupyWallStreet. It works because the name contains everything you need to know: the tactic and the target.

The name is also modular. You can create your own offshoot in your own city. The name is built for it: Occupy Los Angeles, Occupy Seattle, Occupy Detroit, Occupy Paris. They are local protests and built locally, and yet through the name they connect to the bigger protest and become part of Occupy Wall Street. Everyone is invited in. You don't have to have the time and money to go to NYC. You can be a teacher or a mother or a high-school kid and just head to your local occupation. So the modular, flexible nature of the name is a big part of making the protest work. We need the right tactics for this historical moment. The financial industry is international, fluid, and not only in NYC. A significant protest needs to mirror that reach. All roads lead to Wall Street, but we feel the effects of Wall Street on every street corner. Certainly in Syracuse, NY, where I live.

I took my seven-year-old daughter to an Occupy Syracuse march. As we walked and chanted through the streets of Armory Square, I felt I was a small part of OWS. But I also realized that when other people saw us walk by, they could connect what they have been seeing on the news to what they now saw in their streets. To hear about rallies and arrests in New York City is impressive, but in some ways it can feel as far away as Cairo. To have it amplified by a local presence means that maybe this protest includes you and your local interests. Maybe this is something different. It helps the movement break through the media noise when you can see it with your own eyes and in your own city.

The modular nature of the name and the way it allows local tentacles to reach everyone feels truly new and powerful to me.

Then there is that word, *occupy*. It isn't Protest Wall Street. Occupy is a much more specific word. It has its roots in the Latin verb *occupare*, which means to seize or capture. So although it is a nonviolent protest, the word is aggressive and warlike. Protesters have long appropriated war terms, and I understand that is a way of appropriating power. I admit I do have a little trouble reconciling the commitment to consensus and democracy with the martial language. Yet I understand that the militaristic connotation of the word projects the anger people feel. It galvanizes people and makes them feel formidable. And it also points to the endless duration that is a big part of an occupation's power.

The duration is a crucial component. The press and the attention of the whole world have come because of the relentless sleeping and living in Zuccotti Park. The protest isn't over when the rally is over. It isn't over when the IMF or the WTO meeting is over. In that way it is more like a sit-in or a strike – all historically very powerful tactics. Occupying means refusing to go away. The longer people stay, the more impressive the statement becomes. It is ongoing, and it collects power as it continues. Our economic injustices are chronic, and so then must be the protest.

To occupy also means to engage someone's attention. Occupy Wall Street means making Wall Street and the corporate power elite understand that the people affected by the binge of unregulated greed are not going away, and they are not going to give up. Occupation also means employment. The Occupy protests give the unemployed something to do. They are occupied with protest, political engagement, and justice. One of my favorite signs from Zuccotti Park reads 'Lost my job, found an occupation.'

Everything we need to know is right there in the name. I don't care that the movement doesn't have specific demands. And I don't care if I disagree with some of the protesters on some of the issues (hey, you with the Ron Paul sign, don't stand so close to me). As long as the protest remains nonviolent, I am happy that it is diverse and inclusive and wide-reaching. Wall Street is occupied, and so are all of us. ◆

occupywriters.com/works/by-dana-spiotta

Occupying the Imagination, Cultivating a New Politics' (Part 5)

Vijay Prashad
23 November 2011

'My heart makes my head swim'
– Frantz Fanon, *Black Skin, White Masks*

Part 5: Occupy

In 1968, just before he was killed, Martin Luther King, Jr, said, 'Only when it is dark enough, can you see the stars.'

It is now dark enough.

Out of the social woodwork emerged the many fragments of the American people to occupy space that is often no longer public. It began in New York, and then has spread outward. The demand of the Occupy Wall Street movement is simple: society has been sundered into two halves, the 1% and the 99%, with the voice of the latter utterly smothered, and the needs of the former tended to by bipartisan courtesy.

Why there is no list of concrete demands is equal to the broad strategy of the movement: (1) it has paused to produce concrete demands because it is first to welcome the immense amount of grievances that circle around the American Town Square; (2) it has refused to allow the political class to engage with it, largely because it does not believe that this political class will be capable of understanding the predicament of the 99%.

Two more reasons to discount the ideology of multiculturalism: Oakland Mayor Jean Quan, one of the founders of Asian American Studies; San Francisco Mayor Ed Lee, one of the main fighters in the I-Hotel struggle in 1977. One sent in the police to run riot through Occupy Oakland, and the other threatened the same in San Francisco. The passion that is pretended is only to obtain advancement.

Occupy is not a panacea, but an opening. It will help us clear the way to a more mature political landscape. It has begun to breathe in the many currents of dissatisfaction and breathe out a new radical imagination. In *Dreams of My Father*, Obama relates how he was motivated by the culture of the civil rights movement. From it he learnt that 'communities had to be created, fought for, tended like gardens'. Social life does not automatically emerge. It has to be worked for. The social condition of 'commute-work-commute-sleep' or of utter disposability does not help forge social bonds. Communities, Obama writes, 'expanded or contracted with the dreams of men – and in the civil rights movement those dreams had been large'.

Out of the many struggles over the past several decades – from anti-prison to anti-sexual violence, from anti-starvation to anti-police brutality – has emerged the Occupy dynamic.

It has broken the chain of despondency and allowed us to imagine new communities. It has broken the idea of American exceptionalism and linked US social distress and protest to the pink tide in Latin America, the Arab Spring and the pre-revolutionary strivings of the *indignados* of Club Med.

This new radical imagination forces us to break with the liberal desires for reform of a structure that can no longer be plastered over, as termites have already eaten into its foundation. It forces us to break with multicultural upward mobility that has both succeeded in breaking the glass ceiling, and at the same time demonstrated its inability to operate on behalf of the multitudes. Neither liberal reform nor multiculturalism. We require something much deeper, something more radical. The answers to our questions and to the condition of bare life are not to be found in being cautious. We need to cultivate the imagination, for those who lack an imagination cannot know what lacks. ◆

leftturn.org/occupying-imagination-cultivating-new-politics

The Oakland Commune

Aaron Bady
5 December 2011

As a site of resistance, 'Wall Street' is a metonym for a system, a transnational apparatus of capital and political oligarchy. We don't have to get too specific, because we all know what we mean when we say 'Wall Street' (even if we don't agree on what that thing actually is). And so while that particular part of Lower Manhattan might be a focal point of a gigantic process of accumulation and dispossession, 'Wall Street' is still just a concrete symbol for that larger and much less tangible process. The fact that so much financial work is actually done elsewhere is not that important; to 'Occupy Wall Street' is to attack and de-legitimize the thing it symbolizes, the ordering structure that builds and rebuilds the world around us, that the rest of us have no choice but to inhabit and endure.

This is why it has meant something very different, from the beginning, to 'Occupy Oakland'. In a just world – in the world the occupiers are trying to usher into existence – there might be no such thing as 'Wall Street' at all, and certainly not in its current form. But Oakland is not a center of finance and power or a locus of political privilege. There is a 'here' here.[1] No one really lives in Wall Street, but those who 'Occupy Oakland' do so because they already did. As a result, when we 'Occupy Oakland', we are engaged much less in a symbolic protest against 'the banks' or 'the 1%' – political actions which are given their shape by the political terrain of protesting abstractions – and much more in a very concrete struggle for a right to the city.

After all, the police who dispersed occupiers with teargas were only doing the sort of thing they had long been accustomed to doing to the poor, transient and/or communities of color that make up a great majority of Oakland's humanity. They used inhuman means of regulating human bodies – the declaration of 'unlawful assembly' – because the city is accustomed to having the power to do so, the effective right to assemble and disassemble Oakland as they see fit. It's that power that's being contested. When a body calling itself the Oakland Commune renames the front yard of city hall after a police shooting victim, sets out to feed and house anyone who stands in line, and refuses to allow the state's purveyors of violence to police them, the challenge is quite direct and legible, a peaceful revolution.

This point is worth lingering on, because it has generally been neglected. You will struggle in vain to find the words 'Oscar Grant Plaza' or 'The Oakland Commune' in most national news reports on Occupy Oakland; even in local Bay Area reporting, those words tend to appear, at most, in quotes made by occupiers. Instead, 'Occupy Oakland' gets made legible by reference, first and foremost, to other occupations, mainly the one in New York. It will be described as more violent, perhaps, or more radical, or the way the police crackdown has been more intense will be noted (and, in some cases, found to be wanting by the guardians of the true spirit of the movement[2]). It is *like* Occupy Wall Street, but *different*.

I'm not saying this is right or wrong, or even making a media critique (though there is much to critique). My point is that using a comparative lens – that mode of analysis by which 'Occupy' is a category, a series of variations on a theme that first emerged in Zuccotti Park – will almost inevitably lead us to overlook the ways that an *autochthonic* Oakland Commune rises up and makes sense of itself, in resolutely local terms, by reference to nothing other than itself. There's a crucial way, in other words, in which Occupying Oakland (or Atlanta, or Philly, or San Jose, or Huntington, WV, etc) is not the same thing as to be a part of the 'Occupy Wall Street' movement: while the former is a reclamation of a very particular shared space, community and history, the latter not only implies that 'Occupy Wall Street' is the original thing – the *important* thing – but it places and understands all the other occupations by reference to that original, like local franchises or copycats who have been inspired by it.

This distinction is especially important, because a certain idealized (and whitewashed) version of #OWS has become a useful narrative for a variety of establishment politicians and critics of both good and false faith. But we need to beware of people who pay theoretical lip service to an idealized 'Occupy Wall Street' brand and then to use the particular shortcomings of its local iteration to condemn it. Oakland mayor Jean Quan, for example, always says that she supports the goals and principles of Occupy Wall Street – a theoretical solidarity, by which she rhetorically positions herself in opposition to abstractions like 'Wall Street' – but this theoretical solidarity has, of course, never translated into any *actual* support for Occupy Oakland. And this is precisely its purpose: a symbolic protest against a symbolic abstraction like 'the banks' is sufficiently meaningless in practice that almost anyone can rhetorically sign on. And once a symbolic protest has been allowed, for the moment, the *nonsymbolic* protest (of breaking a law against open flames or camping in public) suddenly becomes all the more illegal by reference to it.

Take Joan Walsh's recent argument in *Salon* that doing practical social justice will get in the way of doing social justice:

'In Oakland, as in other cities, the camps have become magnets for the symptoms of the social injustice they're protesting: homelessness, drugs, mental illness and crime. Dreamers and do-gooders in the groups genuinely believe the movement has to help society's victims as it tries to change the world. Some think that's part of creating the alternate society that is going to gradually annex the rest of us. I admire those people, but I think the shameful problems of our larger society will capsize this movement if it attempts to solve them on its own, rather than channeling energy into changing a political structure that creates and ignores these human tragedies. Meanwhile, the more the camps attract troubled and violent people, the more they alienate the vast majority of the 99% the Occupy movement is trying to speak for, and leave those comfortable with violence and disorder in control.'[3]

The logic of capitalist realism is overwhelming here – in which the desire to include homeless people is 'admirable' but unrealistic – but what interests me in such rhetoric (and Walsh is pretty representative) is the explicit privileging of 'the movement' over the claims of those it seeks to speak for. Not only have the homeless and chronically unemployed suddenly ceased to be a part of 'the vast majority of the 99%', but she's telling a revisionary history. Homeless people were sleeping in Frank Ogawa Plaza long before Occupy Oakland showed up and renamed it; to push them out because they're not wanted – because to include them would be too difficult – would be to replicate the logic of the city managers themselves. It is to Occupy Oakland's credit that they never did; all were welcome to be present and to be part of the camp. And those who were there, before the city tore it down, know that the pulsing heart of the camp was never primarily the General Assembly. It was the kitchen.

And this was what I found inspiring from the beginning: in a community as utterly divided by class, race, politics, language and gender as Oakland, people reflecting so much of that variety of difference were getting together to hammer together some kind of common and communal purpose, to declare that everyone who inhabited the same space was, in an important sense, *there* together. We ate together, we listened together, we spoke together, and we were teargassed together; in the days when Frank Ogawa Plaza became Oscar Grant Plaza, that tiny stretch of Oakland was perhaps the least segregated neighborhood in the city, and the *only* place in the city where I would ever have the conversations I had with the people I did.

In a way, I'm idealizing it, both because it sometimes lived up to that ideal, and because having it as an ideal reminds us that more is possible than we find to be imaginable.[4] Problems are solvable, and we are capable of confronting them. *You* are capable of being the person who steps up when some crisis arises organically out of the dysfunctions we've inherited from the societies we have no choice but to occupy. This is not the easy triumphalism of Yes We Can, but the hard responsibility of Yes, We Must that we are forced to look in the face when the problems we'd like to avoid don't go away. And this is clearly the job ahead of us.

This is why putting up tents in Oakland was not a symbolic protest, not a part of the movement that can be allowed to die. To put up a tent and sleep in it, in violation of city ordinances, is a tiny way to claim the right *to make the city ourselves*. And since we are, as people, a function of the cities we build to remake ourselves as a people, as David Harvey puts it quite nicely, putting up a tent in this way is the very definition of the right to the city:

'The right to the city is far more than the individual liberty to access urban resources: it is a right to change ourselves by changing the city. It is, moreover, a common rather than an individual right since this transformation inevitably depends upon the exercise of a collective power to reshape the processes of urbanization. The freedom to make and remake our cities and ourselves is, I want to argue, one of the most precious yet most neglected of our human rights.'[5]

The construction of a thing called 'The Oakland Commune' at a plaza that was renamed after Oscar Grant was, in this sense, not a franchise of Occupy Wall Street but a revolutionary defense of that particular space, the demand that *we who occupy it* have the right to decide what will be made of it.

* * *

At this point, then, we have to talk about Oakland itself, about what 'Oscar Grant' means to the people who made that name the center of their protest (or what it would mean if Occupy Oakland renamed itself 'Decolonize and Liberate Oakland.'[6]) The broad and racialized social restructuring that Oakland has undergone in the last half century – an 'urban renewal', after the end of segregation, that has melded seamlessly into suburbanization and gentrification – is a process that has analogs in cities across the United States. But the Bay Area is also unique, and the fact that Oscar Grant was a young African American man traveling on the Bay Area Rapid Transit (BART) system – and was shot and killed by a police officer charged with policing BART – is a perfect symbol of the forms of differential inclusion through which Oakland has been formed and reformed (as this blogger describes too precisely for me to need to replicate[7]).

After all, is Oakland really a city? It might once have been clearly distinct from San Francisco, Berkeley, San Leandro, Castro Valley, Emeryville, Piedmont and Alameda (to name only the Bay Area municipalities on its borders), but it clearly is no longer. To put it more firmly, to pretend that Oakland is anything but a thoroughly well-integrated unit within the vast urban system that wraps itself around the San Francisco Bay is to allow ourselves to be mystified by the very structures of economic and political segregation that we oppose. Woven together by the BART system and by a series of freeways that allow commuters from the hills and bedroom communities in Contra Costa and Alameda counties to pass over or under Oakland's once-vibrant flatland communities – that have been left economically stagnant as a result – on their way to San Francisco, whatever is 'there' in Oakland is there because of how the Greater Bay Area has been designed around it, how it was reshaped by its differential inclusion.

When BART and the freeways were built in the 1950s and 1960s, this differentiating inclusion was made painfully clear by the massive displacement and demolition of primarily African-American communities in West Oakland that their construction required: once the heart of Oakland's African-American community, West Oakland's most thriving commercial and residential districts were torn down to make room for the transportation corridors that linked the expanding suburban fringe to San Francisco's thriving downtown and financial district.

In fact, it would not be much of an exaggeration to argue that 'Oakland' is what's left behind when you carve away the most capital-rich parts of the Bay Area, a single, relatively poor and non-white gerrymandered remainder. As the industries that once employed Oakland's middle class have foundered and gone elsewhere in the last 50 years, Oakland's most affluent residents fled to Alameda, San

Leandro, Hayward, Orinda, Lafayette, Concord or suburban enclaves where their taxes would do nothing for the (increasingly non-white) Oakland they left behind. And even as new sites of industry and development have emerged just outside its borders – in Emeryville, for example, home of Pixar, or in Alameda, adjacent to but external to Oakland itself – the astoundingly affluent island city of Piedmont remains officially external to the impoverished city of Oakland all around it, a kind of reverse Bantustan of millionaires. Named one of the '25 Top-Earning Towns' by *CNN Money* in 2007, its tax rolls need contribute nothing to the schools and communities around it, and do not.

To tell the story of post-war Oakland – as the Bay Area has exploded around it – is to tell a story of political and economic exclusion. But while that story might have begun at the end of official Jim Crow segregation (when the Oakland Police Department notoriously recruited white police officers from the deep South to police its fast-growing black population), Oakland's constitution through exclusion certainly didn't end there. As part of the gentrifying flood of white Oakland residents that have progressively lightened Oakland's demographic makeup in the last 10 years, I can testify that the lines separating where it is 'safe' and desirable to live – and where it is not – are as well understood as the red line that separated black and white Oakland in the 1960s.

All of this is necessary background for understanding why, from the beginning, Occupy Oakland has been the kind of radically inclusive space that it's been, why the beating revolutionary heart of the camp has not been its library or information tent – or even the General Assembly – but the kitchen that fed thousands of hungry Oaklanders every day, or the grassy space of Frank Ogawa Plaza where Downtown Oakland's substantial homeless population could find a home. Local history is necessary for understanding why the occupants of the 'Oakland Commune' have focused less on national economic issues than on the right to the city of Oakland which has, for so long, been denied them. Occupy Oakland has set its sights resolutely local from the very beginning; while anti-bank rhetoric and actions have not been absent, of course, activists at Occupy Oakland have targeted the five elementary schools that Alameda County recently voted to close, for example, and are moving in recent weeks towards defending neighborhood homes from foreclosure.

In other words, a close focus on local Oakland history is necessary background for understanding why this local orientation is so *important*, why the many calls to stop focusing on the camp and refocus on the economic issues – Wall Street! The Banks! Political Corruption! – are missing something utterly crucial about what is happening around us. ◆

possible-futures.org/2011/12/05/oakland-commune/

1 Link to an article about the Gertrude Stein epigram often misconstrued as a description of Oakland: http://nin.tl/HbwDTP 2 See, for example, Micah White's critique of Occupy Cal: http://nin.tl/Hcjc3m 3 http://nin.tl/GUMNlX 4 See video of Judith Butler speaking at Occupy Washington Square Park: youtube.com/watch?v=rYfLZsb9by4 5 http://nin.tl/HfGogs 6 See proposal to rename Occupy Oakland at http://nin.tl/H9qoyt 7 http://nin.tl/H96xLN

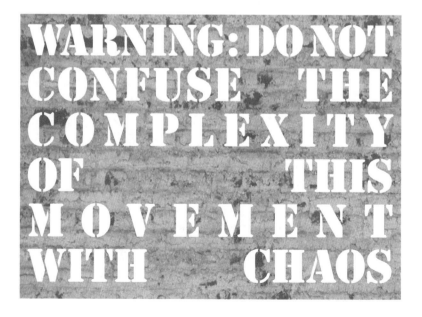

the class implications of 'know your history'

Sarah Jaffe
3 October 2011

It's been bothering me lately, in regard to Occupy Wall Street. The critiques – so many of them are well-meaning, and so many of them are calling for the protesters to have read this or that pet theorist, to have studied the history of protest movements, to have been connected to organizers on the ground.

And the thing is: we live in a society that is structured specifically so that 'the 99%', most of us, DON'T do that. You don't read Gramsci in public high schools. Fuck, I'm a leftist with a Master's degree and I STILL haven't read Gramsci. Yes, I know enough to understand the political implications of the term 'occupy' besides sit-ins – but most people don't, because they haven't spent the last six years reading feminist blogs and all the theory and history they could get their hands on. They are struggling to get by.

Most people are not connected to community organizers on the ground because there are no community organizers on the ground in most neighborhoods. The only reason I know a lot of the people doing the work in NYC is because I worked for a TV show that featured a lot of them. A TV show that wasn't watched by nearly as many people as the ones who watch the nightly network news.

Which plays into the question of why the protesters call for mainstream media coverage. It is wonderful to have an alternative media. I work in it, I believe in it, I love what I do and I wouldn't trade it for a mainstream media job (and yes, I've actually had the opportunities to do so).

But my mom doesn't read AlterNet – not even my writing. My uncle doesn't watch Democracy Now.

I had a conversation with the cab driver who picked me up yesterday – yes, I'm going into Thomas Friedman territory I KNOW, LEAVE ME ALONE – about Occupy Wall Street. Why? Because it was on the AM news radio station he listens to. And he had comments and thoughts about the arrests and was shocked when I told him one of my colleagues, a reporter, was arrested. That guy found out about it because the mainstream media covered it.

So many times the Left would rather be pure than win battles. We would rather be self-assured that we are right, that we always use the appropriate language, that we have read the right theorists and the right histories and our friends are refreshingly diverse and we recycle and buy long-lasting lightbulbs.

But right now, Occupy Wall Street is getting in people's heads. It's doing it by being there, day after day, week after week (now Week 3). It's creating a space, a church of dissent, as Matt Stoller called it, where you can go and make friends, where you can be fed – ANYONE can grab a free meal, which is absolutely a draw for unemployed people struggling to make ends meet – and where you can borrow books from an ever-growing library, where you can join a teach-in – Nobel laureate economist Joseph Stiglitz was there yesterday explaining economics to people – and where you can learn.

It's not perfect. Of course it's not perfect. The incident on the bridge was a clusterfuck and 700+ people spent a night kettled in the rain and then in jail because of it.

But it's attracting people beyond the usual suspects, and it's creating a space where you can learn. Because most people? They get radicalized when something happens to them. They get angry when they can't pay the rent but they hear that Bank of America got bailed out – and then turned around and charged them $5 to use their debit card. That's not pure or perfect or theory or nice. It's true, though.

So what does it say about us, when we say 'They don't know their history!' Who was supposed to teach it to them? 'They don't know the community groups on the ground' – how would they, unless an organizer came to their door? And we all know how woefully underfunded community organizations are. We all know how they've been endlessly attacked by the Right for just these reasons. Just like public education.

End rant. Probably not, actually. But for now. ◆

champagnecandy.tumblr.com/post/10980384207/the-class-implications-of-know-your-history

Arriving at Occupy LA
Cops and dogs have more of a place than people with dis-abilities!

Emma Rosenthal
9 October 2011

I made it down to Occupy LA yesterday, after a week of attempting online to assure that such an effort would not be a major misuse of my time and energy and wouldn't be dangerous or humiliating. (It's not easy for many people with dis-abilities [PWDs] to get ourselves out of the house; it takes real planning.) I had been tweeting, facebooking and blogging and getting first-hand reports from friends and family who had made the trek to the event.

I had spent hours on the phone and in person with some of the organizers. I was brutally harassed and insulted on both Facebook and Twitter for even suggesting that outreach to this significant 20% of the 99% be a consideration, and that our participation be more than passive, that our inclusion must have agency and that we must be able to inform this movement.

After a series of attempts at contributing to this event hit a cruel brick wall, I used harsh words, strong words and militant words. That's what activists **do**! That's what marginalized people must **do**, to be heard. We are not asking for handouts (food, medicine, tent space is all free and **easily available** at Occupy LA, for everyone **but** people with dis-abilities). We are demanding that our skills, voices, opinions, ideas, power be present as equal contributors in the movement.

In previous blog posts, I documented my efforts to offer resources for dis-ability inclusion, and attempts to help the committee that was working on this (if there is one). I was finally contacted by Cassie from 'finance' who informed me that she had bought six accessible porta potties and they would be there the next day (it – one – porta potty, didn't arrive for several days, forcing PWDs to leave the event in search of a bathroom more than a block away). We talked for hours on the phone. Cassie told me she also worked in the welcome tent and to come see her when I finally made it to Occupy LA. She gave me the contact information for Cheryl, the person who was 'in charge of dis-ability access', who a google search revealed was a medical marijuana access activist, but whose twitter account ended after the last election cycle. I sent her a tweet, decided to call her later when I was feeling less burnt out, or figured I would attempt to find her when I got to the event, I was just so disappointed in my efforts so far, and the incredible energy it took just to get porta potties. At no time did she ever attempt to reach me.

From the beginning of my attempts to work with Occupy LA, the excuses I got were rote, almost like talking to cult members. 'We are a leaderless group, We are a few people trying to do so much. We are a nascent movement.' So, over the course of the week, and at the event itself, I offered. I offered to work on logistics, on dis-ability access, on social media and on finance. I suggested they needed a page on their web page with a list of committees, contact persons and meeting times. I also told them they needed a page on their web page on logistics, with special outreach to PWDs – information that included parking, bathrooms, what to bring, perhaps a map of the occupation village, etc. I told them they needed sign-language interpreters and outreach, outreach, outreach. I told them that when people asked questions to social media they needed prompt connection to the appropriate person who could respond in a timely manner and that people offering suggestions should not be subjected to a barrage of hate and abuse. Again, the mantra: 'We are a leaderless group, We are a few people trying to do so much.' One thing Cassie and others had told me was to come down and see for myself. That what was on the twitter feed bore little resemblance to what was happening on the ground.

So, I headed out on Saturday, which was the first day I could get assistance and would be prepared for whatever obstacles I might encounter. I hoped that perhaps I was being too hard on this effort, that it was probably not as bad as I imagined.

Boy was I wrong!!! **Nothing** was accessible. **No single key aspect of this event is inclusive of people with dis-abilities!!!**

The entire park around city hall, with one narrow exception, has a curb that prevents wheelchairs and scooters from entering any portion of the park except the walkways!!! **The welcome tent, the food tent, the media tent, workshops, committee meetings, the library (we had brought books to contribute, but not being able to get to the library, I declined contributing), the first aid tent – so the people who might be most in need of medical attention, can't** get it! – the stage, and even the wheelchair-accessible porta potty, were situated so PWDs in wheelchairs would not have access. PWDs are limited in our participation to sitting in the walkway, watching everyone else interact. We are to need nothing, or hope for charitable assistance, and hope we're not in the way. (We get accused of that, a lot!)

I was told online, more than once, 'I have seen people in wheelchairs out here.'

One twitterer, who set up a sock puppet account just to harass me, accused me of not standing (sic) by other PWDs who attended the event, as if my lack of presence, so unwelcome as it was, was a betrayal to those who were happy and brave and were part of this **farce!!!** (**I mean campout!**)

So, then I had to ask myself – is my passive presence simply bearing false 'witness' of inclusion??? Would people say, 'See, *Emma Rosenthal was there, they even*' (maybe if I was lucky) '*allowed her to speak from the foot of the stairs. Sad – so sad – pity–pity–pity – she couldn't make it up the stairs to the stage.*' *And would I want to address a crowd where no sign language was available to sisters and brothers in the struggle, who are deaf?*

I finally did meet up with Cheryl, the person 'in charge' of access, she was giving a tour of the (inaccessible) campout – because a map wouldn't have sufficed? I found out where most things were, and I couldn't even access most of the territory of the park. She had a slew of excuses for the **total** lack of access, I offered to go on the tour. She told me to wait some undesignated amount of time. She would give me my tour later. She wouldn't let me get a word in edgewise, controlling me and the conversation the way a cop controls a crime scene or an interrogation. She was very, very good at **that** (and perhaps that's why she was there, really – to keep anything significant from happening). She also gave me the mantra 'We are a leaderless group, We are a few people trying to do so much. We are a nascent movement.' Of course they're not leaderless, there's plenty of leadership, it's just not accountable.

After my bad cop experience with Cheryl, someone who identified herself as Jeannie, ran up to me, handed me her card, and gave me the good cop approach. She acted like she knew of me, but said she didn't. She let me know she was in charge of social media, but hadn't seen any of my tweets and facebook posts. (How is that even remotely possible?) And she was eager to get my help on any of the committees I wanted to work on. She was very concerned, explained to me again: 'We are a leaderless group, We are a few people trying to do so much.

Images from an exclusive movement

A 'wheelchair-accessible' porta potty – up a step, inaccessible via wheelchair.

Curbless segment of the Park, just a few yards from where event organizers placed the inaccessible porta potty. They should have placed it here.

Close-up of step to first aid tent at Occupy LA, with signage that says 'step up step down' on green tarp with red tape (no, really, it is really red tape!)

Tables for organizations at Occupy LA – up a curb, making staffing at such a table difficult for a person in a wheelchair.

We are a nascent movement.' It was eerie, like they had all worked together to get their story straight, whenever anyone suggested any improvements. Jeannie was very encouraging, but full of excuses. 'Cheryl was working very hard, and of course the mantra 'We are a leaderless....' She also told me that they were having things **stolen by homeless people**, and that **the event had been infiltrated**. Well, this is where the conversation went totally downhill. At first I thought she was talking about how the cops had infiltrated the event, but it turned out that she was referring to activists who had been pushing for a statement opposing police brutality. These were her infiltrators. She told me the police were an important part of the 99% (apparently more important than PWDs) and that the cops working on this event were our friends, and really good guys, she knew them personally. (I bet she does!!) When I told her the cops weren't part of the 99%, she yelled at me not to call her, and she ran away. (So much for democracy, justice, and leaderless action.)

All of the 'leaderless leaders' I spoke to at Occupy LA were white 30-50 year olds. Neither my partner, activist Andy Griggs, nor I had ever seen any of them in any leadership capacity in any organization or event in Los Angeles.

While I was there, I did see and speak with three other people with ambulatory dis-abilities: one person with a walker, aside from Andy, and two other people in wheelchairs. None of them was happy with our lack/level of inclusion.

At one point I just fell apart, and was consoled by a stranger named Ryan, as well as by my partner, Andy, and my friends Kathleen, Cindy, and Tamara, who was serving at the First Aid station. (She put a call out for plywood for ramps.) I want to thank them for helping me metabolize my rage. I was approached by other strangers, who were also willing to help. But all were powerless to really address issues of equitable and empowered access.

The class struggle is vast, and I would rather find a small stream and flow firmly with the currents, then get caught up in a stagnant eddy in some huge river that has no place for me, nor appreciation of even the most simplest aspects of my humanity. The amount of abuse and isolation is infuriating, and I don't need environments that negate my existence while I'm fed platitudes to 'think positive'. The level of rage I reached just isn't good for anyone. So, unless there are huge changes in the entire movement, I won't be back. ◆

inbedwithfridakahlo.wordpress.com/2011/10/09/arriving-at-occupyla-cops-and-dogs-have-more-of-a-place-than-people-with-dis-abilities/

change comes from connection across difference, not by erasing difference
(excerpt)
Larisa Mann
26 November 2011

The biggest problem for people who DO care about the occupations (which I do) is framing #ows and the occupations as an exceptional struggle unconnected with the continuing struggles in this country and internationally around displacement and police violence.

It is blistering ignorance to claim police brutality towards #ows is unique/unprecedented. Letting the words 'police brutality' come out your mouth without acknowledging its daily reality for communities of color and poor communities in this country is beyond ignorant. It is racist.

You don't say 'I got raped at Macy's' when they charge you too much money for your new couch. Because the word has a MEANING that comes from its history up to now, and that meaning is based in people's bodily experience.

So too framing #ows as exceptional erases the way that all aspects of government, including DHS (and ICE, for another example)[1] are co-ordinated already in the service of violently repressing the majority who have so little power. This includes immigrants, pacifists, people of Arab descent, other people of color, environmental activists, you name it. It's not new.

Anyway, the point is, the main revolutionary (or at least seriously resistant) potential of #ows lies in the possiblity to co-ordinate with these pre-existing communities and movements. In fact, I think the main reason it is threatening at all to the powers-that-be is in the ways it is making connections with those communities. The more #ows finds common cause (through actually participating in common struggle through shared goals) with existing marginalized communities, the more of a threat it is.

Ignoring these connections actively damages the potential for #ows to foster positive change. Such an argument makes it harder for communities rightfully concerned that #ows will not include them to believe that it can include them.

To put it another way, framing #ows different from other struggles mis-identifies the cause of the crackdown as something unique to #ows, rather than as a response to the fact that #ows may be approaching a common struggle with others. As my scientist friend @debcha put it on twitter: 'a real test of a model is not its explanatory power but its predictive power. a non-conspiracy model is more fruitful.' Or as I put it: 'for actually building a movement (not armchair quarterbacking), identifying the cause shapes allies, tactics & thus outcomes.'

In slightly less-twitterfied form: if you don't identify these common causes at the outset, then your solutions and your tactics will not serve the people broadly defined. Solving the problem for a few means you have not identified the problem. The problem is not evil masterminds co-ordinating everything, but mechanisms that frame how we see the world so that we unknowingly consent to (or knowingly have to put up with) inequality within it. If you identify the problem as the first, you actually do the second. ◆

djripley.tumblr.com/post/13371481036/change-comes-from-connection-across-difference-not-by

1 Department of Homeland Security; and Immigration and Customs Enforcement.

Stop the Tether Ball

Sara Paretsky
24 October 2011

I was among the thousands who marched down New York's Fifth Avenue on 26 August 1970. We carried posters demanding pay equity, passage of the Equal Rights Amendment, free abortion on demand, or an end to rape. Like the people in Occupy Wall Street, and the other Occupy groups around the country, we didn't have a set agenda. We were frustrated after millennia of a subordinated status and we were exhilarated by our camaraderie; we knew that in Iowa City, Lawrence, Kansas, and all over the west coast others were joining the demonstrations.

I remember looking up at a private men's club along the route. A trio who might have been drawn by Thomas Nast was standing at the window, holding highball glasses, their faces reddened by whiskey, looking down at us with mingled incredulity and scorn. We cheered and marched on.

During the next decade, we achieved some of our goals, had frustrating defeats over others, never reached pay equity, but what we did do was change the conversation about women in America, just as Birmingham and Selma changed how we talked about race. I look at Occupy Wall Street, or DC or Chicago – my current home – and hope the conversation about wealth, privilege, and a decent life in America is about to start changing.

In the 1980s, when I worked in the insurance industry, I read an op-ed piece in the *National Underwriter* by a health-insurance executive. He said that just as Americans had learned to accept two different tiers of education – good for the wealthy and miserable for the rest – so we would learn to accept two tiers of healthcare. I thought this was so outrageous I wrote a book about it (*Bitter Medicine*), but the executive was correct: we swallowed two-tier medical care right alongside shockingly awful schools as if both were manna from heaven.

In that same decade, as American business owners began shutting down factories here to send work to the cheapest places possible – even to slave-labor camps in Burma – the Chicago *Tribune* chided Danville, Illinois, workers who wouldn't agree to cut their pay to 10 dollars an hour. The plant was moved forthwith to Mexico. *Try living on $20,000 a year*, I wrote in one of my endless unpublished letters to the editor. *Now support a family on that income.*

For over 30 years, the dominant voices in America have shouted that the only functions the government should regulate are women's reproductive health, and access by the poor to daycare or healthcare (then US Senator Rick Santorum proclaimed that women on welfare, required since 1996 by TANF[1] to find work when their newborns were six weeks old, didn't need help with child or healthcare because 'It never hurt anyone to struggle a little.')

We don't need libraries, because if you want a book or a computer you ought to buy your own. We don't need clean air or water for the country as a whole – those are a privilege for the wealthy. Who don't need to pay taxes. As Leona Helmsley famously put it, 'Only little people pay taxes.'

We little people subsidize the roads, the police, the fire protection and the public safety for the Koch brothers. We little people buy gold-plated healthcare for Congress, which includes 244 millionaires, many of whom are working hard to deprive the rest of us of a modest shadow of the coverage we buy for them.

When I look at Zuccotti or McPherson or Grant Park, I'm not surprised the Occupiers don't have a fixed agenda. For decades, we've been like a tether ball in a schoolyard, pummeled by so much abuse from so many different directions that we've just spun around in circles. Now, the Occupiers are stopping the ball, and demanding that we play a new game, one where the 1% don't get to pummel the 99%.

The Preamble to our Constitution cites six purposes of the document that made us a nation. Two of them are 'to establish justice' and 'to promote the general welfare'. It's high time we turned our conversation in America toward how to achieve those goals. ◆

occupywriters.com/works/by-sara-paretsky

---

1 Temporary Assistance for Needy Families, a US government program.

Direct action

Occupy/Decolonize has been defined by bold street actions nearly as much as by widespread encampments. This section gathers analyses of the movement's approach to direct action and contributions to discussions of strategy.

Staughton Lynd, drawing on decades of experience as activist, organizer and strategist, expresses his worries about the future of the movement as it heads into a 'long hot Spring' of mobilization. His immediate concern is Occupy's impending confrontation with the G8 and NATO summit meetings, both initially announced for Chicago. While the G8 meeting has retreated to Camp David, as we go to press, NATO is still expected in Chicago. Recalling experiences of co-optation and internecine warfare within earlier social movements, he urges us to 'act within a wide strategic context, and engage in more than tactical exercises' — and 'to be gentle with ourselves and one another, recognizing the special difficulties of this task'.

In her call for participation in the Oakland General Strike of 2 November 2011, **Michelle Ty** gives a thorough account of the meaning of 'the general strike'; she details the specific conditions of Occupy Oakland, the general strike's relevance to public education, and the plan of action. The 'pepper spray cop', Lieutenant John Pike, and his boss, UC Davis Chancellor Linda PB Katehi, quickly became the faces of liberal willingness to use violence against the Occupy/Decolonize movement after Pike's attack on seated student demonstrators. The **UC Davis Bicycle Barricade** collective go beyond growing calls for their removal, proposing that nothing short of structural change, within the university as outside, will do and arguing that internal repression cannot be separated from other forms of complicity with violence, like UC Davis' involvement in agribusiness operations both in the US and in US-occupied Afghanistan.

After the successful shut-down of the Port of Oakland during the Oakland General Strike, **West Coast Occupy/Decolonize groups** called for a Pacific Coast port blockade. The call was in part a response to specific requests to Occupy for solidarity with the labor struggles of port truck drivers in Los Angeles and longshore workers in Longview, Washington. The proposed coast-wide shut-down quickly sparked fierce debate both within the labor movement and Occupy over the relationship between workplace- and community-centered organizing and actions. Foreshadowing the 6 December 2011 National Day of Action to Occupy Our Homes, **Mike Konczal** proposes that Occupy/Decolonize adopt strategies developed since 2008 by 'foreclosure fighters'. By doing so, he argues, Occupy can bring the struggle directly to the banks, winning material victories, mobilizing broad support and building a base of power in a range of communities.

A Letter To Other Occupiers

Staughton Lynd
28 February 2012

Greetings. I write from Niles, Ohio, near Youngstown. I take part in Occupy Youngstown (OY). I was asked to make some 'keynote' remarks on the occasion of OY's first public meeting on 15 October 2011. I am a member of the legal team that filed suit after our tent and burn barrel were confiscated on 10-11 November. I am helping to create the OY Free University where working groups explore a variety of future projects.

I do not write to comment on recent events in Oakland. Our younger daughter lived for a few years in a co-operative house situated on the border between Berkeley and Oakland. For part of that time Martha worked at a public school in Oakland where most of the children were Hispanic. A can company wanted to take the school's recreation yard. In protest, parents courageously kept their children out of school, causing the school's public funding to drop precipitously. As I understand it, in the end the parents prevailed and got a new rec yard.

That was many years ago. It sticks in my mind as an example of the sort of activity, reaching out to the communities in which we live, that I hope Occupiers are undertaking all over the country.

I

Every local Occupy movement of which I am aware has begun to explore the terrain beyond the downtown public square, asking, what is to be done next?

This is as it should be and we need to be gentle with ourselves and one another, recognizing the special difficulties of this task. The European middle class, before taking state power from feudal governments, built a network of new institutions within the shell of the old society: free cities, guilds, Protestant congregations, banks and corporations, and, finally, parliaments. It appears to be much more difficult to construct such prefigurative enclaves within capitalism, a more tightly knit social fabric.

I sense that, because of this difficulty in building long-term institutions, in much of the Occupy universe there is now an emphasis on protests, marches, 'days' for this or that, symbolic but temporary occupations, and other tactics of the moment, rather than on a strategy of building ongoing new institutions and dual power.

I have a particular concern about the impending confrontation in Chicago in May between the forces of Occupy and capitalist globalization. My fears are rooted in a history that may seem to many of you irrelevant. If so, stroke my fevered brow and assure me that you have no intention of letting Occupy crash and burn in the way that both the Student Nonviolent Co-ordinating Committee (SNCC) and Students for a Democratic Society (SDS) did at the end of the Sixties.

II
Here, in brief, is the history that I pray we will not repeat.

In August 1964, rank-and-file African Americans in the Mississippi Freedom Democratic Party (MFDP), staff of SNCC, and many summer volunteers, traveled to the convention of the national Democratic Party in Atlantic City to demand that the inter-racial delegates of the MFDP should be seated in place of the all-white delegates from the 'regular,' segregationist Mississippi Democrats. It was an apocalyptic moment, made especially riveting by the televised testimony of Fannie Lou Hamer.

But politically speaking, many who made the trip from the Deep South never found their way back there. A variety of causes were at work but one was that it seemed tedious to return from the mountaintop experience up North to the apparently more humdrum day-to-day movement work in Mississippi. The so-called Congressional Challenge that followed the traumatic events in Atlantic City caused many activists to continue to spend time away from local communities in which they had been living and working.

Bear with me if I continue this ancient Movement history.

In November 1965, there was a gathering in Washington DC of representatives from a myriad of ad hoc student groups formed to oppose the Vietnam war. During the weeks before this occasion several friends warned me that different Left groups were preparing to do battle for control of the new antiwar movement. I assured them that their fears were needless: that kind of thing might have happened in the 1930s, but we were a new Left, committed to listening to one another and to learning from our collective experience.

I was wrong. From the opening gavel, both Communists and Trotskyists sought to take control of the new activist network. In the process they seriously disillusioned many young persons who, perhaps involved in their first political protest, had come long distances in the hope of creating a common front against the war.

Paul Booth of SDS called this meeting 'the crazy convention'. I remember sleeping on the floor of somebody's apartment next to Dave Dellinger as the two of us sought to refocus attention on what was happening in Vietnam. I recall pleading near the end of the occasion with members of the Young Socialist Alliance (YSA) to be allowed into a locked hotel room where, apparently having lost on the convention floor, they were forming a new national organization.

SDS faced the identical problem at the end of the 1960s with the Progressive Labor party (PL). Essentially what PL did was to caucus beforehand, to adopt tactics for promoting its line within a larger and more diffuse organization, and then, without any interest in what others might have to say, ramming through its predecided resolutions. After a season of hateful harangues and organizational division, very little remained.

Some Occupiers may respond, 'But we're not trying to take over anything! We only want to be able to follow our own consciences!' Sadly, though, the impact of Marxist-Leninist vanguardism and unrestrained individualism on a larger body of variegated protesters may be pretty much the same. In each case there may be a fixed belief that one knows the Truth and has correctly determined What Is To Be Done, which makes it an unnecessary waste of time to Listen To The Experience Of Others. Those who hold these attitudes are likely to act in a way that will wound or even destroy the larger Movement that gives them a platform.

In the period between Seattle in 1999 and September 11, 2001, many activists were into a pattern of behavior that might unkindly be described as summit-hopping. Two young men from Chicago who had been in Seattle stayed in our basement for a night on their way to the next encounter with globalization in Quebec. I was struck by the fact that, as they explained themselves, when they came back to Chicago from Seattle they had been somewhat at a loss about what to do next. As each successive summit (Quebec, Genoa, Cancún) presented itself, they expected to be off to confront the Powers That Be in a new location, leaving in suspended state whatever beginnings they were nurturing in their local communities. So far as an outsider like myself could discern, there did not seem to be a long-term strategy directed toward creating an 'otro mundo', a qualitatively new society.

This brings me to the forthcoming confrontation in Chicago in May. My wife Alice and I were living in Chicago in 1968. I was arrested and briefly jailed. Although many in the Movement considered the Chicago events to be a great victory, I believe it is the consensus of historians that the national perception of what happened in Chicago contributed to Nixon's victory in the November 1968 election. More important, as some of us foresaw, these predominantly Northern activists, like their SNCC predecessors, appeared to have great difficulty in picking up again the slow work of 'accompanying' in local communities.

I dread the possibility of a re-run of this sequence of events in 2012.

III

It may seem to some readers that 'Staughton is once again pushing his nonviolence rap'. However, although I am concerned that small groups in the Occupy Movement may contribute to unnecessary violence in Chicago, it is not violence as such that most worries me.

While I have all my life been personally committed to nonviolence, I have never attempted to impose this personal belief on movements in which I took part. Perhaps this is because, as an historian, I perceive certain situations for which I have not been able to imagine a nonviolent resolution.

The most challenging of these is slavery. At the time of the American Revolution there were about 600,000 slaves in the British colonies that became the United States. In the Civil War, more than 600,000 Union and Confederate soldiers were killed. It was literally true that, as President Lincoln put it in his Second Inaugural Address, every drop of blood drawn by the lash had to be 'sunk' (repaid) by a drop of blood drawn by the sword.

Similarly, I cannot imagine telling Zapatistas that they should not be prepared to defend themselves if attacked by the Mexican army or paramilitaries. I believe that self-defense in these circumstances meets the criteria for a 'just' use of violence set out by Archbishop Oscar Romero of El Salvador in his Pastoral Letters.

My fundamental concern is that the rhetoric of the Occupy Movement includes two propositions in tension with each other. We appear to say, on the one hand, that we must seek consensus, but on the other hand that, once a General Assembly is over, individuals and grouplets are free to do their own thing.

A careful distinction is required. In general, I endorse the idea of individuals or small groups carrying out actions that the group as a whole has not, or has not yet, endorsed. I believe that such actions are like experiments. Everyone involved, those who act and those who closely observe, learns from experiences of this kind. Indeed, I have compared what happens in such episodes to the parable of the Sower in the New Testament. We are the seeds. We may be cast onto stony soil, on earth that lends itself only to thistles, or into fertile ground. Whatever our separate experiences, we must lay aside the impulse to defend our prowess as organizers and periodically pool our new knowledge, bad as well as good, so as to learn from each other and better shape a common strategy.

The danger I see is that rather than conceptualizing small group actions as a learning process, in the manner I have tried to describe, we might drift into the premature conclusion that nonviolence and consensus-seeking are for the General Assembly, but once we are out on the street sterner methods are required.

We have a little more than two months before Chicago in May. Unlike Seattle, the folks on the other side will not be unprepared. On 18 January, the Chicago City Council overwhelmingly passed two ordinances pushed by [Mayor Rahm] Emanuel that restrict protest rules and expand the mayor's power to police the summits. Among other things, they increase fines for violating parade rules, allow the city to deputize police officers from outside Chicago for temporary duty and change the requirements for obtaining protest permits. Large signs and banners must now be approved, sidewalk protests require a permit, and permission for 'large parades' will only be granted to those with a $1-million liability insurance policy. These are permanent changes in city law.[1]

It would be tragic if we failed to make good use of the precious period of time before all this must be confronted.

IV

So what do I recommend? I am 82 and no longer able to practice some of what I preach, but, for what they may be worth, here are some responses to that question.

We need to act within a wide strategic context, and engage in more than tactical exercises.

We need to invite local people to join our ranks and institutions. We cannot hope to win the trust of others, especially others different from ourselves in class background, cultural preferences, race or gender, unless we stay long enough to win that trust one day at a time. We must be prepared to spend years in communities where there may not be many fellow radicals.

In thinking about our own lives, and how we can contribute over what Nicaraguans call a 'long trajectory', we need to acquire skills that poor and oppressed persons perceive to be needed.

We should understand consensus and nonviolence not as rigid rules, or as boundaries never to be crossed, but as a core or center from which our common actions radiate. Consensus is not just a style of conducting meetings. It seeks to avoid the common human tendency to say, after an action that runs into trouble, 'I told you so'. The practice of consensus envisions that discussion should continue until everyone in the circle is prepared to proceed with a group decision. Perhaps different ones of us have varying degrees of enthusiasm or even serious apprehensions. Anyone who has such misgivings should voice his or her concern because it may be an issue that needs to be addressed. But we must talk things out to a point where as a group we can say, 'We are doing this together.'

Likewise, nonviolence is under some circumstances the most promising way of challenging authority. Trotsky describes in his history of the Russian Revolution how, on International Women's Day, 1917, hundreds of women in St Petersburg left their work in textile factories demanding Peace and Bread. The women confronted the Cossacks, the policemen on horseback, in the streets. Unarmed, the women approached the riders, saying in effect: 'We have the same interests you do. Our husbands and sons are no different from yourselves. Don't ride us down!' And the Cossacks repeatedly refused to charge.

After all, policemen and correctional officers are also part of the 99%. When I visit prisoners at the supermaximum security prison in Youngstown, more than one officer has called out, 'Remember me, Staughton? I used to be your client.' When they could not find other work in our depressed city, which has the highest rate of poverty in the United States, many former steelworkers and truck drivers took prison jobs.

Nelson Mandela befriended a guard at Robben Island whose particular assignment was to watch over him. The officer, James Gregory, has written a book about it sub-titled *Nelson Mandela: My Prisoner, My Friend*. Mr Gregory had a seat near the front at Mr Mandela's inauguration.

The same logic applies to soldiers in a volunteer army. Thus one Occupier has written, 'A thoughtful soldier, a soldier with a conscience, is the 1%'s worst nightmare.'[2]

In the end, I think, consensus decision-making and nonviolence both have to do with building a community of trust. One of my most chilling memories is to have heard a national officer of SDS talk to a large public meeting in Chicago about 'icing' and 'offing' persons with whom one disagreed. Actual murder of political comrades apparently took place in El Salvador, the United States and, so I am told, Ireland.

Everything depends on whether two persons who differ about what should next be done nevertheless trust each other to proceed within the invisible boundaries of their common commitment.

A principal lesson of the 1960s is that maintenance and nurturing of that kind of trust becomes more difficult as a movement or organization grows larger. Here the Zapatistas have something to teach us. They do have a form of representative government in that delegates from different villages are elected to attend co-ordinating assemblies. But all governing is done within the cultural context of the ancient Mayan practice of 'mandar obediciendo', that is, governing in obedience to those who are represented. Thus, after the uprising of 1 January 1994, negotiations began with emissaries from the national government. If a question arose as to which the Zapatista delegates were not instructed, they informed their counterparts that they had to go back to the villages for direction.

All this lies down the road. For the moment, let's remind ourselves of the sentiment attributed by Charles Payne to residents working with SNCC in the Mississippi Delta half a century ago: they understood that 'maintaining a sense of community was itself an act of resistance'. ◆

zcommunications.org/a-letter-to-other-occupiers-by-staughton-lynd

1 'Managing Dissent in Chicago,' *In These Times*, March 2012. **2** *The Occupy Wall Street Journal*, Nov 2011.

The Coming General Strike

Michelle Ty
31 October 2011

As someone who rarely likes to make an imposition on people's time, I am writing this letter to entreat you to consider setting aside some of your hours this Wednesday – and with these hours to support the general strike that was called for by Occupy Oakland.

For the sake of conceptual clarity, we might begin by noting that what makes a strike 'general' has little to do with surpassing some quantitative threshold of participants. What is implied in the adjective is not strictly about size – how 'big' the strike is – but rather designates a political action that is qualitatively different from the typical labor strike.

According to [Walter] Benjamin (who himself is drawing from Georges Sorel), there are two essentially different kinds of strikes. In the *political strike*, partisans withhold labor, with the hope that their action – which interestingly is an *omission* of action – will cause an employer to make certain concessions that the strikers have specified beforehand. Because it is assumed that participants are ready to resume work once certain demands have been met, the strike can be thought of as the means to a determinate end (usually some form of material gain).

By contrast, the general strike is what Benjamin describes as 'pure means'. Such an action differs from the paradigm of political activity that seeks only immediately practicable goals – like wage increases, health benefits and certain modifications to the workplace. The premise of the general strike is this: work will not resume once this or that concession is made; instead, people will show their 'determination to resume only a *wholly transformed work*' [my italics]. In a characteristically wonderful phrase, Benjamin writes that the general strike 'not so much causes as consummates'.

Likely, one can already see why, for the 'occupy movement' that refuses to articulate 'moderate' demands, the general strike would be an apt form of resistance.

But before rushing into a consideration of the upcoming general strike that is just a day away, it is perhaps worthwhile to counterpoint Benjamin's conception with that of Rosa Luxemburg, who cautioned that the 'abstract, unhistorical view of the mass strike' would all too easily lose sight of the circumstances that made such actions possible.

When she wrote about the general strike in 1906, she had the Russian Revolution on the mind. From her point of view, the 1905 strikes marked a 'new epoch in the development of the labor movement' and was the first time the idea of the mass strike – a mature form of the general strike – had been successfully realized. Here is an excerpt from her historical account of these events, which is quite astonishing if read with care:

> The spring of 1903 gave the answer to the defeated strikes in Rostov and Tichoretzkaia; the whole of South Russia in May, June, and July was aflame. Baku, Tiflis, Batum, Elizavetgrad, Odessa, Kiev, Nicholaiev and Ekaterinoslav were in a general strike in the literal meaning of those words. But here again, *the movement did not arise on any preconceived plan from one to another; it flowed together from individual points in each one from a different cause and in a different form…* In Tiflis the strike was begun by 2,000 commercial employees who had a working day of from six o'clock in the morning to eleven at night. On the fourth of July they all left their shops and made a circuit of the town to demand from the proprietors of the shops that they close their premises. The victory was complete; the commercial employees won a working day of from eight in the morning to eight in the evening, and they were immediately joined by all the factories, workshops and offices. The newspapers did not appear, and tramway traffic could not be carried on… In Elisavetgrad on 4 July a strike began in all the factories with purely economic demands. These were mostly conceded, and the strike ended on the 14th. Two weeks later, however, it broke out again. The bakers this time gave the word and they were joined by the bricklayers, the joiners, the dyers, the mill workers, and finally all factory workers. [my italics]

At the very least, the imagination should now be aroused. A 6am to 11pm shift – utterly outrageous. One has the image, too, of the city's bakers, rolling pins in hand, sending text messages to the bricklayers, reputed to be active tweeters, who then go on to spread word of the strike to the mill workers. Soon enough, all factory workers have their two feet in the street.

The conclusions that Luxemburg drew from her involvement in the revolution are worth repeating. For the ease of your eyes, some of these ideas are laid out in bullet form.

* It is absurd to conceive of a general strike as an isolated act; it is, rather, an 'indication, the rallying idea, of a whole period of the class struggle'.
* Often, the general strike can be seen to oscillate with smaller-scale economic strikes – or what, in Benjaminian terms, would be called the *political strike* for economic gain. Thus, economic and political struggles seem to pass into each other and to be mutually animating.
* Although planning is involved in a general strike, a general strike cannot be 'planned'. Its success cannot be entirely guaranteed by conscious initiative and direction. Rather, its fruition depends largely on a degree of spontaneity.

A word on this last point: Luxemburg's emphasis on the necessity of spontaneity should not be interpreted merely as a caricatured expression of Romantic ideology. Her insistence on acknowledging the role of accident in history is itself a critique of a theory that would suggest that history is made up of the decisions of a few. Even a most cursory survey of the events of the Arab Spring or, for an example closer to home, the building occupations in California, would seem to corroborate her hypothesis.

As the above passage illustrates well, Luxemburg noticed that the most significant events of the popular movement were not orchestrated or produced artificially but were often triggered by little, accidental occurrences, which – like the first dapple of color on the canvas – are to a degree unforeseeable. Without downplaying the importance of organization, Luxemburg insists that a mass strike cannot be called at will, and that the form it takes cannot be determined in advance.

To conclude our preliminary understanding of the general strike, we can say that it is characterized by a cross-sectoral cessation of labor and animated by the conviction that what is wrong with the present state of things cannot be set straight by a finite set of 'feasible' modifications; instead, some yet-to-be-determined structural transformation must take place. The general strike involves some element of spontaneity and, when consummated, results in a marked disruption of the functioning of business, and therefore the city, state, nation or world.

With Benjamin and Luxemburg as historico-philosophical touchstones, we can now begin an inquiry about the coming general strike of 2 November.

* * *

The last general strike in the United States took place some time ago, here in Oakland in 1946. This was the same year that Gertrude Stein died, and a year following a wave of protests against the bombing of Japan. The 1946 strike was initiated by a few hundred clerks, mostly women, who were working in retail. In December, a relatively small strike prevented delivery trucks from supplying goods to two large department stores in downtown Oakland. The police exercised force to break up picket lines, and soon, several other labor organizations joined the strikers in solidarity.

More than a hundred thousand employees walked out of their jobs – sailors were among the first – and a 'workers' holiday' was declared (the force of this figure is only felt when one recalls that, at the time, the total population of Oakland's workforce was about 200,000). All stores were instructed to close, with the exception of pharmacies and food markets. Jukeboxes were set out in the streets and played tunes for free. By day two, the strikers demanded the resignation of the mayor.

That was in 1946. Since then, the practice of the general strike has been relatively dormant in America. The question must be asked, *why a general strike now? Why here?*

Although I am hardly qualified to supply what is necessary to answer these questions adequately – namely an analysis of the objective conditions from which this strike emerges – I can offer some thoughts about why such a strike should be supported and why, to put it simply, the general strike matters.

* * *

There are times when it seems that the chasm between theory and practice cannot be traversed, and times, like last week, when it seems that they manage to find their way to each other, all on their own. Times, that is, when the day itself seems to impose upon you questions of a 'theoretical' nature.

What does it mean to enclose public space in order to prohibit *public* space from being publicly used? This question was posed by the fences that were erected downtown, to prevent people from reclaiming a plaza that is ostensibly accessible to all.

We might also wonder (as Weber and others have), why it is that the state can lay claim to the exclusive right to the 'legitimate' use of force? And, given that the police do claim that their acts of physical violence are sanctioned, we might ask, from where does this sanction come?

As you have undoubtedly heard, the Oakland police raided the peaceful encampment at Frank Ogawa Plaza last Tuesday – at five in the morning. Dressed in riot gear, the police destroyed tents and confiscated property, including medical supplies. Ninety-seven people were arrested. When, that evening, people gathered at the library and decided to reclaim the plaza, the police reacted with an even greater show of force. Against a crowd of unarmed civilians, they deployed rubber bullets, flash grenades, and fired not one, but six rounds of teargas. In the fray, a projectile fired by an officer hit an Iraq war veteran, Scott Olsen, resulting in a fractured skull and the impairment of his faculty of speech.

Some have argued that the protesters were forewarned that 'chemical agents would be used', that harm would come to them if they remained. But, as even the most rudimentary playground wisdom will attest, announcing one's intention to strike out at another does not mean that doing so is okay.

The evening following the confrontation with police, over 3,000 people congregated for a general assembly, during which the general strike was first proposed.

In this skeletal recapitulation of a now-familiar narrative, I want to call attention to the strange temporal dynamics at work in the local enforcement of law. The occupation of Oakland began on 10 October; an eviction notice was not issued until the 20th. On the 10th, the encampment was supported by the city; 10 days later it was condemned. What was, at one point on Tuesday, recognized as a peaceful demonstration, by nightfall was declared an 'unlawful assembly'. What should be evident, here, is that something awry is happening to the separation between law and its enforcement. That the very same act that is initially assessed not to be in violation of the law can later, without any structural transformation of the act, be persecuted as an illegality, suggests that the law enforcement is not merely preserving the law given by the people, but that it is actually attempting to instate the law. This act of law-making by law enforcement does not derive its power from the people, but forcefully institutes law primarily by means of the threat of violence. This would seem a clear violation of democratic principles.

On occasion, concrete experience can bring unprecedented clarity to abstract contradictions. When, on Tuesday night, a police sergeant announced that he was 'declaring this to be an unlawful assembly in the name of the people of California', one woman in the crowd retorted, with some fervor, *We are the people of California*. Apart from the fact that such a comment reveals a sense of humor under duress that I personally find charming, the incident did make palpable the incongruity between a state that acts in 'the name of the people' and the people themselves.

A consequence of recent events is that, for many Bay Area residents, this contradiction, which one might readily acknowledge as a fact, has lately been *felt*, heard and seen. The prevalence of gas masks, a somewhat recent fashion trend, testifies visually to felt experience. Recalling Luxemburg's reflections earlier discussed, these October events, which include developments in the occupation of Wall Street, might be thought of as the relatively small occurrences that flow 'rapidly to a raging sea'.

The recent occupation of Oakland emerges, too, from a backdrop of various unresolved local and statewide issues that were exacerbated by the financial crisis of 2008 and surfaced acutely in the past year – the gang injunctions that impose curfews in designated areas populated mostly by ethnic minorities, the closure of state parks and public libraries, the rise of California's unemployment rate to over 12 per cent, the shooting of Oscar Grant by the BART[1] police, to name a few. Occupy Oakland also speaks to those state-level problems that have been percolating for decades. Although it is only one of numerous causes, many single out Proposition 13 (1978), which limits property taxes, as a significant factor that contributed to the unnecessary inflation of the state budget deficit, and the resultant enervation of public services, including California's state education system.

* * *

From its inception, Occupy Oakland conceived of itself as a response to its local history of resistance, as well as to the occupation under way on the east coast. In part because it has decidedly formed itself as part of a national movement, many of the reasons to support the Oakland general strike coincide with arguments in favor of the occupation of Wall Street.

I will not rehearse the many motives that have now become buzzwords for the movement (i.e., 'corporate greed'; the 99%). I will, however, suggest a few other, perhaps less familiar considerations, regarding these nationwide efforts.

1) To deny the legitimacy of a movement on the grounds that it does not make (practicable) demands is to deny political praxis the

right to theoretical reflection.

Such a view restricts politics to the smaller realm of practical activity, then falsely asserts their coincidence. Although the Occupy movement is often ridiculed for being directionless, it would seem even more absurd to insist that people are entitled to make feasible demands, yet denied any say over what constitutes feasibility. Popular politics should be permitted to devote itself to something that is not strictly immediately practical, but would actually be able to determine what the limitations of practical activity are (an assessment of aims, means, method).

It also might be added that, as in the moment of articulation, something is lost in the very act of definition. Something is lost when the constitutive power of people is constituted in discursive prescriptions and a set of norms. The point is perhaps most easily made by appealing to that experience, which you no doubt have had, in which something is felt yet remains unspoken. That moment of bringing to words what had before only existed, spread out like a mist, does confer upon something a new reality but also robs it of what it might have been.

2) The reaction of the state suggests an unfortunate predicament: although the state, in the name of austerity, is increasingly reluctant to provide for the welfare of citizens, it also prohibits citizens from providing for the welfare of one another, including those people who are not recognized as citizens.

When the Occupy Oakland encampment was first being set up, its priorities were telling. Medics and medical supplies were among the first things to be secured. Along with that, the camp ensured the provision of food, a library, a free school, a source of sustainable energy (a stationary bike powered a generator), a garden – and eventually daily classes in yoga and meditation.

Healthcare, education, sustenance, energy, and well-being. There is a sense that these things must not be provided for free. In Austin, occupiers were arrested for criminal trespassing (!) when they set up a food table in front of the City Hall. In Zucotti Park, firefighters confiscated gas canisters and generators that powered electronic devices and kept people warm. In more distant history, the FBI denounced as 'communist' the Black Panthers' social program that served free breakfast to children.

3) From the second point, we might arrive at a third, namely *the rejection of the idea that what is extra-legal is necessarily illegal.* The

occupy movement, among other things, is attempting to make possible a politics that is not subjected to the mill of legal process. If the formation and regulation of law is often influenced by private interests, it would make sense for people to try to form a political process outside of a legal system that no longer reflects popular sovereignty.

4) To support the general strike would indicate support for labor rights more generally, which, in the past year especially, have been diminished in the United States. Labor rights, one can recall, are things that protect people who do not have any other resources to ensure their livelihood, apart for their own work and time.

Admittedly, I suffer from a feeling of enthusiasm that some noses might snub as naiveté. And though I am willing to admit the possibility that the strong impression made on me could have to do, in part, with historical myopia, I do think something remarkable is happening here and, as a result, that remarkable things are happening elsewhere.

The immediate and attentive international response to local events is noteworthy. Within a day of the OPD's show of police brutality, activists in Egypt announced their solidarity with California and organized a march on Tahrir Square, issuing a statement that 'Oakland and Tahrir are one hand'. New York responded quickly, too, with donations and a solidarity protest. Yesterday, the Philippine Airlines Employees' Association issued a statement of support and are now planning to occupy airports in Cebu and Manila as a sign that they stand 'shoulder to shoulder with the Occupy Oakland Protesters'.

A chant that has recently grown popular draws together two places with a copula: 'Oakland is Tahrir'; 'Oakland is Greece'; 'Oakland is New York'; 'Oakland is Denver'. Of course one should take careful note of where comparisons illuminate and where they only obfuscate important differences. The assertion of an unequivocal parallelism between Egypt and Oakland fails almost instantly in that there is an unmistakable difference between the occupations here and the struggle against dictatorial regimes in the Middle East. That said, such international alignments do draw attention to some shared economic conditions – and speak to the notion that the most pressing problems extend well beyond the borders of the nation-state and have much to do with the workings of global finance and uneven economic development across the world.

So then, we might say that the copula keeps distinct what it draws together.

* * *

Among the several reasons for supporting the general strike that we have considered, I have left out the one that may hit home most closely – that is, the insistence on the importance of accessible education.

Although the defense of public education may seem a remote or peripheral concern of the Occupy movement, the connection between the two is indisputable. There is a financial pipeline that travels from public universities directly to Wall Street, and what is trafficked through this pipeline is not anything positive – rather it is debt. This year, student debt hit the trillion-dollar mark, surpassing credit-card debt in magnitude. As Bob Meister has put it, student loans are one of the last legal forms of subprime lending – the practice of lending money to people, knowing that it is unlikely that they will be able to pay it back. Now that debt has been securitized – can be sold as an asset – it has become possible, on a large scale, to convert debt (future labor) into a source of profit.

Nietzsche reminds us that the relationship between creditor and debtor depends on the wager of the body as collateral. The creditor lends what the borrower does not have. As a guarantee of repayment, the debtor agrees that in the event of default, the lender can inflict harm on the body as method of compensation. Although the workings of this principle of exchange have become abstract – and even spectral – at root, the economy still operates in quite the same fashion. Those who lack resources are forced to take out loans in order to provide for basic needs, like education, all while the cost of these basic needs becomes increasingly prohibitive; as a result of this unwise, but necessary borrowing, bodies are put on the line (the working body that can never seem to catch up to the interest that it owes; the sleeping body that is displaced from its shelter).

In response to speculative finance's guise of being wholly immaterial, the form of political action called for by the general strike – the congregation of bodies – gives corporeal expression to what would otherwise remain abstract and therefore somewhat remote.

There is much else to say regarding how public education has played the double role of being a great casualty of privatization as well as its very conduit. One could point to the questionable investment policies of the UC [University of California] Regents; the increasing ratio of managerial to faculty positions in the university; the still-escalating cost of student fees; the UC's borrowing of money from banks and its pledge to raise tuition as a means of keeping its bond rating high; the liquidation of minority departments to cut expenses; the layoffs and furloughs imposed in the name of a fiscal emergency; the closure of libraries and schools; the rise of the for-profit education sector; the influence of the private sector on scholarly research; the uneven accessibility of education that seems to follow closely racial lines.

But perhaps all this talk is for another day.

Since its announcement, the general strike has been endorsed by the UAW, the union that represents Berkeley staff and graduate students. The Berkeley Federation of Teachers has also invited members to participate. And, as of yesterday, the Oakland Teachers Association endorsed the strike, after the board came to a unanimous vote.

* * *

The Plan

The Oakland general strike was called for on Wednesday 26 October, during the general assembly that convened at seven o'clock in the evening. When I say that a strike was called, what I mean is that the strike was discussed and voted upon by the people who attended, and that anyone was welcome to attend.

The official proposal calls for the city to be shut down; encourages workers not to attend work and students to walk out of school. The event is called a general strike *and* a mass day of action so that organizations that would otherwise be penalized for officially endorsing a strike can lend their support.

Protests will be held at Oscar Grant Plaza (14th and Broadway) at nine, noon, and at five. They have opted to schedule multiple mass convergences so that those who cannot leave the workplace can participate in the evening.

The evening plan, as I understand it, is to march south from the plaza to the Port of Oakland and to arrive before the change of shifts that will take place at seven o'clock. They plan to shut down the port, which happens to be the fifth-busiest container port in the country. This is hardly an impossible task. In 2008, union workers and protesters who opposed the Iraq war successfully shut down much of Oakland's port. More recently, 10 ports in the East Bay were shut down by workers demonstrating in solidarity with Wisconsin and Ohio.

In Berkeley, people will congregate at 11am at Sproul Plaza. The hope is to gather at least a couple hundred people so that a march to Oakland, through the streets, will be possible. There will be another convergence at four o'clock in the afternoon, but it seems that the earlier meeting may be the better option.

* * *

Among the most trenchant objections to participating in the strike is that it would seem imprudent to insist on the priority of education by encouraging students and teachers to abandon their schools. Though the point is well taken, it does seem to reveal some short-sightedness in that the worry about missing one day of school is incommensurate with the very possible loss of the whole prospect of affordable education.

And, of course, there is also that old objection about the inefficacy of protest, the possibility that the lion's roar may turn into little more than the paper tiger's whimper. To the repeated question, 'What will a strike actually do?', we might recall Benjamin's analysis, which suggests that such a question fails to understand something fundamental about the general strike. In addition, we could also heed the experiential wisdom of Luxemburg, who writes: 'After every foaming wave of political action a fructifying deposit remains behind from which a thousand stalks of economic struggle shoot forth.'

So yes, there is a real possibility that your hours ultimately may be of little consequence. That said, it does seem that to live by entangling heart and mind only with those things that are sure successes would guarantee little more than the very atrophy of life. And though I'm perfectly aware of how odd and rather perverse it is to close with the words of Wordsworth, I ventriloquize him in order to issue a different sort of call: 'Up, up! My friend and quit your books!' ◆

Fondly,
Michelle Ty

The version printed here restores several paragraphs that were cut from the text that circulated publicly. My apologies for being unable to furnish proper citations under the pressure of time. References will gladly be provided upon request. Written with the support of 21 UC Berkeley colleagues.

zunguzungu.wordpress.com/2011/11/01/the-day-before-the-day-of-action/

1 Bay Area Rapid Transit.

No Cops, No Bosses

UC Davis Bicycle Barricade
20 November 2011

By now much of the world has seen video and photos of Lt John Pike of the UC Davis police department as he discharged a canister of burning chemicals into the faces of students seated in the center of the university quad. Most viewers are outraged, and justifiably so. Much of the outrage has been directed at John Pike. He deserves it. But we should remind ourselves that Friday's police violence was only an aberration because it happened on a university campus not easily assimilable to the stereotype of 'Berkeley radicals' and to students who are perceived or portrayed as mostly white and as resisting passively. Whiteness is brought up here, not to chastise those who only now denounce police violence that has been routinely applied to non-white communities and individuals – this itself is a misperception of Friday's events: a majority of those arrested were not white – but to invite readers, new and old, to extend the critique of police violence beyond the walls of the university to the communities whose life it damages every single day.

Friday's punitive violence, as terrible as it was, is not an example of bad policing. *It is an example of policing.*

We've seen this kind of violence used before on California campuses, and not just in response to the anti-privatization protests and occupations of the past two years. We're seeing it used now to suppress dissent in cities across the world, from Oakland to Cairo.

When UC Davis police chief Annette Spicuzza says she is 'very proud' of her officers, who 'did a great job', she is convinced that this is true. It's not simply a public-relations strategy, it's a reflection of the fact that her officers did what cops are expected to do: employ violence against those who challenge authority.

This is why we do not demand the dismissal of Lt John Pike, although it would be welcome.

Our demand is COPS OFF CAMPUS. Period.

Chancellor Linda PB Katehi is working feverishly to control the media narrative about Friday's police attack on protesters. She tried to hold a press conference yesterday, but we shut it down with our voices and bodies. It's telling that the press conference was held in a building meant to accommodate satellite trucks and internet broadcasting, but whose size and peripheral location bar students from attending. Katehi's press conference was meant to calm a national public outraged by her use of force against students. Addressing students and, more importantly, listening to them, was not part of her agenda. We were locked out of the building yesterday, but we let ourselves in and stopped the propaganda session.

Although we posed no danger to her, Katehi refused to leave the building for two hours, perhaps waiting for rain, or nightfall, before walking past a silent wall of students and ducking into her luxury automobile. She could have addressed students there, of course, but she preferred the leather-lined cocoon of the car and the comforts of a phone interview with CNN, conducted immediately after she left.

For Katehi, students are a nuisance, an obstacle standing in the way of her plans to privatize and internationalize the campus. This is apparent in the email missives that she sends to everyone, trying to justify her use of force. She invokes safety and health concerns.

[T]he encampment violated regulations designed to protect the health and safety of students, staff and faculty.

Here, the health and safety OF STUDENTS become empty abstractions that must be protected FROM STUDENTS.

Similarly, in the Chancellor's tiresome rhetoric about the university's mission and standards, the word EXCELLENCE loses any educational significance it may have had; it becomes a quantifiable property of the university, indistinguishable from reputation or ranking. 'Excellence must be maintained,' recite the administrators. Like health and safety, it must be protected from students, whose disruptive protests mar the university's image. The careful construction of this image often takes the form of actual construction – the so-called capital projects, the gleaming buildings featured so prominently on university websites.

The fee increases, pepper spray, beatings, arrests and student disciplinary procedures of the last two years are not the unfortunate consequences of a dismal budgetary situation. *They are the primary vehicles for maintaining 'excellence'.*

Katehi makes repeated references to the presence of non-students among the protesters who were attacked by police, as if community members and alumni had no right to set foot on the campus of a PUBLIC university, as if they had no stake in the fate of a PUBLIC university. Our administrators prefer the university's connections to the public to be mediated by formal contracts with agribusiness giants. They prefer alumni to mail checks from a distance. They prefer that the city not interfere with its project to increase the size of the student body and expand its physical footprint. They prefer visitors to be chaperoned through campus on tours that highlight statistics, amenities and, most of all, the buildings – the shiny new buildings and construction projects financed by student debt. Against the administration's attempts to keep the community at a distance, the students of the University of California, Davis, invite alumni, community members and everyone else to the Quad on Monday, 21 November at noon, for a conversation about the university's future. We ask Davis residents to support us in our struggle against a university administration at war with students and with the notion of a public university.

We second calls for Katehi's resignation. She must go. But we don't want to replace her with another Regental appointee or an interim chancellor. We don't want to replace her.

The administration, as a managerial class for whom the ideal university is a massive corporation in imperialist partnership with other massive corporations and banks,[1] will never accede to our demands for self-management, greater student and community participation in university governance, and better working conditions. The administration at UC Davis and every other UC campus has proven that, when faced with these demands, they will unleash violence in our learning spaces.

We demand the abolition of the administration and the transfer of all their functions to workers, students and faculty.

As a necessary precondition to self-management and for our safety, we demand that UCPD be disbanded and that the University be declared a sanctuary space, free of interference from law-enforcement personnel. Universities outside the United States already enjoy this freedom. We must demand it here.

Cops and administrators off campus! ◆

bicyclebarricade.wordpress.com/2011/11/20/no-cops-no-bosses/

1 Links to sources on UC Davis' partnerships: http://nin.tl/GSnY4s ; http://nin.tl/GT6Ali ; http://nin.tl/GSo641

Clarification on Nature of Call for West Coast Port Blockade

Occupy Oakland Port Blockade Working Group
27 November 2011

West coast Occupy movements plan to blockade west coast ports on 12 December. This decision is not affected by a recent memo written by International Longshore and Warehouse Union (ILWU) President, Robert McEllrath, and quoted by the *Longshore and Shipping News*. Occupy Oakland's working group on the port blockade wants to clarify the situation, so that there is no confusion on intent and support for this significant action.

1. The port blockade is being called for by the west coast Occupy movements

2. The blockade is in solidarity with the ILWU local in Longview, WA, which is fighting a move by giant grain and shipping companies to bust the union, so they can have cheaper labor. The port action is also to support LA port truckers' drive for union recognition at SSA, a port terminal operator – 51-per-cent owned by Goldman Sachs. The blockade is also intended to disrupt the profits of the 1% by showing solidarity with those in the 99% who are under direct attack by corporate tyranny – exerting the collective muscle of the west coast occupies.

3. The ILWU rank and file have historically honored community picket lines in the port – for example, they refused to cross community picket lines to unload cargo from apartheid South Africa. They refused to cross picket lines at an Israeli ship protesting the Israeli blockade of Palestinians in Gaza.

4. The ILWU did not call for the 2 November general strike in Oakland, either. However, they did not cross the picket lines, set up by tens of thousands of people, including labor, community and student groups,

at the Oakland ports. They have a history of honoring such picket lines.

5. The fact that the ILWU Coast Committee cautioned its members that if a similar situation develops on 12 Dec, longshoremen should *stand by* (our emphasis) in a safe area and await a decision by employers to call for an arbitrator. This is similar to past situations where ILWU members have honored community picket lines. It allows the ILWU a legal out, not to cross the lines, if the picket lines are large enough to pose a threat to their safety, as interpreted by the arbitrator.

6. ILWU Local 21, Longview, Washington, was strongly heartened and encouraged by the overwhelming support shown for them by the historic 2 November port shutdown in Oakland. Their local president spoke at Oakland Occupy's rally last Saturday, thanking us for our support. He and other ILWU rank and file members marched with us that day. ◆

westcoastportshutdown.org/content/clarification-nature-call-west-coast-port-blockade

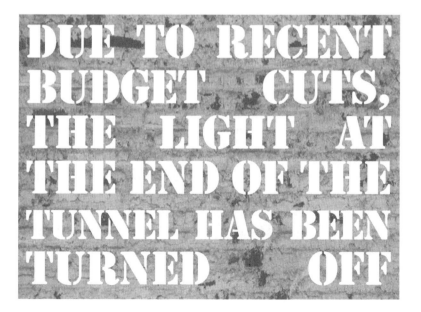

DUE TO RECENT BUDGET CUTS, THE LIGHT AT THE END OF THE TUNNEL HAS BEEN TURNED OFF

The Sword and the Shield: Occupy Foreclosures

Mike Konczal
19 October 2011

As people think a bit more critically about what it means to 'occupy' contested spaces that blur the public/private and the legal boundaries of claims between the 99% and the 1%, and as they also think through some things local Occupy Wall Street might do next, I would humbly suggest they check out the activism models surrounding Project: No One Leaves. It exists in many places, especially in Massachusetts – check out the Springfield version of it[1] – and grows out of activism pioneered by City Life Vida Urbana. It is similar to activism done by the group New Bottom Line and other foreclosure fighters. Here is PBS covering them.[2]

Its major goal is to mobilize as many resources as possible towards protecting those going through foreclosure and keeping them in their homes as long as possible, in order to give them maximum bargaining power against the banks. For those focused on 'weapons of the weak', this moment – where banks and creditors use state power to conduct massive amounts of foreclosures, thus impoverishing poor neighborhoods through a financialized rationality – is a crucial site of resistance.

> From the [Springfield] webpage: '*Post-Foreclosure Eviction Defense*. We mobilize tenants and former homeowners living in recently or about to be foreclosed homes (bank tenants) to stop evictions, protect Springfield's housing and communities, and mobilize bank tenants to fight back against major lending institutions and banks that are tearing our communities apart.'

Their model – a two-step process known as the Sword and the Shield, works:

> '**The Sword**. Encouraging residents to stay in their homes, and to make their stories public, we organize blockades, vigils and other

public actions to exert public pressure on the banks. The sword works together with:

'The Shield: We inform bank tenants of their rights and work with legal services & progressive lawyers, to use aggressive post-foreclosure eviction defense to get eviction cases dismissed, win large move-out settlements (if it makes sense for that family/person), and force the banks to reconsider foreclosure evictions.'

They use public action through blockades, protests and marches, along with smart legal advice on how to maximize legal resistance to forced removal. Beyond the fact that it is a major space of contention, it is also a great way to mobilize people. And as JW Mason notes, there is power in having a clear opponent as well as a special type of bargaining power people might not realize they have:

'Homeowners who still have title have a lot to lose and are understandably anxious to meet whatever conditions the lender or servicer sets. But once the foreclosure has happened, the homeowner, paradoxically, is in a stronger negotiating position; if they're going to have to leave anyway, they have nothing to lose by dragging the process out, while for the bank, delay and bad publicity can be costly. So the idea is to help people in this situation organize to put pressure – both in court and through protest or civil disobedience – on the banks to agree to let them stay on as tenants more or less permanently, at a market rent.'[3]

But there's another important thing about No One Leaves: They're angry. The focus isn't just on the legal rights of people facing foreclosure, or their real chance to stay in their homes if they organize and stick together, it's on fighting the banks. There's a very clear sense that this is not just a *problem to be solved*, but that *the banks are the enemy*. I was especially struck by one middle-aged guy who'd lost the home he'd lived in for some 20 years to foreclosure. 'At this point, I don't even care if I get to stay,' he said. 'Look, I know I'm probably going to have to leave eventually. I just want to make this as slow, and expensive, and *painful*, for Bank of America as I can.' Everyone in the room cheered.

Slow, expensive and painful indeed – it's like the person can put the bank through their own version of HAMP [Home Affordable Modification Program]. Economics note: 'But wait, aren't foreclosures healthy for the economy? Mitt Romney thinks so.'[4] According to the latest research using discontinuities across state lines, 'estimates suggest that foreclosures were responsible for 15-30 per cent of the decline in residential investment from 2007 to 2009 and 20-40 per cent of the decline in auto sales over the same period'.[5] This research is being debated, but the opposite – that quicker foreclosures help the macroeconomy – isn't found there, or anywhere else.

So does this fit well? Given the rampant fraud and abuses in the current foreclosure chain, from manufacturing documents to 'robo-signing' to fee-stacking to everything else, the Obama administration's refusal to support a serious investigation is a major example of the government-financial alliance and two-tier system of justice that those in Occupy Wall Street hate. Occupy Wall Street likes to pick spaces that are legally contestable – like private-public parks – that draw attention to real conflicts between those with power and those without, and a resident post-foreclosure is one of those spaces.

It also allows Occupy Wall Street to tap into already existing networks of foreclosure fighters. It is a type of demand that is actionable without leaving the movement looking powerless by asking Congress to do anything – these battles can be fought now. And it ultimately gets at the banks in a way occupations normally don't – banks may or may not feel that they aren't appreciated enough by these protests, but they'll definitely be mad if someone is disrupting their foreclosure mills through occupation and refusal to leave. ◆

rortybomb.wordpress.com/2011/10/19/the-sword-and-the-shield-occupy-foreclosures/

1 http://nin.tl/GTCuMO 2 http://nin.tl/H9loei 3 http://nin.tl/HeXEm0l 4 http://nin.tl/H9onDB
5 http://nin.tl/HeYT4q

Town planning

One of the greatest successes of Occupy/Decolonize has been its creation of an autonomous infrastructure to meet participant needs. This has been one of the most visible ways in which the movement models the world it is creating.

Juxtaposing the Bloomberg administration's preparation for what would in the end be a failed attempt to evict OWS from Liberty Plaza in October 2011 with the workings of the encampment itself, **Sarah Jaffe** gives a detailed look at the infrastructure of OWS. She makes clear the connections between material – truck-mounted solar panels; the gray-water system – and immaterial – childcare; medical care – infrastructures and the encampment's response to the threatened eviction. **Hannah Chadeyane Appel** conveys the visceral power and the difficulties of the people's microphone, one of the defining features of Occupy/Decolonize. Nodding to Chuck D of Public Enemy's famous description of hip hop as 'CNN for Black people', **Sara Marcus** makes the case that livestream embodies the strategic and political shift Occupy represents by decentering the big event and replacing it with 'the banality of life in a democratic public space', thus disrupting the 'frictionless' spectacle of capitalism and restoring linear time in the TiVo age. **Jaime Omar Yassin** argues that creating 'an ad hoc community based on voluntary work' is itself a revolution. Moving from an ode to the Occupy Oakland kitchen to a consideration of the encampment's future in the face of an eviction threat, he 'sheds his role as documentarian and 'simply participat[es]'. **Morrigan Phillips** aims directly at the idea of 'the 99%', insisting that 'Occupy is not a poor people's movement' and asking what it would mean were it to become one.

Occupy Wall Street Prepares for Crackdown

Will Bloomberg try to tear it all down?

Sarah Jaffe
13 October 2011

'If Bloomberg really cared about sanitation here he wouldn't have blocked portapotties and dumpsters.'

Free healthcare, a sanitation team, a public library, solar power, and free childcare are just a few of the services the Occupy Wall Street protesters are providing.

On Thursday afternoon Occupy Wall Street called an emergency General Assembly (GA) down at Liberty Plaza to deal with the announcement that Friday will see a cleanup of the park by the City, starting at 7am. Representatives of Brookfield, the company that owns the park, said in the clean-up notice that everything left behind will be thrown away. On Thursday it was also revealed that Brookfield had sent a letter to police commissioner Ray Kelly asking the NYPD help clear out the protestors. A group of New York civil-liberties lawyers warned the CEO of Brookfield that forcing protesters from the park violates their first amendment rights, stating: 'Under the guise of cleaning the Park you are threatening fundamental constitutional rights. There is no basis in the law for your request for police intervention, nor have you cited any. Such police action without a prior court order would be unconstitutional.'

The densely packed crowd is aware that reports are circulating that they will not be allowed to bring any gear back into the park after it's been cleaned, and they are discussing next steps.

'We have been self-governing and self-organized and taking care of our space,' the woman facilitating the GA calls through the people's microphone earlier today. 'Today we clean to call their bluff.' The sanitation team is calling for all hands to clean the park, and indeed all morning volunteers have been picking up trash with gloved hands. The willingness of the protesters to embrace such tasks is part of the reason they've been successful in camping out for nearly a month.

Occupy Wall Street, as many have noted, isn't just a protest, it's a reclamation of public space, a new commons for people who feel left out and left behind by the current system. Arun Gupta, editor of the *Indypendent* and one of those who helped create the *Occupied Wall Street Journal* newspaper, says: 'You have this uncommodified radical public space right in the heart of global capital. There is no money being exchanged, and that's remarkable in a city that is kind of the height of the idea that we exist to consume.'

He points out that the people claimed the space, and from there came up with the idea of the 'We are the 99%' slogan that has taken hold across the country. 'The mere presence itself,' in the square, he notes, 'became almost the politics of it. It's through the space that we can bring real democracy into being.'

Symbolically snatching that space back just shouting distance from the New York Stock Exchange and holding on to it would be protest enough, but inside that space the protesters built a model for the communities they'd like to see. They created infrastructure, and the infrastructure they chose to build stands in stark contrast to the hacking and slashing at public infrastructure spending done over the last 30 or so years and rapidly accelerated in the age of austerity.

'People who couldn't afford food or healthcare, that's no longer the case. They can come here and get what they need,' says Red, a street medic at the medical station. 'It's probably my favorite part of this movement.'

Red explains that the medical station is staffed by anywhere from 5 to 12 people at a time, some of whom are EMTs[1] or trained medics, others are nurses or doctors. 'We have five or six doctors that rotate in and out,' he says. 'They work for free; sometimes they stay up all night.'

The medical station can't provide every bit of healthcare that people might need, of course – it's hardly set up for surgery or treatment of serious illnesses. But they're surprisingly well stocked, with donations from 1199 SEIU[2] and the National Nurses United as well as supplies bought with cash donations. In a country that still balks at the idea of 'socialized medicine', having a place where one can get a free doctor visit is all too rare.

It's not just healthcare and free food that the occupiers are modeling in the park, it's everything from greener lifestyle techniques to support for arts and books.

The People's Library might be the most impressive structure in the park. It's now extended from the concrete benches along one wall onto tables, and the books have been stickered, labeled and had their barcodes scanned and cataloged onto the web.[3] This, as libraries across the US face budget cuts and closure.

'Our working group has 15 or 20 people,' Betsy Fagin, a Brooklyn librarian who is currently not working, tells me. Instead, she spends her days at Liberty Plaza, labeling and cataloging books, and her nights working on the online catalog. 'We have a librarian in Indiana who is cataloging online for us,' she notes. As of Tuesday 11 October, the library had around 400 records, and more donations are coming in all the time. (That's Day 25 of the occupation, according to a board that also provides a weather report, a donations count of more than $40,000 and an arrest count of 834 plus.)

On Tuesday, as I make my way through the park, there's a sign declaring the Arts and Culture space, and a man carrying a 'Roving Help Desk' sign. A man with a broom and dustpan is sweeping up, and another scuttles to bring paper towels to wipe up some coffee that's spilled a bit too near some sleeping bags.

Over the weekend, the computers throughout the plaza (at the media station as well as the 'Internet café' and phone-charging station) were powered not by the generators that have kept them going most of the time, but by a solar panel-laden truck brought up by Greenpeace.

Robert Gardner, whose business card describes him as a 'Coal Campaigner' for the organization, explains: 'It's a two-kilowatt array on the truck, which rolls down. I'd take up the whole street if I could,' gesturing to the panels. It provides 50 kilowatt-hours of storage, he tells me, and can provide for the energy use of an average American home – or for several laptop computers and cellphones as well as a few lights that stay on as the late-night crowd works. Greenpeace normally uses the truck as a campaign tool to demonstrate clean energy, he says, but they heard the occupation was using gas generators and came up to donate clean power and lend their support.

That's not the only way the occupation is modeling more earth-friendly technologies. The kitchen, which now has several racks of dishes and supplies, has created a gray-water system to filter the water used to wash the dishes before using it to water the plaza's flowers.

It's not just the New York occupation that is creating institutions to provide care. Jamieson Robbins, who has been involved with Occupy Dallas and Occupy Fort Worth in Texas, tells me: 'The experience that I've had with my three-year-old daughter out at Occupy Dallas and now Occupy Fort Worth has been nothing short

of fantastic. Several days before our first march, discussion began on OccupyDallas.org about children being involved. Many people felt that having children present at our march was a liability and many were waiting to see how it goes before bringing out their young ones.

'I, and many others, thought about it a little differently. I think people should involve their families, their friends, their co-workers, their neighbors, but most of all their children. What are we fighting for if not for the chance to one day answer the question, "Grandma, what was Occupy Wall Street?", with "It was the beginning of change, my love. The country wasn't always the way it is now." Not only that, but what a fantastic statement to onlookers to see not just hippies and anarchists, but families with their children's futures at stake.'

'Now, I'm proud to say that Occupy Dallas, even under threat from city council to either buy a million-dollar insurance policy or face eviction, has set up a permanent "Occuplay" child center within Pioneer Park.'

The shifting, growing infrastructure at the occupations around the country is taking shape differently in different places.

Street medic Red says, 'It really restores your faith that there's some level of decency left in our culture.'

And it appears to be exactly what will be targeted by the mayor, the police and the wealthy park owners. The infrastructure is exactly what makes Occupy Wall Street different from other protest actions, and by cleaning the park and trying to dismantle that infrastructure they're attempting to reduce the occupation's symbolic power.

'We are now creating a society that we envision for the world. Being responsible for ourselves is at the heart of that,' the People's Microphone rumbles. ◆

alternet.org/story/152694/occupy_wall_st._prepares_for_crackdown_--_will_bloomberg_try_to_tear_it_all_down/

1 Emergency Medical Technician, or paramedic. 2 The healthcare division of the Service Employees Industrial Union, headquartered in New York City. 3 http://peopleslibrary.wordpress.com/catalog/

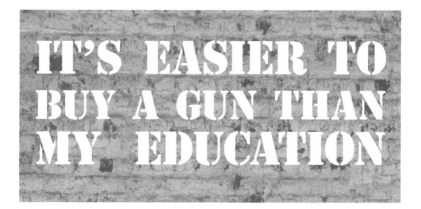

The People's Microphone

Hannah Chadeyane Appel
13 October 2011

'**M**ic check!' The shouted exclamation punctuates the days at Occupy Wall Street (OWS). A lone voice yells it from somewhere in the crowd, soliciting the hoped-for response, 'mic check!' yelled back by all within earshot of the initial call. Often the response is weak the first time around. Maybe the caller is surrounded by people new to the movement, who aren't yet familiar with the rituals, or don't yet feel comfortable making them their own; maybe the voices around her are tired, from so many days and weeks of the people's microphone. But with a second, often more insistent call, *'mic check!'* the surrounding voices rise in response, **'mic check!'**

Amplified sound requires a permit in New York City for which OWS has applied repeatedly, and been denied. While this ordinance is unevenly enforced across the city's landscape, violating it in Liberty Park would give the police an expedient rationale to end the occupation. Yet messages still have to be communicated to thousands of people, whether during decentralized days of small-group work or during the nightly General Assembly meeting at 7pm. The people's microphone is the solution. Perhaps tracing a genealogy to the phrase's use in hip hop, the call of 'mic check!' followed by its response, **'mic check!'** from all who heard, begins what is one of the most definitive experiences of communication at the occupation – the repetition and amplification of one another's voices.

'There will be–' shouts a caller,
'there will be–' responds the collective,
'a teach in–' she continues,
'a teach in–' we respond
'on co-operative economies–'
'on co-operative economies–'
'under the red sculpture–'
'under the red sculpture–'

'in 10 minutes!'

'in 10 minutes!'

Amplified by the voices of many, the voice of one can spread through the crowd without amplified sound.

The people's mic is available to anyone in the park at any time, and it becomes both a tool of radical equalization and an embodied ritual of spending time in the movement. Cornel West, Slavoj Žižek, Joseph Stiglitz, Naomi Klein, Russell Simmons, Michael Moore and other public figures who have come to the park to express solidarity all used the people's mic, speaking in short bursts and pausing as they listened to the amplified chant/echoes of their words spreading through the assembly. When particularly large crowds gather – on the weekends or in nightly General Assembly meetings – there can be two and sometimes even three 'generations' of amplification, so that the original utterance echoes outward into the far reaches of the crowd. In talking to MSNBC about his experience at Liberty Park, Joe Stiglitz commented on the people's mic: 'we have too little regulation of banks, but too much regulation of our democratic processes. I could not talk yesterday with a normal bullhorn. I've talked [to activists and gatherings] in other places, and this is the first time that there's been that kind of restraint to communicating with a large group… This is not the way other countries have allowed their demonstrations to communicate with each other.'

Stiglitz's criticism on the strictures of democratic processes juxtaposed with the libertine deregulation of financial processes is well taken, and it points us to the ways in which the people's microphone is a synecdoche for the larger issues at stake: Occupy Wall Street aims to show that despite living in a democracy that has been *radically* attenuated by the financialization of everything from our personhood (credit scores) to our citizenship (private campaign finance), we can and will speak back. Our numbers will amplify us if our money will not.

And yet at the same time, as an inhabited practice, the people's microphone is *difficult*. It is strenuous and cumbersome, vulnerable to fatigue and a lack of mass participation. An otherwise brief announcement, sent over the people's mic to a large crowd, can take 10 minutes or more. Attention spans wane; voices get hoarse; rhythm gets off and instead of a unison echo, people's words get jumbled into a polyphony of partial repetition. And other noises are everywhere. The vigorous drumming and chanting that continues from morning until night in the down-slope corner of Liberty Park does not stop during the General Assembly, in deference to radical democratic ethics in which everyone can freely express their participation without being policed by others. In addition, there is a city work crew which begins to jackhammer an adjacent sidewalk every evening shortly after the 7pm meeting time. (Talk about passive resistance! Lovely to see the city having to resort to weapons of the weak.) With its difficulties and aural competitors then, the people's mic seems also to be a lesson in the burdens of direct democracy, a lesson in the obstinacy required for intentional, durable citizenship.

At the General Assembly on 11 October, a young man who introduced himself as Ian ('Hi, I'm Ian,' **'Hi, I'm Ian'**) explained that he had developed an app for the movement.

'It amplifies my voice–'
'It amplifies my voice–'
'through your phone!'
'through your phone!'
In other words, were his idea to be implemented, people could call his number for free access to the application, and then sit together in smaller groups in order to hear what was being said, without having to yell. Perhaps it will be an elegant solution to the problem of amplification. Undoubtedly, it will come with its own difficulties and exclusions, and require its own forms of obstinacy. But the cry of 'mic check!' – one voice seeking many – will surely endure. ◆

socialtextjournal.org/blog/2011/10/dispatches-from-an-occupation-the-peoples-microphone.php

C-SPAN for Radicals

Sara Marcus
21 October 2011

*M*onday, *17 October:* It is 12.30am on the dot. The live video feed from Zuccotti Park has just frozen, as it does from time to time. At last there is silence in my apartment, and I can begin to write.

I keep the video window open despite the interruption, but some apparently do not: the odometer at the bottom of the frame, measuring the number of real-time viewers, cascades downward, spinning like a dying slot machine. Livestream viewers are an impatient bunch, it seems. When the plummet slows, though, it turns out that only a hundred or so have left, of over a thousand people. The rest of us would rather watch a blank screen, waiting for the stream to return, than give up hope.

An hour ago, restless and browsing Twitter, I learned that the protesters had just won a minor skirmish with the police. Some cops had come to take down the medical tent. Everybody linked arms and formed a human chain around the tent. Jesse Jackson magically appeared. The cops left.

I tune in to the livestream in time to see a guy re-enacting the confrontation with funny voices and hand puppets, his hands pursing into Muppet-like visages. 'You can't have any structures here!' one hand squeaks. 'Fuck you, this is our park and our medical tent!' the other retorts.

Has anybody else seen these amazing puppets? I search Twitter and get into a conversation with somebody who goes by Weeddude. Weeddude thinks the livestream is too unprofessional. Weeddude objects to the hand puppets.

I happen to believe that hand puppets are the key to the coming revolution. Scratch that – the *present* revolution.

Watching the livestream inclines one to make such sweeping statements.

* * *

The livestream is addictive. 'Nothing ever happens,' says my friend who has been too sick to make it down to the park but has been watching the stream for days on end. 'But something *might* happen, so you have to keep watching just in case.' It's the anti-Tivo: on it, time runs only forward, and if you miss seeing an event – a confrontation with police, a meeting, a concert – it's hard to go back to it. Although many segments are saved, and the most recent ones are easily available on the site, they're titled only with a date and time, nothing descriptive or searchable, and in most of the segments nothing happens anyway. (If there were titles, they would be things like 'People mill about on a brisk morning' and 'Man with cigarette frowns at a computer'.) The archived segments are there, but we're not encouraged to watch them.

In a world where the past seems infinitely accessible, the livestream provides a rare dose of linear time. In a movement where the desirability of progress is taken for granted but the idea of particular goals is looked on with suspicion, the livestream may be the perfect mode of documentation.

* * *

Most mornings, the camera sits simply on its tripod, registering the daytime bustle in a jerky, distorted strobe of motion. If it's a windy day, the gusts come across as a blown-out rush of digital noise and feedback, like something you'd hear at a festival of difficult electronic music. My friend compares these long stretches of tripod-mounted inaction to a structuralist film, in which you might see just, say, a fire burning for four hours, forcing you to be hyperaware of the presence of the film itself.

In the evenings, the General Assembly meetings are broadcast live – C-SPAN for radicals. The people's microphone turns dry bits of activist bureaucracy into poetry, or process art:

> What we're gonna do now
> Is break into groups of about twenty
> Read the proposal
> Designate one person
> To take notes
> And report back
> On what you love about the proposal
> And what you'd like to see changed about the proposal
> Then after small groups
> Each group
> Will be able to report back

For one to two minutes
And your notes will be sent
To the structure working group

After the GA meetings wrap up, Livestream puts down the C-SPAN and picks up the *Wayne's World*. It's too dark for a tripod-mounted camera to capture much of anything, so anchors take over: dudes (and it is almost always dudes) who can't figure out the autofocus, aim the camera unwittingly right at their navels, repeatedly indulge in the funny-only-once joke of speaking the people's-microphone buzz phrase 'mic check' into an actual microphone. In a chat-room panel to the right of the video window, conversation unfurls at a dizzying pace, sometimes ignoring the action on camera, sometimes responding to it, sometimes driving it. 'What's my major,' says a New School student, peering down at his laptop to read the questions being lobbed at him from Arkansas, Ottawa, Laguna Beach. 'Global studies with a concentration in social justice.' Sometimes the chat scrolls by too fast to read any of it, countering the slow sameness of the video. 'Am I single. Yes. Where's Dwayne. Dwayne's not here.'

Dwayne is the guy who did the puppets. He is model-beautiful, with an artful goatee and a graceful gathering of long dreadlocks, and he's terrific on camera. Everybody misses Dwayne.

The most-accessed images from Occupy Wall Street, of course, are not these fleeting livestream dramas; they're the cellphone shots of women being pepper-sprayed, men being punched, and they fit easily into a long history of activist video. But the livestream decenters the big event in favor of the casual banality of everyday life in a democratic public space. This transfer of function is possible in large part because the immortalization of the big event, and of the police misconduct that comes with it, has been so effectively farmed out to thousands of citizen videographers. It's hardly necessary any more to have an official video-activist team affiliated with the movement to organize documentation of actions, as was once common. (Indeed, the livestream is spectacularly ill suited to fulfill that function: when protesters were being arrested en masse on the Brooklyn Bridge, over 19,000 people tried to watch the live video online, and the feed sputtered and went down for long stretches of time.)

The livestream's redirection of our attention from single zap action to ongoing occupation parallels precisely the evolution of tactics represented by these protests. If structural film's long eventless expanses and experimental video art's intentional glitches and errors (I think, for instance, of Joan Jonas's glorious *Vertical Roll* [1972], in which that once-common televisual hiccup incessantly interrupts a video image) can teach us how to understand the livestream, perhaps the livestream is teaching us how to understand Occupy Wall Street. The movement is, as so many have observed, one that fetishizes process. (It can hardly be an accident that among the most professionally produced segments to emerge from the movement so far is an eight-minute mini-documentary about consensus.[1]) Yes, the occupiers' process is inefficient. But efficiency has helped bring about our current crisis, with money and jobs zipping frictionlessly around the globe, people sliding past one another encased in cars or in iPhone reveries. The protests remind us of this. They – and the livestream more than any other mode of observing the movement, short of going in person to a site of occupation – insist on the value of the slow and the processual, the wisdom inside every individual (recall consensus's Quaker roots), the righteousness of sitting awhile with questions instead of hastening to swathe ourselves in the moth-eaten false security of answers.

I am seduced by these ideas, but not completely. It's now Thursday night. I can't stop watching the General Assembly meeting, which is so enormous that the people's mic has to repeat everything twice, a pair of waves rippling back from the center. Hundreds of people have split off into smaller circles to discuss the possibility of a more streamlined decision-making structure. Watching from my living room as the breakout groups commence their report-backs, I feel wistful, homesick.

The next item on the agenda is a proposal from the park's barely tolerated drum circle that the GA give them $8,000 to replace stolen instruments and an unspecified amount to help fund a second occupation site specifically for drummers. In effect, they are asking the GA to buy them off. I mute the stream. When I return half an hour later, the debate is still raging. I wonder whether the drummers might actually be infiltrators from the police. Another half hour later, I read on Twitter: 'Drummer who didn't get money from GA tonight now yelling, cursing at members of GA at Zuccotti Park.'

'Where's Occupydwayne?' one chat-room participant writes plaintively. From time to time, somebody types in a plea for the puppets to return. I know how they feel. ◆

lareviewofbooks.org/post/11738084396/c-span-for-radicals

1 See the Meerkat Media Collective's video, Consensus (Direct Democracy @ Occupy Wall Street) at youtube.com/watch?v=6dtD8RnGaRQ

Occupy Oakland, Day 8
Solving global problems in a downtown microcosm (excerpt)

Jaime Omar Yassin
18 October 2011

I committed myself to spending a significant amount of time at night at Ogawa yesterday. This meant shedding my documentarian role, and simply participating. That was more difficult than I intended for a couple of reasons. In the first place, I felt awkward in taking up space and time, while not having yet invested any labor or risk in Ogawa (besides a bushel of apples I picked off the tree in the backyard and transported there via bike). I made a conscious effort to have regular conversations with people and participate, which reminded me how much more easy it is to talk to someone when you have the excuse of an interview and have the unspoken privilege of managing the conversation. I had some great conversations with some interesting people, at random, as usual; but I interacted as a human being and not as a historical recording device, so I probably won't be writing much about those.

One thing I did want to write about was the revolutionary power of the kitchen at Occupy Oakland. At some point, the idea of having a place where people could grab some food while they occupied, developed into the idea of a permanent and round-the-clock food-creating infrastructure, which would hydrate and feed all who came up, regardless of their affiliation with the camp [...]

The camp participants I spoke to remarked in wonder how organic the process had been, and that the idea had not come from any one person or strategy. In my view, that's what's created the incredible diversity of the camp, which now houses a large homeless population, and draws in a large number of local residents – hungry, peckish or simply curious – who then interact with each other and with the activists there [...]

The resulting meeting of minds has been a real joy to witness. I hope I'm not overstating the case, but I truly believe that if Oakland Occupy – and more broadly most of the Occupy Movements – has any value at all it's in this capacity of creating a place where the previously apolitical or politically unsophisticated can learn from each other and others, and become politicized without the confines of an ideology/goal or institution.

I spoke to an African woman who happened to be in line with me and, although she didn't understand the dynamics of the occupy, nor why the police were letting occupiers stay at Ogawa, she was nevertheless grateful for the space, because it brought together so many happy, smiling people.

The process of this kind of community-building and attendant politicization, and the harder work of creating and sustaining an ad hoc community based on voluntary work, is its own revolution. Over the years, I've noted that there are some very big flaws in our notions of what constitutes political struggle, effective strategies, and ways of interacting with the local and federal governments. Sanctioned and hallowed by time, these have become traditional, rather than effective, and often the equivalent of marching in a circle, yelling and then going home. Before we get down to the brass tacks of how to leverage growing political participation in a previously apolitical populace, I hope this kind of association gets a chance to grow into at least some of its full potential. But in any case, as one person I spoke to yesterday put it, Occupy Oakland had 'solved the problem of hunger and homelessness in downtown Oakland'.

That's not to say there aren't other problems. A scuffle last night showed the power of confusion and emotion among a very small group to disrupt an entire community, and it brought up serious questions of how to manage a community without state or outside intervention, which is an ongoing and thorny conversation amongst many groups at the encampment, from what I've gathered. But another way, I think, of looking at it is as the price to pay for taking complete responsibility for one's community.

In a neighborhood, when people get into serious mess, others often don't involve themselves. Despite the fact that it's their community, they delegate the authority of problem solving to outside professionals who don't live in the community, or they simply ignore it. It's easier to do that, it depersonalizes issues. But it also shuts people off from each other. Their problem-solving and interpersonal skills decrease as a result. Watching people try to deal with a potential fight last night, was like watching someone rise out of a coma and begin to learn to use their extremities again, of dealing with each other one to one. That is not only a valuable skill, but a cognitive structure worth acquiring. It's difficult, but we've gotten used to ignoring the difficulties in our community, or delegating the solutions to others, both locally and nationally.

City Hall intrudes

Speaking of difficulty. The city has sent a letter to the Occupy Oakland community, asking for a series of concessions with a threat to kick out occupiers by force on Wednesday if the demands aren't met. A group of occupiers set about to write a response to the letter; the letter was pretty hilarious and basically told the city to screw itself and that there would be no *quid pro quo* as that would run counter to the philosophy of an occupation. They presented the letter as a resolution to respond to the city. That led to a heated discussion of whether there should be any response at all – the outcome of that was another vote. The General Assembly voted to not respond at all to the letter; although, as it was pointed out to me, that could change tonight in another assembly resolution.

One of the writers of the letter insisted that the purpose of the letter wasn't as negotiation, but as a message to the city and world about the purpose and nature of the occupation, and the baselessness of the city's ostensible concerns. I agreed with him, though I was in the minority last night.

I'm not sure what will happen on Wednesday. A small group of occupiers branched out to Snow Park, a small green area close to Lake Merritt, early this morning, and have begun occupying there. It's possible that, in the event of losing the struggle to stay at Ogawa, the occupation could continue there or in another place. Occupy Oakland maintains the idea that autonomous actions and movements are encouraged outside of the group – and that includes, I suppose, restarting Occupy Oakland elsewhere, or spreading it out when it's gotten too unwieldy, or even starting new kinds of political occupations. ◆

hyphenatedrepublic.wordpress.com/2011/10/18/occupy-oakland-day-8-solving-global-problems-in-a-downtown-microcosm/

Room for the Poor

Morrigan Phillips
12 February 2012

Solidarity means that even if you win, you stand with everyone until everyone wins.

Poverty is, as the most basic definition states, the lack of resources sufficient for someone to live comfortably in society. For many, credit cards and loans have kept them in reasonable enough comfort that they have been able to put off acknowledging the grim realities of our economic system. Much of this myth of comfort and stability has fallen apart in recent years as the economic crisis has pushed more people into the uncomfortable position of realizing how close they are to a financial crisis of their own. Meanwhile, according to new poverty measures and census data, rates of poverty, particularly in rural communities and urban communities of color, have risen to a 52-year high.

Complicated financial games and doublespeak mask much of what has been fueling the financial crisis. But as more and more people have found themselves with no work, no money and mounting debt problems, the financial tricks and gimmicks that have been keeping this wreck going seem more like smoke and mirrors.

Fueled by outrage over economic gluttony and seeming impunity on Wall Street, the Occupy moment took hold of a piece of anger lying deep in the hearts of masses of people. The proverbial pinch was being felt by too many. Pop! A would-be movement sprang forth representing those for whom the promise of prosperity in exchange for hard work had been made and broken.

It should be made clear that Occupy Wall Street and the multitude of Occupies that have come alive around the US are not orchestrated nor primarily constituted by financially comfortable, gainfully employed, resource-rich individuals. Plenty of unemployed, underemployed and broke-ass people are taking on roles of organizers within Occupies. There are also those who rely on various forms of public assistance, both safety net programs like public housing and social security programs like unemployment. Further, the camps drew many from those forgotten and neglected corners of our communities: the houseless, those with mental health issues and substance use problems. Where camps remain, these communities' members also remain.

But to be clear – Occupy is not a poor people's movement. 'How long are you broke before you are poor?' This was the question, posed by a Unitarian Universalist minister and organizer in Boston, Jason Lydon, while walking from one meeting to another. He, like many, feels being broke, struggling with cashflow and financial uncertainty, as being a different identity than that of being poor.

As Occupy Wall Street and then the local Occupy Boston began to gain their legs and solidify their place in the public discourse, so too did an analysis. Corporate personhood, bank bailouts, executive bonuses and general Wall Street excess at the expense of democracy were at the top of the list of grievances. Personal stories have been told: stories of unemployment lasting two or more years, home foreclosures, bankruptcy due to medical expenses, untenable student loan debts and more.

These are the stories of people for whom the promise of security was broken. These too are those who are broke but for whom that sense of being able to live comfortably in society is somewhat attainable. But for thousands, a promise of security was never made. No part of the system has ever worked in their favor and for decades the economy has failed them in boom or bust.

Amidst seeming abundance of stuff and prosperity, the poor make a patchwork living that is a shadow of what many are able to attain. In our overly commercialized and consumption-driven society, being poor can mean being left out and left behind. Left to create and build as best one can with limited resources but never looking like everyone else. Never seeing your life reflected back to you on TV, in the news, in advertisements. Not even close. This alone makes it less likely that the poor will take up in protest with Occupy. The society that Occupiers are mounting a defense of never included the poor in the same way.

But that does not mean the poor will not organize and rise up. Poor people's movements have played, and continue to play, an important role in social and community change work. Here is a small list of examples out of a deep and rich history:

Coalition of Immokalee Workers
The National Welfare Rights Movement
Domestic Workers Bill of Rights
Take Back the Land
City Life/Vida Urbana: anti-foreclosure organizing in Boston
United Farm Workers
The unemployed workers' movement during the Great Depression
Poor People's Campaign organized by Martin Luther King, Jr, and
    the Southern Christian Leadership Conference
Poor People's Economic Human Rights Campaign
All of Us or None: an organization of prisoners, former prisoners
    and felons, to combat discrimination
Formerly Incarcerated and Convicted People's Movement
Western Regional Advocacy Project

Statistically speaking, the poor hold the space at the bottom of the 99%, earning less than $22,314 for a family of four. For an individual, the poverty threshold comes in at $10,890 a year in earnings, or around $900 a month. For most federal and state programs, individuals are eligible for assistance within 200% to 300% of the federal poverty line. More than a reflection of earnings, the poor are a class unto themselves. The poor not only have precarious livelihoods that experience frequent economic disruption but also live in communities where there is generally less stability. Poor communities are often isolated either by location (i.e. rural isolation) or through systematic disenfranchisement. Examples include poor public transportation options, the closing of public hospitals in poor communities, and a lack of supermarkets, parks, walkable streets and sound infrastructure.

Making room for the poor
In his State of the Union Address President Obama mentioned poverty only once, and that was in passing. Presidential hopeful Mitt Romney recently said he is 'not concerned about the very poor'. In today's political discourse, it is the loss of the middle-class dream that is most lamented. Every political candidate, pundit and journalist seems to be looking to champion the middle class. But no one wants to champion the poor or even acknowledge their existence. This goes, too, for much of the discourse emerging from the Occupy movement.

Just as much of society excludes the collective experience of the poor, so too has Occupy. From the very beginning of Occupy Boston, there was a striking lack of an analysis of poverty being present in the discussions and messaging of actions. Demands and grievances have focused on personal gains rather then collective objectives: a middle-class desire for debt relief; the focus on individual corporations or banks rather than on the system of capitalism; a practice of policing individuals without a larger reflection on provocateurs and a collective reflection on the societal disrespect toward the mentally ill, homeless or substance addicted. So what would an analysis of poverty within Occupy look like?

Historical reference points. Messaging and demands would be rooted in a historical analysis of years of cuts to social welfare spending and the toll those cuts have taken on communities of color in the US. Economic recovery, when it does come, often leaves scars in poor communities that look like cuts to social service and public welfare spending, including funding for economic development, housing, food assistance, aid to the elderly, education and job training. Additionally, since the Reagan era, poor communities have been blamed, bullied, marginalized and subjected to slander in the media.

An understanding that this is not the first nor last moment in which people will face economic hardships: things have been getting worse on the ground for decades. This too is not the first time people have risen up (see above for just a sampling of poor people's movements). Both the political and popular discourse around poverty in the United States has always boiled down to the 'deserving' and 'undeserving' poor. The US welfare state was birthed out of a legacy of Elizabethan Poor Laws which placed the onus of one's poverty squarely on one's shoulders. The only ones deserving of assistance were widows with children and anyone who could not work. The influence of this philosophy is felt throughout the history of the creation of the very limited US welfare state. There is no culture of poverty. But there is a culture of reluctance and outright disdain for aid to the poor in American political discourse.

The meme of the 1% and the 99% would be more actively developed and nuanced. The 99% includes people earning upwards of $400,000 a year. It also includes people who went to Harvard and, while likely buried in debt, they have social access and privilege not enjoyed by many. The idea that the 99% meme is useful and popular should not overshadow the importance of examining power and privilege within the 99%. For example, the foreclosure crisis is amounting to the largest loss of land in the black community since the African slave trade tore people from their land.

Unemployment among black men is at Depression-era levels. Again, economic hardship hits some communities harder due to historical disenfranchisement, oppression and economic exclusion. Economic inequality is better represented in the US by looking at the 10% at the top versus the bottom 20%.

Moving beyond individual interests to a collective understanding of shared interests for economic justice. Protecting and improving social safety net and entitlement programs such as unemployment insurance, food stamps, foreclosure protection and other social safety net programs, needs to be the context in which other demands such as financial industry regulation and an end to corporate personhood are placed. Messaging and tactics deployed against direct attacks to the social safety net that hit poor communities the hardest, with that distinctive Occupy analysis that ties economic hardship to big finance, could be powerful. A move in this direction would also create an opening for solutions to immediate needs of people now and in the long term. There is a history worth noting in the US of social movements winning demands that aid those in the middle more so as to relieve the pressure and slow the movement. Solidarity means that even if you win, you stand with everyone until everyone wins.

Thinking global and local. The analysis that Occupy is formulating should invoke economic justice and economic rights and be born from the messages that have been raised up by poor people's movements in the US and Global South for decades. Further, there needs to be the acknowledgement that the relative prosperity here in the US relies on the exploitation and subjugation of the Global South.

A shift in praxis, or how the lessons and skills of Occupy are learned and acted upon. The way in which the economic crisis is conceived of and organized against needs to be informed by a systemic analysis of power, culture, history and economics that moves deeper into a social-change model, one that re-envisions how our society meets the needs of everyone. Ending corporate personhood, for example, will not restore funding to much-needed programs and services. It will not restore dignity and comfort to those left in the cold each night by homelessness. Only a cultural and societal change that internalizes an analysis of poverty and the poor will do that.

Diversity of organizing structures to be inclusive of people of homeless and other economically stigmatized communities. Much of the conflict that consumed the Dewey Square Occupy Boston camp revolved around the role homeless people played in the camp. Sometimes called junkies, other times called trouble, from the get-go there was little capacity within the camp to deal with the challenges. The typical structures of Occupy – with the General Assemblies, consensus process and working-group structures – have limits when it comes to being inclusive of people who live in those dim and oft-forgotten parts of society. The promise of meals every day, protection in numbers and community drew the homeless to Occupy camps. For those struggling with mental health issues, living on the streets or in the shelter system and those whose struggle is compounded with substance use and addiction live frustrating lives every day. Occupy camps also offered the promise of a space to be a part of addressing their needs.

But organizing structures that were built at Occupy Boston mostly showed the divide between the priorities of the middle of the 99% and the needs of the bottom 10%. Violent and admittedly unstable personalities were present at Occupy Boston, but it was those personalities among the houseless (houseless, not homeless, is the preferred term of members of the community active in Occupy Boston) population that drew the most scorn. Plenty of young white, housed and comfortable men showed outright oppressive tendencies. But it was not these participants in Occupy Boston at whom the Good Neighbor Agreement was directed. Solutions have been sought within the established process and almost exclusively targeted problematic personalities within the houseless community. What is more, use of the police and criminal justice system has been viewed as an acceptable option without discussion of the role these forces play in the oppression and criminalization of homelessness. There are many organizing models and many examples of empowering organizing work that don't rely on forcing marginalized and unheard communities with varying capacities to fit into our preferred process. Occupy needs to examine how its processes can and often do recreate the societal norm of excluding the voices of people living on the fringes.

An analysis of the Prison Industrial Complex (PIC) and its role in poor communities. The PIC, the criminal justice system and the police serve as methods of oppression and destruction in poor communities. The 99% analysis needs to acknowledge that for the bottom 10%-20% the police, prison guards and other agents of the criminal justice system are not allies and are certainly not 'in it together' with poor communities of color. This is not about income but about the role these agents play in the criminalization of poverty. The approach to addressing inequality and societal disparities must not only look at income but also at the roles people play in the systems of inequality. Occupy for Prisoners is an excellent example of solidarity between Occupy Oakland and prison-abolition activists in recognition that there are many thousands locked up on the inside that cannot join us in our meetings or in the streets as we fight for justice.

At the end of the day, Occupy needs to own who and what it is. It does not need to be a poor people's movement. Plenty of people active in Occupies throughout the country are hurting and letting that hurt fuel their rage and conviction. But it will not serve anyone for Occupy to continue without an analysis of poverty. This is about the top 10% versus the bottom 20%. Occupy can choose to align itself with either. But an Occupy movement that joins its interests with the interests of a poor people's movement in a shared vision of economic justice would be remarkable and bold.

In turn, anti-poverty activists, organizers and community members need to dig deep and assess how the many voices, campaigns, organizations, groups and networks can be joined in a great new national anti-poverty poor people's movement for economic justice.

We all deserve better, but what is better for some should not come without, or at the expense of, the poor. ◆

infrontandcenter.wordpress.com/2012/02/10/room-for-the-poor/

Elsewhere

Drawing inspiration from movements elsewhere in the world, from the Zapatistas to Spain's indignadxs[1] to the Arab Revolution, Occupy/Decolonize is a US movement within a global upsurge. Its name has been adopted worldwide as a sign of affinity among projects – some predating it – that share hallmarks defined by a common practice: a participatory ethos; directly democratic decision-making structures; a refusal to respond to the demand for demands; determination to resist the present global social and economic order. This shared practice leads to shared tensions and debates, shared sources of optimism and pleasure, shared questions. These writers remind us that the global cross-fertilization of Occupy grows out of the constant circulation of ideas and practices.

Sam Halvorsen contrasts his experiences in Porto Alegre, Brazil, among Occupy activists and at the Thematic Social Forum on Capitalist Crisis, Social & Economic Justice, and considers what it would mean to have 'a truly 'global' movement'. Tim Gee, Kerry-anne Mendoza and Steven Maclean describe day-to-day encounters at Occupy London and Occupy sites across northern England; take positions in discussions of homelessness and 'disruption'; and show the texture of the movement in the UK. Each of the tactics and strategies of Occupy/Decolonize has a specific history that moves across borders. Michael Richmond's consideration of the tradition linking the masked anonymity of 'Captain Swing' to the Guy Fawkes masks of Anonymous tells one such tale. Tim Gee, pursuing another movement lineage, revisits the history of protest camping. Gianpaolo Baiocchi and Ernesto Ganuza's summation of the first year of Spain's 15-M movement of indignadxs, from plaza encampments onwards tells another. Finally, Emmanuel Iduma evokes the texture of resistance and the particularity of being a writer participating in the Nigerian revolution. Contesting both corporate media descriptions of 'Facebook protesters' and the idea that there is, or can be, such a thing as 'normalcy', Iduma calls upon us 'to transcribe the language of a dream into the spoken word of reality' – 'there is change lurking everywhere'.

1 Indignadxs is the preferred gender-neutral form for indignados, especially on the Latin American Left.

Occupying Everywhere: A Global Movement?

Sam Halvorsen
11 February 2012

Having just spent a week with occupiers, indignants, and social movements from across the world, I have been thinking lots about what it means to have a truly 'global' movement. I would like to sketch two different outlines of what this may mean based on my experiences as participant in a large social forum on the one hand, and my contrasting experience with a local Occupy group on the other.

The 24th to 29th of January 2012 saw the Thematic Social Forum take place in Porto Alegre, part of the 11-year-old World Social Forum process, which was considered by many to be an integral component of the global justice movement that flourished last decade. Following the explosion of Occupy around the world, they decided to invite a few individuals from the movement to participate in various discussions about the capitalist crisis and social and ecological justice. Whilst I learned from and shared ideas with numerous activists, in particular from the Global South, I could not help but feel that the Forum itself was an old model for our contemporary 'world' movement.

The Forum process was centered around a series of panels and talks, in which speakers would sit at a table and talk to their audience, before answering questions. I participated in numerous of these, and enjoyed responding to some of the critiques posed about the Occupy movement (how can you hope to change the world without taking power? being the most common). However, as I left the air-conditioned rooms and rigid chairs of the Forum's space and moved into the Occupy camp outside, I realized just how limited their process was.

It is not simply the model of panel-audience interaction in an institutionalized setting, but it is the whole concept of pre-determining who should speak and how they must do so. The Forum was set up at a time when the decentralized networked movements that spanned the Global North and South were being celebrated. It was based precisely on the importance of global social movements. However, 11 years on, the whole concept of 'social movements' seems to have been reified and transformed into an essential and yet at the same time completely ignored concept in the Forum. A list of established trade unions, NGO coalitions and long-standing 'movements' are called upon to debate the state of the contemporary crisis and the social response. Doing so ignores the wide plethora of activists who are constantly experimenting with responses to crisis, yet do not hold the flag of any specific organization.

Speaking to Occupy activists in Brazil, it is clear that for every similarity we have a difference. Crucially, however, we are united in our commitment to the process of social change, in which we seek to constantly (re)create open spaces for dialogue and action. Sadly the Forum seems to have forgotten this, and perhaps one reason for inviting occupiers was precisely to give it a new breath of life. A global movement for the Forum is based on an unproblematic clustering of external 'social movements' that come together for question and answer sessions. A global movement for Occupy however, is to ask what a global movement might mean for us, as individuals and collections of individuals. We do not want to find the answer to this question, for it is question itself that guides us.

A global Occupy movement, if we can call it that, is a patchwork of experiences and imaginations taking place in the minds and actions of individuals and collections of individuals worldwide. It is an open space for direct action that grounds itself in very particular contexts. Constantly (re)territorializing itself in diverse corners of the world, Occupy has taken us beyond the 'network' of the World Social Forum and into a truly global movement, full of very real places. The camp in Porto Alegre is one of them, and so is St Paul's courtyard in London. These places, which exist as much in our mind as our actions, are at once together and apart, and no panel will ever be able to answer what it is that brings us together. This is why we occupy. ◆

theoccupiedtimes.co.uk/?p=2340

Occupy the North

Tim Gee
20 December 2011

When I was a child, Wigan Pier was a museum with clog dancing, a mock Victorian schoolroom and a boat down the canal to a cotton mill. Last week I visited again. But this time it was empty. The one sign of life was a pub, appropriately called The Orwell.

'What's happened?' I asked the bartender.

'Oh, you know,' came the reply, 'budget cuts.'

In *The Road to Wigan Pier*, George Orwell is an outsider looking in to The North. I am not. Going north is going home. But it now looks different. And it isn't just me that has changed.

My visit to Wigan followed a series of talks and workshops in Salford, Stockport, Manchester, Leeds, Huddersfield, Bradford, Durham, Newcastle and Liverpool. In conversation after conversation, two words were to be heard again and again. Why is the Churchtown museum in Southport shut? Budget cuts. Why is the youth service in Leeds being delivered through a mobile van? Budget cuts. The only silver lining is that the shocks are inspiring people to take to the streets together to campaign for a better world.

This has manifested itself in various ways, but by far the most visual are the Occupy camps: liberated spaces that physically and psychologically defy clone town corporate high streets and sanitized financial districts. There were rarely more than 20 people at the four that I visited, but I left with no doubt that within them are the seeds of something new.

At some sites I facilitated workshops which began by asking people to name one campaign they have been involved in before. The replies were striking. There were a few experienced activists there but, for the vast majority, Occupy was the first political thing they had ever done.

My questions as to what motivated people to get involved were answered at length. One person told me he had applied for more than 80 jobs and not got one of them. Another man dreamt of opening a café, but with no capital, jobs hard to come by and access to affordable education closed down, didn't see how he could do so. Another person told me he'd been consistently applying for jobs for three years. Staying full-time at the camp, and visibly shivering in the Merseyside wind, he told me being involved in Occupy was the best thing he had ever done and he intended to see it through to the end.

There was no sense of tension here between the employed and the unemployed within the camps or beyond them. Among the many images that stick are lorry drivers honking their support, a photographer presenting the Newcastle camp with a picture he'd taken, and some cake decorators promising a cake. I arrived in Liverpool on 30 November – the day of national public service sector strikes – and the city center was alive with banners, flags, whistles, *vuvuzelas* and the city's Socialist Singers. By far the largest cheer of the rally went to the Occupy campers braving so many challenges to make their voices heard.

Those challenges are by no means small. The first is the weather and the constant struggle to stop tents from blowing away when there is no grass to peg them in to. As I prepared to begin my workshop at Occupy Newcastle, the sleeping tent almost blew away, triggering an all-hands-on-deck effort to retrieve and re-secure it with ropes, rocks and water butts. The day after my visit to Occupy Leeds, a camper told me that the tent I had facilitated my workshop in hadn't survived. The night before my visit to Occupy Liverpool everyone had got soaked in the rain. But still the protesters continue.

Another challenge is safety. The Occupy Manchester camp had to move from its first site because of the challenge of passing drunk people, some of whom sought to stay. By the time I reached them, every camp I visited had adopted a no-alcohol policy.

Another safety challenge is more political. I heard stories of fascists from the English Defence League attacking camps with bricks and threatening to burn tents. In Liverpool I encountered them myself. As the five or six men approached the site, I joined a defensive line around the camp. The EDL's strategy seemed to be to goad one of us into hitting them, to give them the excuse to start a fight. A couple of them started addressing campers by name, searching for weak points. Another snatched a phone from a camper which we succeeded in retrieving. A couple of women then moved in between the lines to de-escalate the situation until the police arrived. Once they had left, a lively debate ensued. Are the police part of the 99%? What about the EDL? The violent passers-by? And if they are part of the 99%, in whose interests is each of them acting?

If one thing is for sure, though, it is in whose interests the government is acting. On the last day of the tour I flicked on the television to be greeted by a very different perspective. In an attempt at spin after the announcement that youth unemployment has risen to record highs, Deputy Prime Minister Nick Clegg was on the news congratulating Starbucks for their plans to expand. I had to rub my eyes. Starbucks, frequently charged with destroying jobs and small businesses through its expansionist tactics, was now being congratulated by the government for 'creating jobs'. There is a word for such a position coined in another Orwell book: doublethink.

The sense of distrust in the words of those who claim to be in authority came across strongly in every conversation. To my mind, the joy of Occupy is that it is a space for seeing beyond the doublethink that prevails in politicians' words and the mainstream media. It is a rejection of the doublethink that cutting jobs and services will create employment. It is a rejection of the doublethink that the way to stop climate change is to consume more. And it is a rejection of the doublethink that the only way to address injustices in society is to join a political party whose policies perpetuate injustice in society.

Everywhere, I asked campers what they would like me to include in the article I was writing. The answer to this question was almost always the same: 'This is a space to discuss and to come up with our own solutions to the problems we face.'

In the 1960s, the Brazilian educationalist Paulo Freire advocated for education and consciousness-raising to be based on discussion and co-learning. What might now be called 'Freirean' methods can be seen as far back as the 1790s, when workers and artisans met to debate with one another whether they should have a say in the running of their country through electoral democracy. Now, in our struggle for economic democracy, people all over the country, and all over the world, are doing so again. ◆

newint.org/blog/2011/12/14/occupy-the-north/

Voices from the Occupation

The homeless and the hungry – modern-day outlaws

Kerry-anne Mendoza
5 January 2012

I heard something on the radio last night which made me furious. It wasn't Diane Abbott[1]... it was the news that Hungary has outlawed homelessness.[2] It is now a criminal offense to find yourself without a home in Budapest. The Occupy Movement exists to be the amplified human megaphone of sanity, in the context of a world gone mad with a bloodlust for 'making it' and victim blaming.

This article discusses the Hungary situation, together with further examples from the UK and how we need to radically alter our conversation, if we want to live in a transformed world where nightmares like this are distant memories.

Guilty of being skint

The story seemed so absurd that, when I awoke this morning ready to write about it, I wondered if I had simply dreamt it. During my fact checking, it not only proved true, but worse. When the story started, I assumed that it was part of a drive to prevent homelessness: Outlaw Homelessness, like a War on Poverty. However, this is not the case. Hungarian capital Budapest has circa 10,000 homeless people attempting to survive in it. The Conservative government has declared this too much for Budapest to bear, and therefore banned it. The law has been passed. Its implications? If you are found homeless in Hungary, you get a warning. If found again, you get a fine of $614 and/or prison.

Now, I'm no fortune teller – but I'm happy to predict that this ludicrous law will be about as effective at stopping homelessness as making short skirts illegal would stop rape.

People are not on the streets of Budapest, freezing and starving to death, because of some legal loophole. People find themselves on the streets for all sorts of reasons. Many are the most vulnerable members of our society, homeless because they couldn't find a place in the world we built. The addicted, people with learning difficulties, the disabled, those fleeing devastation at home or elsewhere in the world, the mentally ill. Then there are people who fall into none of the above, who perhaps once passed the mumbling homeless man on the street corner, irritated by his incessant reminder that all is not well in the world. Then, living from payday to payday, suddenly found themselves on the other side of the divide. How long does it take to look that shabby? For people to stop opening doors for you? To fail to stop and check if you are OK if you are crying – because you are clearly too far gone already? To step over you, as you shiver in your sleeping bag?

Homeless people are not a species separate from those with homes. People aren't born with a homeless gene. Anyone who finds themselves, for whatever reason, unable to pay for it – doesn't get a home. End of story. There are safety nets, and they have holes in, and not everybody gets caught.

How dare you be disadvantaged?

For Free Marketeers, Neoliberals and Libertarians alike – it is not 'our' job to put a safety net up in the first place. Each person should be free to be responsible for their own destiny and that's that. It's that good old-fashioned 'a real man makes his own luck' sort of thinking. The benefit of viewing the world this way if you have money and others don't, is that you deserve it, and they don't. Nothing to do with you, that famine, or that housing shortage, or all those other poor and destitute. They had the same opportunity you did, they just blew it.

This argument is so fundamentally bogus that sometimes it is not even clear where to start in deconstructing it. First, anyone who thinks the world today is an even playing field must have an attack of the crazy eye. The game is rigged.

So, it's not just Hungary. It's everywhere. And in order to perpetuate this myth, the real and unignorable problems (like homelessness in Hungary) get thrown into a seemingly lively, but blind debate – inevitably resulting in botched 'solutions' which almost always have the victim as culprit.

Stop paying Johnny Foreigner

This morning's news cycle was full of the idea that provision of overseas aid should be attached to conditions on the country receiving the aid – such as privatization, trade liberalization, oh and human rights.[3] A plethora of eager comments and calls in, crying out: 'We should be spending this money at home' and 'Why are we paying for those mad mullahs to hate us?' Of course, anyone who had the chance to pick up a book on the matter of overseas aid would know that, once again, this is victim blaming with no context.

This idea is as old as aid. In fact, after the colonial period (let's pretend for a moment it ended) the IMF and World Bank were established to provide 'crisis' loans and loans for 'reconstruction and development'. The idea was to turn the old colonies into liberal democracies. However, rather quickly, the established economies of the world realized they were onto a loser. What they needed were the resources and the low-cost labor they were used to from their colonies, and just enough of the world wealthy enough to buy things.

The mercenary lending practices of these banks is infamous; eye-watering rates of interest and conditions which have established the so-called first, second and third worlds. The IMF imposes Structural Adjustment Programs on its debtors, effectively overriding any attempt at democracy. Yes, you can have this loan – but you will need to sell off all of your public services, slash public spending, let foreign investors buy up your land... oh and don't open this one up to a vote. What then happens? The obvious: more people in the country fall into poverty as they lose their jobs, they can't afford to send their children to private school and the state can no longer afford to run an education system, health is privatized so people start dying of treatable illnesses – and you have a call for foreign aid to help educate the children, heal the sick and feed the starving. Countries get decimated. Hollowed out for their resources. First Africa, then Latin America... and now they're coming for Europe.[4]

There would be no need for the aid, if this cycle were stopped. Original loans have been paid back multiple times over – this debt is a racket. It is called The Debt Trap.

Some figures for you. Between 1982 and 1990, $927 billion was loaned from rich countries to poor ones – but $1,345 billion was paid back in debt service alone. Furthermore, the debtor states began the 1990s 60 per cent more in debt than they were in 1982.[5] By 1997, world debt had grown to over $2.2 trillion, with $250 billion paid in interest to creditor nations that one year.

The IMF is the wonga.com of the international economy. Except Wonga didn't nick all your stuff in the first place, then give you a loan to try to start buying it back.

But of course, the corporate media isn't having that debate. We are supposed to argue about the conditions to attach to our benevolent foreign aid. A word to the wise: it might be considerably easier for citizens across the world to focus on addressing human rights issues and equality if they weren't subordinated by tyrants and dictators whose sole purpose is to keep those repayments coming our way.

Once again, we don't look at the problem and blame the victims.

People are living too long

There have also been a rash of stories recently in the UK, scapegoating old people for just about every economic woe we have. First, there are too many pensioners and we can't afford them – so they need to pay more, work for longer and get less.[6] Then, a report by the Intergenerational Foundation told us that the housing crisis was down to these pesky old-timers living in houses that were 'too big' and were therefore off limits to young families.[7] That's right, it's not a property bubble. It's not that all the council houses were sold off to bribe some working-class people into thinking they were Tories. It's nothing to do with extortionate house prices and unachievable deposits. No.

As people get to the age where they have worked for perhaps 50 years, they are overnight made redundant. If you have a recognized job – good. If you fall into any bracket outside of that, for whatever reason – bad.

There are always particular points of shame for every generation, where the following one looks back and says 'how did they let that happen?' For our generation, one will certainly be our treatment of the elderly. We have made battery hens illegal, but battery old people persist – sitting in chairs pointed at daytime television in soulless nursing homes, or shivering in their own cold homes unable to afford to put the heating on, struggling to care for their partners as their carer services are scrapped due to 'austerity', malnourished as their meals-on-wheels service is abandoned, terrified to go to the shops in case they get mugged for the change in their wallet. A whole generation that paid its taxes arrives at the point at which they may make some use of the investment only to find the world has forgotten their contribution and now sees them as an unwanted and unnecessary expense.

I don't know about you, but I found my grandparents really useful while I was growing up. They provided me with a personal history which I could listen to, learn from, critique and make my own way on the back of. They worked, and then they retired and then they worked again as my grandparents. They owed me nothing.

Again... this is not up for discussion. It's their fault they're too old and useless to be anything other than a burden on the state.

So how about restructuring our economy to work with the demographics we have, rather than start blaming our demographic reality for our broken economy? The economy is there to serve us, not the other way round. Our current approach is as absurd as solving the problem of your shoes being too tight by chopping off your toes. It is the shoe which needs to fit the foot, not the foot the shoe.

A little bit of thought goes a long way

It seems to me that much of the issue we have right now is a lack of critical thinking, imagination and empathy. One of the things which struck me hardest when I first arrived on an Occupy camp was the freedom to find my way of contributing – and to have that recognized and valued no more or less than anyone else's.

So much contribution in our world is just not valued, because it doesn't register as a financial value. If you can't or don't want to spend your life doing a job, arriving at a place at an agreed time, in an agreed outfit, leaving at an agreed time, and behaving in an agreed manner in exchange for an agreed wage, you are unemployed.

Being a childminder is a career, being a mother isn't. Being a farmer is a career, growing your own food in an allotment isn't. Being a social worker is a career, being a primary carer isn't. I know a lot of people without jobs; I don't know anybody who doesn't work.

From Hungary's homeless, to UK pensioners, to the next vulnerable group we choose to hang the responsibility for the current uncertainty and fear in the world upon – the underlying truth remains. We built a world that doesn't work, and now it's got so bad it is harder to ignore it. People don't want to see the homeless man picking food out of the bin, or the lonely old woman, or the fly-covered African child or the hoodies on the street, or the tent cities. It's like a constant poke in the side – things aren't working, what are you going to do about it? People want to keep their eyes averted, keep what they've got and 'just chill'.

Well, tough. We need you. For a society that spends so much time paying lip service to 'self reliance', we seem to be far too keen to have someone else – the government, the free market, the Occupy Movement – solve this for us. The situation is such, that no one really knows how to make it better or what to do next. That's the reality. So politicians make stupid knee-jerk policies, and many people pretend like nothing is happening.

A whole other group are looking around and saying – OK, we need to think this through. There is a breakdown, at a global level, with local impacts. Whether it's homelessness, unemployment, fraud and corruption, your local school, library or hospital closing, pension cuts, racism, sexism, ageism, domestic violence, sexual violence, drugs, politics, government, anarchy, consensus, listening, being heard, talking, love, economics, ecology, war, peace, ego, competition, co-operation... millions of people around the world are discussing openly and earnestly how we got here, what our world could look like, and how we want to build it.

This is so much bigger than Banking. We are taking on ourselves and, by extension, the world. Everyone is invited. In this simple act, we can stop blaming the victims, and start creating a world worthy of our collective imagination. ◆

scriptonitedaily.org/2012/01/voices-from-occupation-homeless-hungry.html

1 See article about accusations of 'reverse racism' directed at the first black woman to be elected to the UK Parliament http://nin.tl/HesOOs 2 http://nin.tl/HhrebG 3 See, for example, http://nin.tl/HkR8MW 4 See the IMF's own coverage of its loan to Greece: http://nin.tl/He6fnS 5 Martin Griffiths & Terry O'Callaghan, *International Relations – The Key Concepts*, Routledge 2008. 6 See, for example, http://nin.tl/HqDAuE 7 http://nin.tl/HU8Q9Y

We Need Caveats On Inclusivity

Steven Maclean
13 February 2012

The Occupy movement is based on some core principles of structure and process: nonviolence, inclusivity, democratic decision-making and a non-hierarchical horizontal structure being the most obvious. I'm a fan of them all, but talking about them – or more accurately, where their limits ought to be – seems almost taboo.

So why might I think we should place limitations on principles I'm in favor of? Well, taking any principle to an extreme can result in undesirable consequences. Absolutist positions are seldom sensible as they tend to ignore complexity and context, but the aspect I think is most problematic for the Occupy movement is *total* inclusivity.

Now I'm not suggesting Occupy ought to be members only, and I realize the importance of outreach and trying to build a critical mass, but that's exactly why I think we need firm caveats on our open-door policy. It's easy to see the consequences of something we do, but we sometimes have blind spots over the consequences of action we choose not to take, and inclusivity if taken to its absolutist logical conclusion would only end up alienating large sections of society.

Here's my thinking. Let's say Gary Glitter[1] rocks up saying: 'Hi guys, I'm here to join your lovely inclusive movement.' Would we welcome him in? If we did, it would immediately rule a lot of people – me included – out. It might seem crass my using Glitter as an example – perhaps I could have invented someone who has shown extreme violence or intimidation toward women in the past, except that has happened without the individuals being told categorically where they can go. So it seems a more extreme example is needed to make the point.

Or what if Nick Griffin[2] fancied doing a session at Tent City University on ethnicity. Presumably some people *are* collectively deemed off limits already, even if it isn't overtly expressed. If so, why maintain the façade?

When you have a set of principles you are prepared to adhere to absolutely, they end up canceling each other out and you achieve none of them. Take free speech and anti-racism; in law, these are balanced to try to ensure the best possible civil rights. Take free speech as an absolutist value and you tolerate all hate speech. Impose total intolerance of racism and you have abolished free speech as a principle.

Inclusivity and nonviolence also need to be balanced if they are to actually have any meaningful effect. If we dare not cast anybody out, we grant them the ability to cause physical harm with an invite to come back and do the same again, something likely to exclude good-minded women and men alike.

We shouldn't fall into the liberal trap of having principles we are terrified to enforce for fear of disregarding another of our principles; stifling us into a position where we fail to implement either to any degree of success. We shouldn't fetishize ideas, nor tactics, but should evaluate their value and limitations, and implement them accordingly.

I've yet to hear it said that someone ought to be excluded from Occupy (though I expect and hope it has happened in unique circumstances) and some might consider it sacrilege to utter the words. We've tolerated people with no desire to actually do anything constructive who continually undermine our efforts and are most likely *agents provocateurs*, and, shamefully, even people who have been aggressive towards women.

I don't think limiting inclusivity means making Occupy a card-carriers' club. Pubs don't tolerate certain behavior without becoming members only. And I don't think it would mean needing to establish rules; any situation could be dealt with individually and democratically. Occupy wouldn't shift from being an open, ethereal movement to a religious doctrine simply because we refuse to tolerate certain behavior.

So let me break what some people have held as a taboo and say it: inclusivity should have caveats, and some people should be excluded. ◆

theoccupiedtimes.co.uk/?p=2271

---

1 1970s British pop star who was convicted of downloading child pornography in 1999 and of having sex with children in Vietnam in 2006. 2 Leader of the far-right British National Party.

Disguising, Mythologizing & Protest

Michael Richmond
31 January 2012

I was a little disconcerted on my first couple of visits to Occupy LSX[1] by the number of people walking around with their faces entirely covered. There is a healthy contingent of Anonymous UK occupiers who wear the iconic Guy Fawkes mask from the *V for Vendetta* film but they can all be seen unmasked at various times – how else are they supposed to have a drink and a smoke? There is also Anon, who is a mainstay of the camp, often greeting visitors in the Info tent. To my knowledge, Anon's face is always covered by his headscarf and his signature ski goggles.

I did, as most people do when they meet anyone, judge Anon by his appearance on first impression. I wondered why he dressed as he did. I have often in the past made similar judgments about Muslim women who fully cover their faces with the *burqa* or leave only their eyes showing with the *niqab*. I feel quite strongly that seeing another person's eyes and face is quite fundamental to being able to relate to them and make a connection. Once I spoke to Anon, and heard him speak at meetings, it was clear that he was full of personality, ideas and sharp one-liners, and other considerations began to matter less.

The ubiquity of masks and disguises at Occupy protests worldwide has made me think about the wider importance of the mythical and the disguise in protest movements historically. When we wear a disguise, even if it's just make-up or some of the clothes we choose to wear, it's usually both to hide or alter a part of our own identity as well as sending a message out to others. The same is probably true in the context of protest.

For example, at the Boston Tea Party in 1773, when a group of colonial Americans boarded a British ship in the middle of the night and threw tons of its valuable tea into Boston Harbor in protest at a new tax imposed from London, these men dressed as Mohawk Native Americans. Their choice of dress has gone down in American history. The latest interpretations as to why they chose to dress this way are, on the one hand, to conceal their identities to guard them from the draconian punishments sure to be meted out on them were the British authorities to catch up with them. And on the other hand, to send out a more symbolic message, namely, 'we are American now', like the American Indian (a bitter irony for the indigenous American community) and like Britain no longer.

There are a couple of fascinating tales of subversive disguise and myth-making in the 19th century. In the late 1820s and early 1830s in southwest France, in the forest region near the Pyrenees, there was a bizarre confrontation brewing between the remote peasant villages of the forests and the modernizing central authorities wanting to systematize what was, to the locals, sacred land. Bands of local men, who became known as the Demoiselles, dressed up in full drag and formed into small guerrilla units attacking any forest rangers or royal authorities who encroached onto their land. It is still something of a mystery as to why these men turned to transvestism in their hour of need but there are suggestions that the use of such disguise drew heavily on both folkloric traditions and the hedonistic celebrations of the carnival. Nevertheless, there's no doubting that it emboldened them in their fight as they held off a much larger enemy for far longer than anyone expected.

A working-class movement in Britain called the Luddites took a slightly different approach to the steady march of capitalism. A phenomenon of the towns and cities of a rapidly industrializing early 19th-century Britain, Luddism, in simple terms, involved thousands of working men destroying and sabotaging the newly invented machines that were putting them out of a job. Much the same as the Demoiselles of the Arièges, the Luddites were left in fear for their way of life and they fought back in what we can see in hindsight were both losing battles.

Where the Luddites interest me is their name. Named after Ned Ludd, a man who may or may not have existed but was rumored to have angrily destroyed a machine a generation earlier, the name took on a mythical significance. Ned Ludd became General Ludd or King Ludd, the personification of the cause, a heroic leader who was said to live in Sherwood Forest, that old stomping ground of another mythical talisman, Robin Hood. It's like that famous line in *The Man Who Shot Liberty Valance*: 'When the legend becomes fact, print the legend.' Essentially it didn't matter who Ned Ludd was or Robin Hood or William Wallace or even Jesus – it's what and who they come to represent. At its height, the Luddite rebellion was engaging more of the British Army than the concurrent war with Napoleon in the Iberian peninsula. But, as dozens of the leaders were captured and either executed or sent to penal exile in Australia, the movement died out.

Enter the rural reprise of the movement and a new mythical embodiment of anti-capitalist rebellion. As new threshing machines looked like spelling the end for many agricultural workers, they took a leaf out of the Luddites' book and began to destroy the new machinery. The Swing Riots of the 1830s, as the widespread agricultural uprising became known, were named after the invented figure of Captain Swing. Adopted as the figurehead of the rebellion, the impressively named Captain Swing's signature appeared at the bottom of hundreds of letters and pamphlets through the south, east and southeast of England, threatening that if they failed to stop the hemorrhaging of rural manual labor then Swing and his followers would continue to take matters into their own hands.

And this is where we can return to Anonymous, because I see a striking resemblance. Then, anyone could sign the name Captain Swing and their message would take on the might of a wave. And now, anyone can post a comment or hack under the name of Anonymous, or set up a camp or Tweet under the name of Occupy, or, on the flipside, commit violence under the banner of al-Qaeda, al-Shabab, etc. What we're talking about here are cells, loosely affiliated networks with no central command or control but thousands of low-level interactions every hour of every day, online and in real life, linked only by a vague set of principles and techniques. This is a paradigm the lumbering hierarchies of the last century struggle to keep pace with – in the same way that the US army has struggled with guerrilla warfare (or 'insurgencies') ever since Vietnam.

For me, the masks of Anonymous say more about the culture that neoliberalism creates than they do about the people who wear them. The mask means more than just anonymity, it is strength in numbers. In one of their calling-card phrases, Anonymous say: 'We are Anonymous, We are legion.' It answers a human need to sometimes be one of many, not just a 'self'. In anonymity, people can hope to escape the exhausting egoism of our age, the atomizing force of late capitalism where the pressure is all on the self and particularly the self-image. Retreating into the crowd can feel like a relief.

But within the theme of disguise there also exists a paranoia and suspicion not just within the Occupy camps but within all direct action movements at the moment. I have been accused of being both undercover police and also an *Evening Standard*[2] reporter! (I don't know which is worse?)

But this paranoia is hardly misplaced because we all know very well that they are out to get us, even in harmless environmentalist groups like the one PC Mark Kennedy disgustingly infiltrated. The establishment are usually guilty of the *most* deceitful disguise and right now they're more rattled and paranoid than ever. For this government, and the New Labour one before it, 'protesters' are an enemy but, as the current system increasingly stumbles around like a dazed prizefighter ready to drop, they are throwing punches more haphazardly than ever. How else can you explain the City of London Police listing Occupy London as a domestic terror threat on the same page as al-Qaeda and the FARC? Protesters are already an 'other', painted as something to be disdained or mocked, but, with a sick and paranoid establishment, anyone with a different ideology now becomes a threat to be kettled, intimidated and beaten into submission. The malign intent of the elite and the police can no longer be disguised, but the swarm is so adaptable and the networks of information so fast that today's activists and 'networked individuals' are always one step ahead. We are not all Anonymous but We are Legion. ◆

theoccupiedtimes.co.uk/?p=2259

1 Occupy the London Stock Exchange. 2 The most established London evening newspaper.

Past Tents
A brief history of protest camping

Tim Gee
30 October 2011

The year 2011 has seen a blossoming of protest camping. First there was the tented city in Egypt's Tahrir Square, then the *indignados* in Spain, then the youth protests in Israel, then Occupy Wall Street in the US. Now, in as many as 950 towns and cities across the world, people have taken to the outdoors and set up tents as part of a global revolt against neoliberalism. On the face of it, camping does not seem like the most likely tactic to bring about the transformation of power relations in society. But it has frequently played a role in movements for change.

More than a century ago, in the context of a financial crisis, thousands of people camped outside the British Embassy in Persia to demand greater democracy and limits on the power of the Shah. Protesters had previously sought sanctuary in a mosque but were threatened with violence by the state. They gave speeches, studied constitutionalism and learnt from one another in their own 'open-air school'. Persia's first elections took place before the year was out.

A more recent example of protest camping took place in the 1980s, when parts of the peace movement established permanent camps outside military bases. By far the most famous was the women's camp on Greenham Common in Berkshire which blockaded, annoyed and hounded the government and military for more than 10 years, until (and after) the missiles were taken away.[1]

Another round of protest camping began in February 1992, when a group of travelers decided to camp on the proposed site of the M3 motorway over Twyford Down. They were soon joined by environmental activists. Together they remained there for the next 10 months. When an alliance of NGOs and activists began making preparations for a campaign at another site – Oxleas Wood near Greenwich – the government got scared and announced that their planned road project there would not be going ahead.

Campaigners kept building the movement and organized protest camps against preparations for the extension of the M11 in Essex and other roads in Newbury, Newcastle and Glasgow to name only a few. Tactics borrowed from anti-logging activists in North America and Australia such as lock-ons, sabotage and tripods (three poles attached together with a person at the top), fused with home-grown ideas suggested by parts of the climbing community, to stretch both the wits and the budgets of the authorities in their efforts to remove them. Due to the heightened publicity and expense, the roads project became untenable. In 1996, the government decided to abandon its plans and axe plans for 77 new roads. The protesters' efforts had paid off.

Perhaps the most well-known recent movement based on protest camping began in 2005 at a purpose-built non-hierarchical eco-village in Scotland to coincide with that year's G8 in Gleneagles. At daily consensus-based meetings, young activists politicized by the Iraq War rubbed shoulders with direct-action old hands from across the world. This was quickly followed by a switch in focus from the summits where decisions were made to the places that CO_2 was emitted. And so preparations for the Camp for Climate Action (Climate Camp) began.

The Climate Camp concept rolls into one the main characteristics of a training camp: autonomous space and sustainable community. Most importantly, the focus is action – either there or thereafter.

The first Climate Camp took place in summer 2006 on land close to a coal-fired power station owned by E.ON called Drax, followed by protests at Heathrow Airport (2007), Kingsnorth Power Station (2008), City of London, Blackheath, Vestas Wind Turbine Factory and Trafalgar Square (2009) and RBS headquarters in Edinburgh (2010). As part of wider campaigns, plans for a third runway at Heathrow and a new power station at Kingsnorth were eventually shelved, while policing was somewhat reformed following the public outcry against the police violence at the 2009 City of London camp. But the movement wasn't only present in England and Scotland. Climate Camps – or their equivalents – were established in countries including Wales, Ireland, the US, Canada, Denmark, Sweden, Switzerland, France, Germany, Belgium, India, New Zealand, Australia, Ghana and Ukraine.

Recent protest camps are not the exclusive preserve of the green movement. The No Borders camp at Calais challenges immigration controls both ideologically and practically. A protest camp at Dale Farm in Essex this year helped catapult the issues of racism against the traveler community onto the front pages and resist bailiffs attempting to evict the site for longer than would have otherwise been the case. In the US, a protest camp outside George W Bush's window instigated by Cindy Sheehan (a mother whose son had been killed in Iraq) was a factor in the turning of public opinion in the country both against the war and against Bush.

Then, of course, there is Egypt, whose 2011 Tahrir Square camp to some extent inspired the current 'Occupy' movement. In an interview with *New Internationalist* earlier this year, activist Gigi Ibrahim called it 'a mini-example of what direct democracy looks like. People took charge of everything – trash, food, security. It was a self-sustaining entity. And in the middle of this, under every tent, on every corner, people were having debates about their demands, the future, how things should go economically and politically. It was fascinating. It was a mirror of what Egypt would look like if it was democratic.' It is likely that anyone who has participated in the recent wave of 'Occupy' camps would be able to recognize this sentiment.

So it can be seen that protest camping can play a role in bringing about social change. Camps can be spaces for people to debate and learn from one another on a large scale, outside of the structures of authority and hegemony that shape ordinary life. But while the awakening of critical consciousness is central to effective struggle, it is not enough. Only by using camps as bases from which direct actions are taken which undermine the interests of the 'haves', are such camps successful in their aims.

Gigi Ibrahim put it thus after the downfall of Mubarak: 'If the struggle wasn't there, if the people didn't take to the streets, if the factories didn't shut down, if workers didn't go on strike, none of this would have happened.' As the 99% takes on the 'global Mubarak' of undemocratic global institutions and financialized capitalism, it is crucial that we heed those words. ◆

http://brightgreenscotland.org/index.php/2011/10/past-tents-a-brief-history-of-protest-camping/

1 See Ann Snitow's 'Greenham Common' at nplusonemag.com/occupygazette3.pdf

No Parties, No Banners
The Spanish experiment with direct democracy

Gianpaolo Baiocchi & Ernesto Ganuza
February 2012

On 15 October last year, 200,000 people marched in Madrid. They were part of a Spanish movement that has come to be known as 15-M – after 15 May, the date of its first action – or the *indignados*. The movement has broad support from the Spanish public, both right and left, with 73 per cent approving in recent polls. Participants and organizers consistently report that 'regular people' and 'first time' protesters, 'not just movement activists', are deeply involved in the assemblies. As Irache, a public school teacher participating in the march, told us: 'The crowd that day came from all walks of life in the city.'

The six-hour march past the city's financial and tourist center to the iconic Puerta del Sol was animated by the now-familiar *indignado* chants: 'If we can't dream, you won't sleep'; 'They don't represent us';

and 'These are our weapons', as protesters lifted their hands in the air, a sign of agreement at assemblies.

Along the route there were more strollers than police. But, at least for North American eyes, what was most striking was the absence of banners. True to the principles of 15-M, almost no one came with signs representing parties, unions, or any other organized groups. The only exceptions were the green T-shirts of the 'Green Tide', an ad hoc movement of teachers and students to defend public education against drastic cutbacks. This group, Irache assured us, was there to support the protest, and not part of 15-M itself.

The lack of banners is essential to the work of the *indignados*. As a movement, 15-M does something novel, bringing people together as equal citizens, not as representatives of particular interests or bearers of particular identities. Claiming broad allegiance – eight million people say they have participated in at least one 15-M event – the movement has broken the barrier between political activists and ordinary citizens. It shares principles of nonviolence and nonpartisanship with the Occupy movement and other peaceful demonstrations around the world. But its central demand – for a direct, deliberative democracy in which citizens debate issues and seek solutions in the absence of representatives – is unique. 15-M represents a striking challenge to traditional political actors – parties, civic associations, unions – and to democratic politics itself.

* * *

15-M has evolved to become a new political subject, distinct from the original internet-based group – *Democracia Real Ya*, or Real Democracy Now (DRY) – that organized the mobilization of 15 May, when about 20,000 people gathered in Puerta del Sol. Three months earlier, on a Sunday night in February, 10 people met in a Madrid bar to began planning the event. They had already been exchanging opinions online about the political and economic situation in Spain. Their meeting ended with both a slogan – 'Real Democracy Now: we are not goods in the hands of politicians and bankers' – and plans to hold a demonstration the week before the municipal elections of 22 May.

Although DRY targeted unemployment and mortgage reforms, the main message was not about the economic crisis but about the breakdown of political accountability and representation. Some commentators on the Left criticized this message as insufficiently radical, but more than 500 organizations and movements supported the 15 May event, even though DRY rejected official collaboration with any political party, union, or other expression of institutionalized political ideology.

The gathering was a success. The widespread disaffection of Spanish citizens took center stage at one of the nation's most visible sites.

That was supposed to be it.

But not all of the participants left the plaza. Initially about 50 decided to stay. By midnight, this group had dwindled to just over 20. They decided to spend the night in the square. Most of the holdouts did not belong to any social movement; they were not seasoned activists or even members of DRY. They stayed, some of them said, because they were 'tired of demonstrations that finish happily and then: nothing'.

A physics PhD student acted as moderator for the group discussions, and a 28-year-old journalist spoke on behalf of the group when the police asked them to leave. They managed to stay in the square until the next morning and, in exchange, guaranteed the police that they were not going to riot or disturb the peace. They organized into small committees to look for food and makeshift mattresses. One of the protesters used a smartphone to spread word of the occupation, with the Twitter hashtag #acampadasol.

The next morning, Monday, the police chased them out, but messages on Twitter and Facebook called for another sleepover that night. This time nearly 200 people attended. The police forcefully removed the occupiers before midnight. By Wednesday nearly a thousand people were camped out. A judicial injunction against the encampment only emboldened the growing movement. On Thursday the numbers increased further and the first tents appeared. Protesters in Barcelona and Seville followed suit, setting up camp in public spaces. By Friday, 20 May, more than 10,000 people were camped in the Puerta del Sol. And many more came on Saturday to express solidarity. Twenty thousand people spent the day holding back the police.

* * *

The central organizing principle of 15-M is individual participation. The movement is infused with a participatory ethos: everyone is expected to take part in all aspects of the group. Strikingly, the movement rejects the principle of representation. Some participants belong to other groups or organizations but, within the movement, individuals do not speak for collectives; they speak in their own voices, for themselves, relying on their own judgments.

This is highly unusual in Spain, which is filled with progressive networks and organizations focusing on diverse interests: housing, the environment, the working class, anarchism, feminism, and many others. Until now, the work of advancing social justice has consisted in suturing together often-fragile coalitions, assuring the right mix of representation at events, and facing the usual controversies that arise when an array of interest groups try to work together.

15-M challenges traditional political actors and democratic politics itself.

15-M has broken with that coalition-politics logic. Assemblies only accept proposals by consensus, and proposals are developed by ad hoc working groups, not permanent institutions committed to single issues. There is no interest-group representation and no bargaining. The decisions that touch all must be accepted by all. And the process is evolving: one very active working group is tasked with improving the decision-making procedure.

Participants in the encampment understand that they are pursuing a new form of politics, a re-conquest of public space for equal citizens, and a radical questioning of the political status quo. This is apparent not only in the way the assemblies make decisions, but in how they talk generally. Every assembly starts with a statement of expectations for participants: be respectful, give only short speeches, keep an open mind and embrace pluralism. All newcomers are welcome and all meeting minutes are public. Everyone is entitled to speak at every assembly, and all are bound by the same rules. There are strict codes to ensure civility. Shouting, insulting and speaking of 'enemies' are forbidden. If someone speaks loudly, the moderator will remind her that she has to be fair and she has to respect others' proposals and ideas. The assemblies always start with an agenda and end on time.

Like the decision-making process, the assemblies are works in progress. Assemblies frequently consider how to avoid the pitfalls of deliberation – sometimes criticized for giving too much power to the educated and articulate – and of consensus – sometimes criticized for privileging the status quo.

These practices pair nicely with theories of direct and deliberative democracy. But the movement as a whole does not explicitly draw on political theory as much as, in the words of one activist, 'conversation in social networks and lots of common sense'. The argument for consensus decision-making is that it opposes the way professional politicians debate and talk, which is seen as instrumental and in the service of narrow interests.

The dedication to individual participation and the refusal of representation were tested almost immediately. Just after the first demonstration, unions, neighborhood associations, social movements and other organizations joined the camp, hoping to express their goals at Puerta del Sol's nightly assemblies. But the campers – *acampados* – consistently rejected these proposals. 15-M addresses 'society as a whole', one of the campers told us in an interview. It 'has nothing to do with the defense of a certain interest, or with the image of one or another sector'.

During the first week, a banner with feminist slogans was taken down. The decision was intensely controversial, and still echoes on the internet. But the reasons for the removal had nothing to do with the cause of feminism. All banners were taken down – banners of trade unions, anarchists, communists and social movements, including DRY itself. Any slogan that branded the assemblies with a group identity was disavowed as a distraction from the movement's political strategy and self-understanding: equal citizens in discussion about the common good. 15-M has even challenged DRY. In many cities, conflict has emerged between the *acampados* and members of DRY, whom many *acampados* see as elitist.

Because of its political innovations, 15-M has been received with ambivalence by urban social movements in Madrid and elsewhere in Spain. Its rejection of banners and its extremely civil mode – both viewed as reformist rather than revolutionary – have aroused particular suspicion. But the movement's popularity has deflected open criticism. Other activists recognize that the high degree of mobilization offers an opportunity. An activist from a social and arts center in Madrid told us: 'If we leave the ghetto, 15-M can help us express our goals and learn a new way to expand.'

The occupation of Puerta del Sol ended in July, but the movement has spread to the city's outer boroughs and across Spain. Anyone can join its working groups via its website. The working groups represent a kind of direct democracy, where people come together as individuals to work on policy solutions to the country's problems. Topics range from proper democratic procedures to financial transparency and mortgage reform. The working group on financial transparency, for example, has uncovered what appears to be evidence of price-fixing on inter-bank lending rates, and the working group on housing and mortgages has been able to stop some evictions. Meanwhile, a working group on assemblies is creating a dispersed deliberative network that will allow people to debate policy from anywhere.

* * *

15-M has shifted the tenor of political debate in Spain, placing disaffection with representative democracy at the center of discussion. And this disaffection extends to all major political actors. Although the movement's policy concerns are closer to preoccupations of the Left, its model of directly deliberative democracy challenges the institutional limits of leftist parties and much of their theoretical imagination.

As with the Occupy movement in the United States, it is hard to know how far 15-M can go in creating change. Spain's recent national elections delivered an overwhelming victory for the rightist Popular Party. Coupled with the results of the most recent provincial and local elections, this victory has put Spain under near-total right-wing dominance for the first time since its transition to democracy. But 15-M remains energetic. Its insistence on deliberation, civility and internal democracy has encouraged erstwhile non-activists to join and play important roles. While 15-M's proposals may deviate from traditional leftist conceptions of social transformation, the movement's rejection of partisanship has empowered the Left at a time when social democratic parties throughout Europe are fighting for their lives.

Occupy bears some similarities to 15-M, especially in the criticisms directed against it: that the movement needs more concrete proposals, institutional allies and tangible targets. And like 15-M, Occupy keeps its distance from political parties, although that charge is perhaps less controversial in the United States, which lacks leftist parties that can win elections.

But there are also large differences. The language of group identity – race, gender, ethnicity – is central to social justice in the United States, and Occupy does not reject group claims. Indeed, by attempting to speak universally, Occupy has at times drawn charges that it may be silencing minority voices. Groups such as Occupy the Hood have made the struggles of people of color their primary focus. Furthermore, because economic inequality has been so central to Occupy's political imagination, unions and union organizers have been more visible than have their counterparts in Spain, and both sides have shown greater receptivity to dialogue, though not without ambivalence.

In spite of the strict ban on special-interest promotion, the *indignados* are not suggesting that unions or other groups have no place in a radically democratic movement. Rather, to play a part, they cannot allow their demands for just democracy to be mere slogans or election strategies. Interest groups need to focus more on speaking for the common good, as some union leaders have

acknowledged in efforts to connect with Occupy. And they need to understand that ossified leadership structures and dependence on political parties are at odds with the larger goal of achieving a genuinely democratic renewal. ◆

bostonreview.net/BR37.1/gianpaolo_baiocchi_ernesto_ganuza_spain_indignados_democracy.php

See, The Nigerian Revolution Has Begun

Emmanuel Iduma
9 January 2012

You tell me that if I speak I will not be heard. No. I will speak and I will be heard. I am not a writer only by talent. I am a writer because I want to be a witness, a real witness.

You recall Edward Said: 'There was something wrong with how I was invented.' Yes, you do. So you understand that I have been out of place for too long. Yet, I am taking the chances of return. When I was invented I was told I was less because I am Nigerian, that I did not have certain opportunities. I will not go to a good school. I will live with the fact of darkness, without electricity. Etc etc. Now I am reinventing my own dialogue, I am taking apart my absence-and-hole-shaped existence. I am filling up the blank spaces. I am writing my story, my essence, my self.

I am a young Nigerian. 'Out of Africa always comes something new,' some ancient Roman historian is supposed to have said. Because I am young I am burdened by the New. I know of the past injustices, the failed sunsets. I know of being labeled, being called a money-monger because I am Ibo, a fraudster because I am Nigerian, futureless because I am African. Yet, I am willing to look to the New, I am willing to constructively forget, to walk through the past and leave the past in the past. I am willing to argue into being this newness I speak about. Because being Nigerian is being New.

Don't think of me as a Facebook protester. I am not. I have gone past updating my status, commenting, posting notes, for the transient reason of being counted amongst a number. I feel embarrassed that you think of me as a young man seeking fame. I am wary of that word. I am wary of being 'liked' by a myriad of people who know nothing of my motivations, my aches, my processes. Instead I am conscious that each Facebook activity or blog post contributes to the historical statements I am making. I will not seek cheap fame. I will contribute to real change.

Which is why I will write and write until my hand is blistered and sore. I will write of the Nigeria I am seeing, of the deconstruction of labels. Of possibilities, of equality, of a new youth. I will write of the shaming of the prodigal fathers, whose failure has been that they forget too easily, too quickly, that no injustice will outmaneuver human resilience, or collective will.

And I am not alone. Look over there, right behind you, by your side, everywhere, the hashtags are ubiquitous. It will fill your head as though multimillion voices are speaking the same words, repeatedly. But I do not want those voices to choke you to death – you will see with your eyes the newness I speak about.

I forgive easily, know this. I am not one to wish for your death, to speak without facts. I will not unfriend you on Facebook, or call for your assassination, or even call you names. How different, then, will I be from you? I am not like you, I am not. I mean it when I say I love peace. I mean it when I say I have not seen a bomb.

The revolution has begun. I am part of it. Do not be fooled that it begins and ends with placards, strikes, Twitter hashtags. I am certainly wiser than that. Yes, I will keep hashtagging, placarding, striking, until I am convinced that I have been destereotyped. Until I am convinced that I am not a matterless blur in the narrative of my country. ◆

blacklooks.org/2012/01/see-the-nigerian-revolution-has-begun/

Is This The End of The Nigerian Revolution?

Emmanuel Iduma
17 January 2012

Something dies in you. You feel disconnected from your dream of a glorious aftermath. For the first time in your life you felt whole, framed within a bigger picture. You spoke, chanted, demanded. You were a witness, you and a million others. You were a revolutionary. Now things have returned to normal. Normal because there are moving cars, stores are open; the street is calloused, as before, by the movement and the people. And the normalcy. You hate that things are normal. This was not what you dreamed of. At all.

But what did you dream?

The horizon of your dream was of a better life, a different form of existence, a tangible and measurable difference. You saw that the debate about fuel subsidy removal was the opportunity to dream of change, because this was a protest above all protests, because this protest seemed naturally logical. But you forgot that in dreaming one does not feel, the night happens so fast, and very soon you are awake.

Are you awake, now?

Do you see that things have really, really, returned to normal? These normal things are the fact of your Nigerianness. All your life, the normal has remained normal, the abuse and the ineptness and the status quo and the cabal. The shift that you thought could happen is an *abnormal*. It takes a lot to make the abnormal happen.

Didn't you know?

When you stood at Ojota chanting, what did you think? It was a dream, yes. But what did you think? Try. Remember. What did you think? When you posted on Facebook about Goodluck Jonathan, Ngozi, Madueke, the Great Nigerian Cabal, what did you think? You were aggrieved, yes. Did you, honestly, see a change in sight?

What did you think would happen? Fuel would be sold again at 65 naira? The president would announce a further 25-per-cent cut in his allowances, that henceforth he would eat in a *buka*? Or were you caught in a mantra, within collective language?

Perhaps you failed to see that all of this, this ad hoc revolution, was simply the beginning of a *shift* of consciousness. It takes a lot, you should know, to transcribe the language of a dream into the spoken word of reality. True, all dreams are translatable, all dreams *are* reality. But within the terrain of the dream and the terrain of reality lie shadows.

What you did was tell the shadows you are beginning to reclaim your reality. Do not feel undermined, betrayed or *normal*. There is no such thing as normalcy; there is change lurking everywhere and those mountebanks from the other side know it. They have seen the rise of *reality*; they have seen, yes. And they know that it is only a matter of time before they are overtaken, overridden, outpoured.

The danger is that you might *normalize*. Because the corruptible have seen that your reality is within your grasp, they introduce elements of normalcy, they end their strike, they compromise. And they claim it is on your behalf, for the sake of security. They might be named 'Labor', 'organized labor', 'government' or whatever other nomenclature they can muster. Do not be fooled. You must not normalize.

Your soul can fly while your feet are on the ground. Know this: there's no one telling you to stop your flight. They can force you away from the street. But your body must not triumph over your soul, your body must not be accustomed to return. The real protest is the protest that happens when you are caught between the shadows and your reality. And that protest happens in a nameless place, where no eyes can see, that moment when you decide that enough is enough.

You have engineered your dream. It is time to engineer your reality.

They will come to you in 2015 again, and say, vote, vote, PDP. Or ACN, CPC, or whatever other conception their destructive ingeniousness has molded. That is when you will exercise your real power. You will demand a real leader, one from your ranks, one who will not migrate to outer space like they have done, one who will not become insensitive to cogent earthly matters.

Because this is not the end of the Nigerian revolution.

Because a revolution does not end.

A revolution only begins. ◆

blacklooks.org/2012/01/is-this-the-end-of-the-nigerian-revolution/

Onward

Rachel Schragis

Flow Chart of the Declaration of the Occupation of NYC

Conceived and drawn by Rachel Schragis, and edited through a crowd-sourcing process in Zuccotti Park facilitated by the artist.

nycga.net/resources/declaration/#flow

Occupy

To employ, make use of.

To keep busy, engage, employ (a person, or the mind, attention, etc.).

To hold possession of; to have in one's possession or power; to hold (a position, office, privilege).

To live in and use (a place) as its tenant or regular inhabitant; to inhabit; to stay or lodge in.

To take possession of, take for one's own use, seize.

To take possession of (a place), esp. by force; to take possession and hold of (a building).

To gain access to and remain in (a building) or on (a piece of land), without authority, as a form of protest.

To take up, use up, fill (space, time, etc.); to be situated, stationed, or seated at or in, to be at or in (a place, position, etc.).

– Oxford English Dictionary

Index

Index

Index

Index

Index

About New Internationalist

We are an independent not-for-profit publishing co-operative. We publish a monthly magazine and a range of books covering current affairs, education, world food, fiction, photography and ethical living, as well as customized products, such as calendars and diaries, for the NGO community.

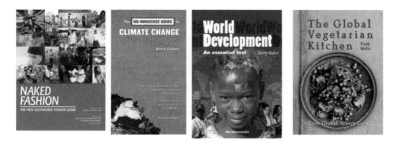

New Internationalist magazine

Agenda: *cutting edge reports*

Argument: *heated debate between experts*

Analysis: *understanding the key issues*

Action: *making change happen*

Alternatives: *inspiring ideas*

Arts: *the best of global culture*

www.newint.org